MW01284309

Kinship and Incestuous Crime in Colonial Guatemala

Kinship and Incestuous Crime in Colonial Guatemala examines social relations in colonial Guatemala through the lens of incest. Using a combination of qualitative and quantitative analyses of incest trials from the Spanish secular courts, this study shows that incest codes were not homogenous nor were its various forms equally condemned. Further, incest codes and the criminal process impacted the articulation of kinship and contributed to the racialization of kin behavior. Colonial actors of all sorts were proficient at using these types of distinctions as they negotiated various crises in their lives. The models of relatedness created within incestuous crime ultimately foreshadowed changes in marriage proscriptions and continued racial polarization following independence from Spain. Overall, this study demonstrates how the lens of incest can add further nuance to our understanding of social relations in a given area. Incest codes force latent divisions between kin to the surface and can provide individuals with multiple avenues to creatively manage interpersonal relationships. They also afford a fruitful arena in which to explore social inequalities in society and mechanisms of culture change. This book will appeal to anyone interested in Latin America or engaged in the fields of kinship, gender, or sexuality studies.

Sarah N. Saffa is currently a Visiting Scholar at Johns Hopkins University.

Routledge Studies in the History of the Americas

For more information about this series, please visit: https://www.routledge.com/Routledge-Studies-in-the-History-of-the-Americas/book-series/RSHAM

Kinship and Incestuous Crime in Colonial Guatemala

Sarah N. Saffa

NEW YORK AND LONDON

First published 2021
by Routledge
52 Vanderbilt Avenue, New York, NY 10017

and by Routledge
2 Park Square, Milton Park, Abingdon, Oxon, OX14 4RN

*Routledge is an imprint of the Taylor & Francis Group, an
informa business*

© 2021 Taylor & Francis

The right of Sarah N. Saffa to be identified as author of this
work has been asserted in accordance with sections 77 and 78
of the Copyright, Designs and Patents Act 1988.

Library of Congress Cataloging-in-Publication Data
Names: Saffa, Sarah N., 1985– author.
Title: Kinship and incestuous crime in colonial Guatemala /
Sarah N. Saffa.
Description: New York, NY : Routledge, an imprint of the
Taylor & Francis Group, an Informa Business, 2021. |
Series: Routledge studies in the history of the americas; 15 |
Includes bibliographical references and index.
Identifiers: LCCN 2020022673 (print) |
LCCN 2020022674 (ebook) | ISBN 9780367464424 (hardback) |
ISBN 9781003028789 (ebook) | ISBN 9781000172621
(adobe pdf) | ISBN 9781000172638 (mobi) |
ISBN 9781000172645 (epub)
Subjects: LCSH: Incest—Law and legislation—Guatemala—
History. | Sex crimes—Law and legislation—Guatemala—
History. | Paternity—Guatemala—History. |
Kinship (Law)—Guatemala—History.
Classification: LCC KGD5564 .S24 2021 (print) |
LCC KGD5564 (ebook) | DDC 345.7281/02536—dc23
LC record available at https://lccn.loc.gov/2020022673
LC ebook record available at https://lccn.loc.gov/2020022674

ISBN: 978-0-367-46442-4 (hbk)
ISBN: 978-1-003-02878-9 (ebk)

Typeset in Sabon
by codeMantra

For Zach
  and
  all of my
  stepframily-in-law

Contents

Figures

Tables

1 Introduction
"I Am Not Your Father"

Introduction

In 1810, José Rumualdo Fuentes denounced his father Vicente to colonial authorities for the rape of his wife—Vicente's daughter-in-law—on two separate occasions.[1] José claimed that Vicente annulled both of their marriages through his actions and requested his exile. In legal jargon, Vicente had committed incest in the first degree. The victim in this case, María Rosalía Surqueah,[2] tried to interrupt the sexual violence, evidently referring to Vicente as her "father" in the process. However, Vicente had retorted that he was not her father, and her efforts to impede his attacks were ultimately unsuccessful. Rosalía believed she was pregnant from their union, though this turned out to not be the case. Vicente initially denied the accusation, suggesting that Rosalía was using him to cover up a sexual relationship with another man. However, he eventually admitted to the crime. Like many victims of sexual assault, Rosalía was equally on trial, and debate ensued as to whether or not she consented to the incest. Both Rosalía and Vicente were Indians, and defense counsel on either side drew from colonial constructions of Indianness in their attempts to exculpate their clients. Still, in the end, Vicente was sentenced to four years of imprisonment and twenty-five lashes, and Rosalía to two months of interior service in the Beaterio de Indias (house of pious Indian laywomen) and spiritual exercises. There was also a mandate for the "habilitation" of their marriages, an ecclesiastical process that allowed spouses to resume married life with one another. As it turns out, the story of this Poqomam Maya family resonated with those of many other families in colonial Guatemala. And, taken together, episodes such as these shed light on the lived experience of kinship and its intersections with a colonial regime.

Westerners[3] today often associate incest with sexual intercourse between close blood relatives, but incest taboos are not uniform across time and space. For Spain and its American colonies, the legal definition of *incesto* ("incest") included sexual relations between various types of individuals. Among them were consanguineous, affinal, and "spiritual" kin—the latter of which were created through the Catholic rites of baptism and confirmation—in addition to members of religious orders and non-Christians. Yet, analysis of incest trials from the Spanish secular courts shows that the definition of incest in colonial Guatemala was not always shared, nor were its various forms equally condemned. Further, incest codes and the criminal process impacted the articulation of kinship, with colonial actors often using the norms and nuances related to incest to their own or another's advantage. These variables also contributed to the racialization of kinship models, as individuals drew from assumptions about a relationship between Indianness and incest, even in the face of evidence to contrary. Overall, incestuous acts and the legal proceedings surrounding them reflected and constituted various aspects of social relations in colonial Guatemala and prefigured elements of social life following independence from Spain.

Theory, Method, and Context

Colonial Guatemala was a region within the viceroyalty of New Spain, which included territories within the southern United States, Mexico, Central America, and the Caribbean and Philippine seas. The Kingdom of Guatemala included the area between modern-day Chiapas and the Costa Rica-Panama border. Territories within today's nations of Guatemala, El Salvador, and Belize roughly formed the province of Guatemala within the larger Kingdom of Guatemala during the seventeenth century. Following the establishment of the intendency system in the late eighteenth century, El Salvador became its own intendency, and the province of Guatemala was reduced to areas within present-day Guatemala and Belize. All of the cases analyzed in this study took place within this province and span the years 1682–1821, the year in which independence from Spain was declared.

Colonial Guatemala was largely made up of indigenous Maya, but Spaniards (born in Spain and the Americas), Africans, and individuals of mixed descent also formed a part of the fabric of colonial society.[4] There were large discrepancies in levels of education such that many individuals were illiterate, while others held professional degrees. Religious indoctrination and scrutiny by Spanish colonial authorities was uneven at best, allowing indigenous and rural areas greater liberty from the enforcement of civil and canon norms. While incest in colonial (and post-independence) New Spain has received some scholarly attention, the colonial Guatemalan region has eluded much analysis.[5] Thus, this study works to fill this gap, providing not only a general framework of incest in the area for the purpose of contextualization and regional comparison but also intimate glimpses into the lives of gendered and racialized kinspersons in colonial Guatemala.

Incest has long been intriguing to anthropologists because such taboos are evidently common to all human societies. Incest is typically understood as a proscription on sexual relations between individuals considered to be too closely related, which will vary depending on cultural and historical context. However, the term used to designate such proscriptions can also be extended to include certain non-kin, as was the case in Spanish law. Explanations for the incest taboo have varied. Some consider biological influences, such as the importance of genetic variation (via outbreeding) to the survival and adaptation of the species (see Fox 1980, 10–1). Others focus on sociocultural factors in which incest taboos serve to reduce the potential for intra-group conflict and promote inter-group alliance.[6] More recently, Françoise Héritier (2002) proposed that the incest taboo derives from a universal human proclivity to categorize things as the same or different, with contact between identical bodily fluids (however defined) being the ultimate criterion for incest. Regardless of the exact mechanisms behind incest taboos, their codification is uniquely human, and they have clearly impacted social experience.

Incest naturally intersects with the concept of kinship or relatedness,[7] a signature subject of the anthropological discipline because of its apparent role in human social organization. For much of anthropology's existence, kinship was conceived of as the sociocultural means of organizing the biological "facts" of procreation. In other words, kinship was ultimately rooted in sexual reproduction. Pushes towards reflexivity within the broader postmodern movement led to criticism that kinship was an ethnocentric construct reflecting a Western worldview. Thus, it was argued that kinship should not be considered to have some pre-social, universal existence.[8] Because of such debate, kinship is now viewed in more optative and fluid terms and as not necessarily tied to so-called blood relations.[9] Generally speaking, there has been a shift to thinking of kinship as a process as opposed to a state of being (see Parkin and Stone 2004; Bamford and Leach 2009). At the same time, biology has reentered the equation with the understanding that human culture is not wholly removed from human evolution. However, biology in this case is seen as one potential factor underlying kinship construction and behavior—not as a universal feature of it (see Stone 2004).

While concepts of relatedness in colonial Guatemalan incest trials in many ways centered on the idea of inalienable blood ties, they were also characterized by a degree of malleability and sensitivity to context. As a result, these cases provide a ripe arena in which to view the coexistence of, and tensions between, these different forms of relating. They necessitate thinking in terms of a kinship calculus in which variables like sexual relations or criminal procedure shape the expression of relatedness in culturally predicated—though not always identical—ways. Indeed, there were times when individuals came to different conclusions about the nature of a relationship.

Analysis of incestuous crime in colonial Guatemala demands a feminist perspective. Feminist anthropologists have often highlighted the role of social processes (e.g. kinship) in the production of gender asymmetries and heteronormativity.[10] In colonial Guatemala, incestuous violence was gendered—victims were always women and girls, whereas perpetrators were exclusively men. Further, incestuous violence was typically enacted by father-types—fathers, stepfathers, and fathers-in-law. Both patterns are consistent with the patriarchal ideals that infused much of colonial Latin America (cf. Herman 2000). The criminal category of incest also reinforced a heteronormative environment. Following various legal codes and the cases of incest that were brought to trial in the Guatemalan secular courts, "incest" only referred to sexual relations between male and female kin.

This topic of investigation also requires an intersectional approach. The experience of Indians in the criminal process was particularly marked. The ways in which Spanish legal authorities and defense counsel regularly portrayed Indians in incest trials linked this sector of the population to this particular crime. Indian actors, for their part, both contradicted and reinforced such representations, which were largely intended to lessen culpability. Indeed, Indians were well aware of the stereotypes Spaniards held about them, and they were able to "appropriate the language of the dominant" (Kulick 1996) for their own ends when on trial. Such generalizations had polarizing effects, which not only legitimated the marginalization of Indians in the minds of Spaniards, but also worked against those who denounced Indian offenders before the Spanish courts. Indian women and girls would have been at a particular disadvantage, considering the gendered nature of incestuous violence in colonial Guatemala.

Obviously, power imbalances will characterize any courtroom situation, and these discrepancies can have impacts outside of it. Following Sally Engle Merry (1991), the processing of cases in courts is one way in which the culture of a dominant group is introduced to a subordinate one. She described such instances as "cultural performances" that create change in sociocultural practices and consciousness (Merry 1991, 892; see also Merry 1994). This is not to say that such introductions lead to a one-to-one cultural transfer in favor of the dominant group. In Susan Kellogg's terms (1995, xxii), law is "an arena of cultural conflict and accommodation" and "a catalyst of cultural change and adaptation." The criminal process in colonial Guatemala would have clarified to incestuous offenders who acted in good faith that their sexual activity was inappropriate from the court's perspective, shaping perceptions of incest and relatedness in the process. It would have shown those who knowingly committed incest the potential legal consequences of such actions, perhaps mounting pressure for future compliance. Some individuals no doubt obliged warnings by magistrates to separate from their sexual partners, but others were tried more than once (Case 17). And, since word of incest trials could spread and punishments could be public, enforcement of incest law (or lack thereof) would have made an impression on other community members as well. To be sure, incest trials triggered conversation and debate about the nature of kinship and incest, which could serve to either reinforce incest law or pave the way for new possibilities.

Use of colonial criminal records for historical reconstruction has both its limitations and its benefits. Factors like power disparities between authorities and witnesses, imperfect translations of non-Spanish-speaking individuals, and the handwritten method of recording and typical third-person rendering of oral testimony have all had the potential to impact what was said during a trial and included in the final written product.[11] At the same time, these documents offer information on individuals who would otherwise be lost to history, sometimes even providing the reader with direct quotes from witnesses or personal letters of accused persons.

Also, though it might be tempting to classify criminals as social outliers, scholars have cautioned against this. For example, Steve J. Stern (1995, 52) found that in colonial Mexico, "episodes of criminal violence represented not so much a rupture that stood apart from normal social dynamics but an excess committed within a recognizable logic of behavior." Richard Boyer (1989) also spoke in terms of "excess," noting how married individuals (particularly women) might be forced to act once marital ideals of reciprocity became too overshadowed by a spouse's mistreatment, whether it came in the form of physical violence, neglect, or otherwise. Guatemalan incest cases likewise reveal behavior that crossed into the realm of the excessive, especially in the figure of the father-offender. In essence, deviant behavior can provide insight into cultural norms despite breaching their limits.

Needless to say, participants in incest trials often contradicted one another. While it remains impossible to fully comprehend what transpired between them—if anything—the arguments they made are still informative. To summarize Marilyn Strathern (2005, 50–1), the cultural resources individuals use in support of a persuasive point must communicate something that is possible, and possible worlds inform actions in the present one. Thus, regardless of whether the statements made in incest trials were accurate, exaggerated, or outright false, they were not completely divorced from the realm of cultural possibility that seeped into the lives of colonial actors.

The criminal records analyzed here are housed at the Archivo General de Centro América (AGCA) in Guatemala City, which I visited during the summers of 2012, 2014, and 2015. Using the archive's *fichero* (card catalog) as a guide, I was able to locate, and then photograph, the documents for this study. During my time at the archive, I consulted drawers 1–2 through 1–23, 1–25, 1–28, and 1–29 in the section of the *fichero* dedicated to civil and criminal records, which is organized chronologically. I later analyzed the digital versions of the documents using a combination of qualitative and quantitative analyses.

Seventy-three of the cases found addressed incest—or what would theoretically constitute incest—as the sole crime or as one of multiple crimes. These cases make up the Incest Case Log located in the Appendix and are cited as Cases 1 through 73 in the main text. Other court records that contained information pertinent to this analysis also appear in the text and are cited accordingly. All of these records stemmed from the Spanish secular courts, and the majority of incest cases were explicitly identified as criminal cases. Criminal proceedings—in contrast to civil proceedings—dealt with offenses that entered the public sphere and had a perceived negative effect on the community (Cutter 1995, 111–3).

Over half of the incest cases were tried in the jurisdictional area of Sacatepéquez, which contained the capitals of Antigua Guatemala (or Santiago de Guatemala) and Nueva Guatemala (modern-day Guatemala City).[12] Incest trials typically involved (illiterate) non-elites, making them especially valuable for the study of subaltern lives. Only 11 out of 164 individuals carried the honorific title of *don* or *doña*.[13] One Indian man was listed as a *principal*, an esteemed status in indigenous communities (Case 21). Indians accounted for forty-six of the actors in incest trials, individuals of mixed descent for thirty-two, and Spaniards for eight.[14] Seventy-eight individuals did not have their race recorded in line with Christopher Lutz's (1994, 103) observation of a growing tendency for race to go unrecorded in notarial records from the late colonial period. Significantly, in contrast to their relatively small representation among defendants in incest trials, ethnic Spanish men dominated positions of power in the Spanish secular courts in Guatemala and throughout the Americas. This was also true of the clergy, members of which regularly featured in incest cases in one way or another.

In colonial Guatemalan incest trials, the words *amancebamiento* ("concubinage"), *concubinato* ("concubinage"), and *ilícita amistad* ("illicit friendship") were frequently used interchangeably.[15] Their main significance here is that they connoted nonmarital (sexual) unions between men and women. As noted above, such unions could take the form of sexual violence. Though modern notions of rape as sexual intercourse with a person without their consent or against their will were relatively absent from colonial jurisprudence (see Komisaruk 2008, 373), the issues of force and consent did arise in some incest trials. This study considered sexual unions to be incestuous rape when there was a clear articulation at some point during the proceedings that a woman or girl was either physically assaulted or otherwise compelled to succumb to a male perpetrator. Though verbs like *estuprar* ("to deflower") and *violar* ("to rape") theoretically connoted forcible sexual relations, in Guatemalan incest cases these verbs (and their linguistic variants) were most consistently used in reference to a loss of virginity and were not a reliable indicator of coercive sexual relations. Verbs like *forzar* ("to force" or "to rape") and *violentar* ("to force"), on the other hand, were explicitly juxtaposed to consensual sexual relations (e.g. Case 65).[16]

Overall, incestuous crime was associated with force or intimidation approximately 27 percent of the time, though this is surely an underrepresentation of the reality of sexual coercion within incestuous relations. Surviving court records are often incomplete, sometimes providing little more than a name of an individual and the crime of which they were accused. Further, the question of consent is rarely simple, and power asymmetries based on factors like gender and generation could have in fact contributed to sexual coercion even when violence or fear was not expressly articulated. The approximate ages of participants in incestuous crime are included in the Incest Case Log, provided that they were available. However, it should be noted that children in colonial Latin America could be attributed sexual agency at a very young age by modern standards. Bianca Premo (2005, 120), for instance, found that girls in colonial Lima were generally considered sexual innocents when they were around eight years of age or younger. As they grew older, the state of their sexual honor became more suspect.

Certain stylistic choices have been made for the sake of consistency and readability. Spanish names and terms appear in their modernized forms in the main text. Indigenous surnames, on the other hand, reflect their colonial spellings because they have largely been preserved out of concern over the legal consequences, particularly with respect to land titles. Also, notaries rarely spelled them consistently, and alternative spellings are included in the endnotes when appropriate. Translated passages follow modern conventions for punctuation and the capitalization of words. I have omitted some words and phrases from translations because they are burdensome to the reader. For example, criminal records are full of qualifiers like "aforementioned" and "said" (e.g. "the aforementioned María"). In translations, this phrase would be simplified to "María." I have also replaced identifiers like "the declarant" or "she who states" with pronouns or a referent's name for the same purpose. On occasion, a referent's name has been inserted into a quoted passage for the sake of clarity. Brackets designate these types of modifications. The original Spanish of translated passages can be found in the endnotes with any available folio numbers and more specific document identification when necessary (some cases in the Incest Case Log spanned multiple documents).

It should also be mentioned that once an actor from a criminal case has been identified by their full name in the main text, they are thenceforward referred to by their first (and/or middle) name only. First names communicate gender identity, a helpful reference point in cases that center around interactions between men and women. Further, being that incest cases dealt with families, various actors could share a surname, making first names more useful for conveying individual identities. Defense counsel are referred to by their surnames once introduced because they were always male and fell outside the principal narrative of the case.

Overview of Chapters

Chapters 2 and 3 set the stage for understanding social relations and incestuous crime in colonial Guatemala. Chapter 2 examines the intersection of incest with two major elements influencing social relations in Spanish America—the system of socioracial categorization and the culture of honor (status or virtue). Chapter 3 further contextualizes incestuous crime through exploration of legal and cultural precedents, jurisdictional issues, and the criminal process, including the special treatment afforded Indian actors in the legal realm. It ends with a discussion of the typical penalties for incestuous crime in colonial Guatemala and their correlations with race, gender, and marital status.

Chapters 4 and 5 discuss broad patterns within incestuous crime and relatedness in colonial Guatemala. Chapter 4 first considers debate among legal professionals regarding whether certain forms of incest were more criminal than others and the types of incest that were typically brought to formal trial. It then examines the ways in which the nature of kin ties could contribute to incestuous crime and factor into various aspects of the criminal process. Chapter 5 illustrates how incest codes came into conflict with the malleable nature of kinship practice in colonial Guatemala. It also demonstrates the ways colonial actors of diverse backgrounds were able to take advantage of kinship and incest as they dealt with (forced) sexual relations, marriage, and conflicts with authority figures.

Chapter 6 focuses on a particular segment of colonial society—the Guatemalan indigenous population. It discusses the intersection of colonial constructions of Indianness, particularly its ignorance aspect, with incestuous crime. It examines strategic usage of the ignorance defense in incest trials and its potential implications. It also demonstrates the ways in which challenges to Indianness were ignored, leaving little room for counternarratives. Chapter 7 summarizes the findings of this study and proposes possible avenues for future research.

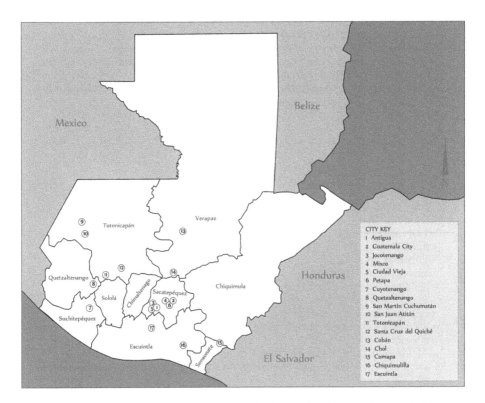

Figure 1.1 Modern Guatemala overlain with late colonial jurisdictional divisions (1785–1821). Jurisdictional information adapted from Komisaruk (2013, xv). Map by Zachary S. Klukkert.

Notes

1 Case 61.
2 Rosalía's surname was also written as Surquiah, Surcheah, Surchiah, Surquial, Zurquig, Surchah, Suchiah, Suaquial, and Sequeh.
3 Carsten (2001, 50) cautioned against drawing stark lines of contrast between Western and non-Western categories. Thus, "Western" is used here as a way to highlight that not all worldviews are influenced by Judeo-Christian values and/or emphasis on the modern scientific method rather than as a way to distinguish between homogenous Western and homogenous non-Western conceptual frameworks.
4 Descendants of indigenous Central Mexican populations also resided in Guatemala. For example, Ciudad Vieja was a community of largely Tlaxcalan ancestry (Komisaruk 2013, 62).
5 For example, Margadant (2001), Rodríguez-Sáenz (2005), Jaffary (2007), and Penyak (2016). Incest cases also surfaced in Castañeda's (1989) treatment of sexual violence and *estupro* (loss of virginity) in Nueva Galicia. The corpus of colonial Guatemalan rape records analyzed by Komisaruk (2008)

also apparently included some incest trials. Guatemalan incest trials are also treated in Saffa (2019).
6 See, for example, Lévi-Strauss (1969) and Goody (1956).
7 In the contributions to Carsten (2000b), the term "relatedness" was adopted and used alongside, or in opposition to, "kinship" to indicate a willingness to embrace indigenous idioms of being related (Carsten 2000a, 4). Here, the term is used interchangeably with "kinship" as a reflection of changes in kinship theory following postmodern critiques.
8 See, especially, Schneider (1984). See also Collier and Yanagisako (1987).
9 See, for example, Weston (1991, 1995), Carsten (2004), and the contributions to Franklin and McKinnon (2001), including Weston (2001), Howell (2001), and Yan (2001). Franklin (2013) showed how biology itself is relativized in the context of in vitro fertilization (IVF).
10 See Ortner (1972), Rosaldo (1974), and Rubin (1975) for early discussion of this topic.
11 For extended discussion of issues related to text production and archives, see, for example, Burns (2010) and Tortorici (2018).
12 The capital moved to Nueva Guatemala following extensive damage to Antigua Guatemala caused by an earthquake in 1773.
13 This title theoretically originated in legitimate descent from high-status parents (Twinam 1999, 4).
14 Domingo Mariano Mejía (Case 46) was identified as both Indian and *mestizo* (of Spanish and Indian descent), but because the Indian identification surfaced more emphatically in the case, it was favored here. Also, doña Teodora Bocanegra (Case 45) was considered Spanish in this study since her title and the identification of her sister as Spanish would have surely resulted in her treatment as such. All information related to racial identification can be found in the Appendix.
15 See Komisaruk (2013, 207) for further discussion of such terms in late colonial Guatemala.
16 For further discussion of rape, deflowerment, and associated terminology, see, for example, Castañeda (1989), Lipsett-Rivera (1997), Komisaruk (2008), and Tortorici (2015).

Bibliography

Bamford, Sandra, and James Leach. 2009. "Introduction: Pedigrees of Knowledge: Anthropology and the Genealogical Method." In *Kinship and Beyond: The Genealogical Model Reconsidered*, edited by Sandra Bamford and James Leach, 1–23. New York and Oxford: Berghahn Books.
Boyer, Richard. 1989. "Women, La Mala Vida, and the Politics of Marriage." In *Sexuality and Marriage in Colonial Latin America*, edited by Asunción Lavrin, 252–86. Lincoln and London: University of Nebraska Press.
Burns, Kathryn. 2010. *Into the Archive: Writing and Power in Colonial Peru*. Durham, NC and London: Duke University Press.
Carsten, Janet. 2000a. "Introduction: Cultures of Relatedness." In *Cultures of Relatedness: New Approaches to the Study of Kinship*, edited by Janet Carsten, 1–36. Cambridge: Cambridge University Press.
———. ed. 2000b. *Cultures of Relatedness: New Approaches to the Study of Kinship*. Cambridge: Cambridge University Press.
———. 2001. "Substantivism, Antisubstantivism, and Anti-antisubstantivism." In *Relative Values: Reconfiguring Kinship Studies*, edited by Sarah Franklin

and Susan McKinnon, 29–53. Durham, NC and London: Duke University Press.

———. 2004. *After Kinship*. Cambridge: Cambridge University Press.

Castañeda, Carmen. 1989. *Violación, estupro, y sexualidad: Nueva Galicia, 1790–1821*. Guadalajara: Hexágono.

Collier, Jane Fishburne, and Sylvia Junko Yanagisako. 1987. "Introduction." In *Gender and Kinship: Essays toward a Unified Analysis*, edited by Jane Fishburne Collier and Sylvia Junko Yanagisako, 1–50. Stanford, CA: Stanford University Press.

Cutter, Charles R. 1995. *The Legal Culture of Northern New Spain, 1700–1810*. Albuquerque: University of New Mexico Press.

Fox, Robin. 1980. *The Red Lamp of Incest*. New York: E. P. Dutton.

Franklin, Sarah. 2013. *Biological Relatives: IVF, Stem Cells, and the Future of Kinship*. Durham, NC and London: Duke University Press.

Franklin, Sarah, and Susan McKinnon, eds. 2001. *Relative Values: Reconfiguring Kinship Studies*. Durham, NC and London: Duke University Press.

Goody, Jack. 1956. "A Comparative Approach to Incest and Adultery." *The British Journal of Sociology* 7 (4): 286–305.

Héritier, Françoise. 2002. *Two Sisters and Their Mother: The Anthropology of Incest*. Translated by Jeanine Herman. New York: Zone Books.

Herman, Judith Lewis. 2000. *Father-Daughter Incest*. Cambridge and London: Harvard University Press.

Howell, Signe. 2001. "Self-Conscious Kinship: Some Contested Values in Norwegian Transnational Adoption." In *Relative Values: Reconfiguring Kinship Studies*, edited by Sarah Franklin and Susan McKinnon, 203–23. Durham, NC and London: Duke University Press.

Jaffary, Nora E. 2007. "Incest, Sexual Virtue, and Mobility in Late Colonial Mexico." In *Gender, Race, and Religion in the Colonization of the Americas*, edited by Nora E. Jaffary, 95–107. Hampshire: Ashgate.

Kellogg, Susan. 1995. *Law and the Transformation of Aztec Culture, 1500–1700*. Norman: University of Oklahoma Press.

Komisaruk, Catherine. 2008. "Rape Narratives, Rape Silences: Sexual Violence and Judicial Testimony in Colonial Guatemala." *Biography* 31 (3): 369–96.

———. 2013. *Labor and Love in Guatemala: The Eve of Independence*. Stanford, CA: Stanford University Press.

Kulick, Don. 1996. "Causing a Commotion." *Anthropology Today* 12 (6): 3–7.

Lévi-Strauss, Claude. 1969. *The Elementary Structures of Kinship*. Boston, MA: Beacon Press.

Lipsett-Rivera, Sonya. 1997. "The Intersection of Rape and Marriage in Late-Colonial and Early-National Mexico." *CLAHR* 6 (4): 559–90.

Lutz, Christopher H. 1994. *Santiago de Guatemala, 1541–1773: City, Caste, and the Colonial Experience*. Norman and London: University of Oklahoma Press.

Margadant, Guillermo Floris. 2001. "El concepto de incesto aplicado por la justicia eclesiástica en la Nueva España y en el México independiente preliberal." In *La sexofobia del clero y cuatro ensayos histórico-jurídicos sobre sexualidad*, edited by Guillermo Floris Margadant, 61–95. México: Miguel Ángel Porrúa.

Merry, Sally Engle. 1991. "Law and Colonialism." *Law and Society Review* 25 (4): 889–922.

———. 1994. "Courts as Performances: Domestic Violence Hearings in a Hawai'i Family Court." In *Contested States: Law, Hegemony and Resistance*, edited by Mindie Lazarus-Black and Susan F. Hirsch, 35–58. New York and London: Routledge.

Ortner, Sherry B. 1972. "Is Female to Male as Nature Is to Culture?" *Feminist Studies* 1 (2): 5–31.

Parkin, Robert, and Linda Stone. 2004. "General Introduction." In *Kinship and Family: An Anthropological Reader*, edited by Robert Parkin and Linda Stone, 1–23. Malden, MA, Oxford, and Carlton: Blackwell Publishing.

Penyak, Lee M. 2016. "Incestuous Natures: Consensual and Forced Relations in Mexico, 1740–1854." In *Sexuality and the Unnatural in Colonial Latin America*, edited by Zeb Tortorici, 162–87. Oakland: University of California Press.

Premo, Bianca. 2005. *Children of the Father King: Youth, Authority, and Legal Minority in Colonial Lima*. Chapel Hill: University of North Carolina Press.

Rodríguez-Sáenz, Eugenia. 2005. "'Tiyita bea lo que me han hecho': estupro y incesto en Costa Rica (1800–1850)." In *El paso del cometa: estado, política social y culturas populares en Costa Rica (1800–1950)*, edited by Iván Molina Jiménez and Steven Palmer, 1–47. San José, Costa Rica: EUNED.

Rosaldo, Michelle Zimbalist. 1974. "Woman, Culture, and Society: A Theoretical Overview." In *Woman, Culture and Society*, edited by Michelle Zimbalist Rosaldo and Louise Lamphere, 17–42. Stanford, CA: Stanford University Press.

Rubin, Gayle. 1975. "The Traffic in Women: Notes on the 'Political Economy' of Sex." In *Toward an Anthropology of Women*, edited by Rayna R. Reiter, 157–210. New York and London: Monthly Review Press.

Saffa, Sarah N. 2019. "'She Was What They Call a "Pepe"': Kinship Practice and Incest Codes in Late Colonial Guatemala." *Journal of Family History* 44 (2): 181–99.

Schneider, David M. 1984. *A Critique of the Study of Kinship*. Ann Arbor: University of Michigan Press.

Stern, Steve J. 1995. *The Secret History of Gender: Women, Men, and Power in Late Colonial Mexico*. Chapel Hill and London: University of North Carolina Press.

Stone, Linda. 2004. "Introduction." In *Kinship and Family: An Anthropological Reader*, edited by Robert Parkin and Linda Stone, 331–41. Malden, MA, Oxford, and Carlton: Blackwell Publishing.

Strathern, Marilyn. 2005. *Kinship, Law and the Unexpected: Relatives Are Always a Surprise*. Cambridge and New York: Cambridge University Press.

Tortorici, Zeb. 2015. "Sexual Violence, Predatory Masculinity, and Medical Testimony in New Spain." *Osiris* 30: 272–94.

———. 2018. *Sins against Nature: Sex and Archives in Colonial New Spain*. Durham, NC and London: Duke University Press.

Twinam, Ann. 1999. *Public Lives, Private Secrets: Gender, Honor, Sexuality, and Illegitimacy in Colonial Spanish America*. Stanford, CA: Stanford University Press.

Weston, Kath. 1991. *Families We Choose: Lesbians, Gays, Kinship*. New York: Columbia University Press.

————. 1995. "Forever Is a Long Time: Romancing the Real in Gay Kinship Ideologies." In *Naturalizing Power: Essays in Feminist Cultural Analysis*, edited by Sylvia Yanagisako and Carol Delaney, 87–110. New York and London: Routledge.

————. 2001. "Kinship, Controversy, and the Sharing of Substance: The Race/Class Politics of Blood Transfusion." In *Relative Values: Reconfiguring Kinship Studies*, edited by Sarah Franklin and Susan McKinnon, 147–74. Durham, NC and London: Duke University Press.

Yan, Yunxiang. 2001. "Practicing Kinship in Rural North China." In *Relative Values: Reconfiguring Kinship Studies*, edited by Sarah Franklin and Susan McKinnon, 224–45. Durham, NC and London: Duke University Press.

2   Social Relations in Colonial Spanish America

Introduction

When the Spanish arrived in the Americas around the turn of the sixteenth century, they used the term *indios* ("people of the Indies" or "Indians") to distinguish native populations from themselves, glossing over the rich cultural diversity among them.[1] As the colonial period moved forward, the process of socioracial categorization—often referred to as the *calidad* (or *casta*) system[2]—became increasingly complex, and it shaped how a person experienced the world in terms of legal standing, marriage options, and more. Spaniards also brought with them Iberian notions of honor, which would soon permeate the Americas, carrying varied degrees of strength depending on time and place. Like *calidad*, the culture of honor bled into everyday interactions, especially with respect to gender, as individuals sought to protect their public reputations. Thus, incestuous crime must be situated within the systems of *calidad* and honor in order to better understand how incestuous relations came to be realized and the ways in which they were documented in court.

The Creation and Challenges of a Two-Republic System

Early Spanish America was in many ways characterized by a system of "two republics," a *república de españoles* ("Republic of Spaniards") and a *república de indios* ("Republic of Indians"). Within this system, Indians were to be kept separate from non-Indians out of concern that the latter would have a negative impact on the former. Those in favor of a two-republic system had a variety of reasons for maintaining this position. Many missionaries viewed Indians as childlike and easily led astray, making them unable to resist or defend themselves against those who wanted to harm them or cause them to sin. Others believed that Indians held the potential for the creation of a society better than that found in Europe when supplied with the proper guidance and isolated from Spanish influence. While the segregationist policies of the two-republic system afforded some advantages to indigenous populations, often allowing them to manage their own affairs through institutions like Indian *cabildos* (town councils), it by no means implied equality between Spaniards and Indians.[3]

Indeed, the colonial period was characterized by numerous disruptions to native cultures and systematic exploitation of Indian labor on the part of Church and Crown. For instance, because scattered settlement patterns proved problematic for the conversion and governance of the indigenous population, the Crown placed friars in charge of creating towns and villages to concentrate the dispersed population into a fewer number of larger areas. Many Indians had been enslaved, and though indigenous slavery was essentially outlawed with the New Laws of the Indies for the Good Treatment and Preservation of the Indians (1542–1543), free Indians were still obligated to provide labor and tribute through the *encomienda* system. Within this system, Indian towns were divvied up and obligated to supply funds and labor either to a royal *encomienda* (in the case of crown towns) or to an individual *encomendero* who had been awarded an *encomienda* for their efforts in colonizing the Americas. Indians who did not carry a tributary status were nevertheless required to pay a tribute known as the *laborío*, which also applied to some non-Indian groups (though never to Spaniards). Further, in response to labor shortages in the late sixteenth century, not only was there increased trade in African slaves but also the establishment of a practice referred to as the *repartimiento de indios*. This institution required that every Indian town send a certain number of individuals to Spanish towns every week where they would be assigned to public works projects or to individual Spaniards who had requested workers. These workers were theoretically reimbursed for their labor, but even in these circumstances, their absence from their own sources of subsistence would have taken an economic toll.[4]

The idealistic notion of a separation between the republics proved challenging in Spanish America. For example, the overseers (*calpixques*) that *encomenderos* often used for directing Indian labor and collecting tribute from the towns under their jurisdiction were rarely Indians. Many were *negros* ("Blacks") or individuals of mixed descent (Sherman 1979, 86). Colonial centers like Antigua Guatemala were especially vulnerable to interactions between Indians and non-Indians (see Lutz 1994; Herrera 2003). Urban migrant workers, such as women employed in domestic service, provided multiple links between Indian and Hispanic spheres (Komisaruk 2013, 65–6). Trade also allowed for intermingling between groups outside the urban environment. European petty dealers established close ties with Indians in the countryside, sometimes becoming godparents of their children so as to enter into a reciprocal relationship of *compadrazgo* (the institution establishing ties between the parents and godparents of a child). Economic ventures in agriculture and animal husbandry also signaled an intrusion by Spaniards, or their African auxiliaries, into the largely native countryside. The majority of permanent workers for these enterprises were black slaves, Indian wage workers, and individuals of mixed descent, with Indian draft laborers arriving during harvest through the institutions of *encomienda* or *repartimiento* (Herrera 2003, 173, 175).

Informal unions and marriage were another realm in which boundaries were muddied. Forced and consensual sexual relations between Spanish men and indigenous women were not uncommon, especially in the first decades of colonization when battles raged and Spanish women were so few in number. The Crown allowed unions between Spaniards and Indians to the extent that they might aid efforts at conversion and governance (see Schwaller 2016, 65–6). Robinson A. Herrera (2007) found that only the most elite men in sixteenth-century Guatemala were able to attract Spanish women as spouses since they were considered the most desirable of marriage partners yet were hard to find. The majority of Spaniards maintained unions with non-Spanish women, who were largely of indigenous descent. In general, native noblewomen were more likely to wed Spaniards than commoner women considering their status and wealth, though the latter did occur. Marriage to wealthy Spaniards declined for both noblewomen and commoner women as the sixteenth century progressed. Indeed, Elizabeth A. Kuznesof (1995) described the evolution of spousal preference among Spanish men in early Spanish America as one in which women with increasingly greater degrees of Spanish ancestry were favored.

It goes without saying that many unions between Spanish men and Indian women resulted in offspring. While these children were theoretically termed *mestizos*, and their presence alone would seem to contradict a two-republic system, the malleability of socioracial categories helped maintain this system to some extent. In early sixteenth-century Guatemala, the two-republic system accommodated *mestizos* by typically assimilating *mestizas* (the daughters of Indian-Spanish unions) and legitimate offspring into the *república de españoles* and other offspring into the *república de indios* (Lutz 1994, 45). Similar patterns occurred elsewhere, with many individuals of mixed descent living as either "tacit *españoles*" or "tacit *indios*" in the early colonial period (Schwaller 2016).

In contrast to Indian-Spanish unions, and in line with the two-republic system, royal policy demonstrated a desire on the part of the Crown to prevent interracial unions with Blacks. In theory, endogamous marriage would keep Blacks separated from indigenous populations and protect indigenous women from sexual assault by African men. It could also serve to pacify slaves and prevent rebellion. Of course, efforts to circumscribe sexual unions and marriage with Blacks were not always successful (Schwaller 2016, 66–9).

In colonial Guatemala, the term *mulato* came to refer to those of either Afro-European or Afro-Indian descent and included those with even a hint of African ancestry. *Mulatos* were problematic for the two-republic system because factors like racial prejudice and phenotypical differences prevented the majority of them from entering either republic. As a result, they laid the foundation for a *casta* (i.e. mixed race) population that neither republic could assimilate. By the turn of the eighteenth century, *castas* had become racially indistinguishable from one another, and they all claimed some degree of Spanish heritage, even if only in a cultural sense. Members of the *casta* population of Antigua Guatemala, which included *mestizos*, free *mulatos* (i.e. not enslaved), and the offspring of unions between them, were eventually designated as *ladinos* (Lutz 1994, 46, 50, 95, 135).

The term *ladino* had (and continues to have) a long history. It was used to describe Indians who had adopted external cultural character-istics that differentiated them from other Indians, particularly with re-gard to Spanish language acquisition (Luján Muñoz 1976, 52; Taracena Arriola 1982, 90), though the term *indio castellano* ("Castilian Indian") could also be utilized. *Ladino* also referred to a Hispanized African slave (Schwaller 2016, 60). In Guatemala, *ladino* could be used to ei-ther distinguish Indians from non-Indians or specify individuals who were neither Indian nor Spaniard (Taracena Arriola 1982, 93–5). Still, Stacey Schwartzkopf (2013) found that while the state promoted use of the categories of Spaniard and *ladino*—in contrast to Indian—more spe-cific terms for ethnic and racial classification continued to be employed alongside *ladino* into the early nineteenth century in some areas.[5]

The intermingling between Indians and non-Indians suggests a com-plete failure of the two-republic system. However, some degree of segre-gation managed to exist due to particular economic factors. Building on Murdo J. MacLeod (1973), Christopher H. Lutz and W. George Lovell (1990) found that highland and lowland areas lying south and east of Antigua Guatemala formed a developed core area, while those lying north and west of it formed an underdeveloped periphery. The core area was richer in resources and more conducive to cash crops than the pe-ripheral area, making it particularly attractive to Spaniards who would come to reside in such areas. Core areas became primarily inhabited by *ladinos*, while peripheral areas only ever saw a Spanish minority. In fact, most Indians in peripheral areas only dealt with Spaniards indirectly through the provision of tribute. Thus, the areas of the periphery may have approximated what the Spanish had in mind in terms of a *república de indios*. Core areas, on the other hand, were more vulnerable to cul-tural transformation.

Of course, attempts to maintain boundaries between Indians and non-Indians were not limited to royal officials. For instance, there were reports of Indians in Central Mexico who supposedly refused to allow *gente de razón* ("people of reason") to reside in their towns (Taylor 1979, 26; Haskett 1991, 17). Among the Tlaxcalans of San Esteban de Nueva

Tlaxcala, marriage to an outsider or racially impure individual represented a threat to ethnic purity (Offutt 1997). Likewise, in an 1802 Guatemalan incest case, the *alcalde mayor* (head magistrate) of Escuintla casually mentioned "the little union that Indians and *ladinos* keep with one another"[6] (Case 31).

Aversion to ethnic and racial outsiders is further alluded to in an 1807 incest case involving a cart driver named Bernardo Quachita[7] and two sisters—María Germana and María de los Ángeles Sánchez—all Indians from Ciudad Vieja (Case 54). As will be discussed further in Chapter 3, when a particular individual had sexual relations with two blood relatives, the various parties became implicated in the crime of incest. María Germana was Bernardo's fiancée, and he was allegedly responsible for impregnating both her and María de los Ángeles. During the trial, defense counsel argued that Bernardo only claimed responsibility for María de los Ángeles's pregnancy out of concern for her honor and reputation. The man who actually impregnated María de los Ángeles was *ladino*, and some townspeople viewed "the woman who copulates with someone outside of her *casta* [i.e. socioracial classification] as the most 'lost' and despicable woman."[8] This apparent cover-up, which was intended to benefit the accused persons in this case, also calls attention to how attempts to maintain racial boundaries could actually encourage incestuous crime to the extent that sexual partners needed to be chosen from a smaller pool of candidates.

Narratives of Difference and Marriage between Kin

Narratives of difference based on race, class, or otherwise could make the quest for suitable marriage partners difficult and require negotiations with civil and ecclesiastical authorities charged with enforcing incest laws. Focusing on the Archdiocese of Mexico in the late colonial period, Nora E. Jaffary (2007) noted a tendency for Spaniards (predominantly *criollos*, or Spaniards born in the Americas) to request episcopal dispensations to marry consanguineous relatives who they would otherwise be unable to marry because of incest prohibitions. The most common argument for such requests was *exigüedad del lugar* ("smallness of the place"). That is, their towns were too small for them to find a spouse of "equal quality," especially in terms of *sangre limpia* ("clean blood"), beyond a particular relative. Jaffary mentioned that Indian couples might also use the "smallness of the place" argument to request similar dispensations. Individuals seeking dispensations due to a shortage of eligible partners were also noted for colonial Medellín (see Rodríguez Jiménez 1988).

Similar themes surfaced in colonial Guatemalan records. In 1796 Nueva Guatemala, the Spaniards doña Margarita Portillo and don Vicente Portillo, the former's uncle, requested permission from the secular courts to marry (AGCA A1.48 Leg. 2759 Exp. 23893). This was in line with a royal order from 1779 requiring that officials of the Treasury seek royal permission to contract marriage (see Rípodas Ardanaz 1977, 351). In order to marry, doña Margarita's "good *calidad*, customs, and circumstances" needed to be proven. She intended to show that her parents acknowledged her as a *hija natural* ("natural daughter") and *hija tenida en tiempo hábil* ("daughter begotten at an able time"). These descriptors meant that one or both of her parents acknowledged her (in this case both), there were no impediments to her parents having married (i.e. kinship, adultery, or religious vocation), and she would have been legitimized had they actually executed the marriage (see Twinam 1999, 2007).[9] Further, she hoped to demonstrate that she was of their same *calidad*—"Spanish, free of all bad race." Following verbal and written evidence (including a baptismal record), permission for the marriage was eventually granted.

Of course, not all couples who requested permission to marry achieved their goal. One bishop even refused to grant a dispensation to a pair of close blood relatives in Venezuela because he did not want to encourage sinful behavior between kin (see Waldron 1989, 159). On the other hand, as noted by Leticia González S. and Ann Jefferson (1995, 101) for nineteenth-century Guatemala, fear that couples would continue in their illicit relationship regardless of a dispensation could have pushed hesitant church authorities to concede to them.

In sum, while colonial policies advocated for a two-republic system in which Indians and non-Indians maintained a degree of separation from one another, everyday economic and social realities complicated its realization. Further, efforts to regulate interpersonal relationships along the lines of race or other status differences had the effect of encouraging relationships between relatives that would be deemed incestuous if they did not result in a church sanctioned marriage.

Honor, Patriarchy, and Incest

Another essential component of social experience in colonial Spanish America related to the culture of honor, a system with roots in Iberia that was transferred to the Americas during colonization. In the Iberian world, honor conveyed notions of both status and virtue. In Spain and some of its colonies, the two words, *honor* and *honra*, were used to distinguish these meanings. *Honor* (or honor-status) was perceived as a relatively static condition stemming from the conditions of one's birth with elites having the most honor-status. In contrast to honor-status, *honra* (or honor-virtue) related to an individual's or family's conduct and, thereby, could be gained or lost (Johnson and Lipsett-Rivera 1998a, 2–4). Catherine Komisaruk (2013, 223) found that *honor* was occasionally used in reference to the honor-virtue of plebeians in late colonial

Guatemala. Guatemalan incest cases similarly demonstrate a degree of ambiguity in the use of these terms (e.g. Case 22, Case 39, Case 45). In an honor culture, an individual's worth and social standing is largely reputational, making honor something to be asserted and defended. Still, should one's honor become compromised, there were often ways to remedy it (Johnson and Lipsett-Rivera 1998a, 6–8).

The way in which honor was defined was gender-dependent. For example, whereas courage, authority, and virility constituted aspects of male honor, female honor was generally based upon modesty and sexual restraint. As the heads of their households, men were expected to control and defend their wives and dependents, and they had the right to punish household members who fell out of line. Real or imagined immorality on the part of female dependents, particularly with regard to sexual behavior, damaged not only a woman's reputation but also that of an individual man or family. Likewise, sexual assaults on women could be largely motivated by a desire to damage the honor of a male kinsman. Thus, men generally demanded sexual fidelity from wives or lovers and sexual chastity from daughters under their care, and they were expected to protect the women in their lives from insult or injury, seeking retribution if necessary. Any failure to assert their claims over female dependents would leave behind a stain of emasculation.[10]

For scholars of Western cultures, the image of a patriarchal family and a sexual double-standard is a familiar one. With the colonization of the Americas, indigenous peoples grappled with Hispanic gender codes in various ways. The degree to which indigenous women's status was negatively impacted by them has been the subject of some debate and certainly would have varied due to factors like class and ethnicity. Some scholars have found it useful to think in terms of gender complementarity or gender parallelism to accommodate the value attributed to women's roles in pre-Hispanic and colonial Mesoamerican gender systems. However, they are careful to point out that these concepts should not be mistaken for romanticized views of gender equality. In fact, hierarchical relations often operated alongside complementary ones. For instance, there is evidence of a general bias towards male leadership at the highest levels of society and even at the level of the household, though there were clearly exceptions. In terms of sexuality, some sources suggest that pre-Hispanic women were more circumscribed than men, but the strong association between female sexual purity and honor, exemplified by the figure of the Virgin Mary, seems to have been a largely European introduction. It appears that adultery was widely condemned among Mesoamerican groups and often punishable by death. However, whereas in the Spanish system, a man was more dishonored by his wife's infidelity than the reverse, it is apparent that the shame of infidelity was less gendered in some areas.[11] Thus, Hispanic and Mesoamerican gender ideals would have found some common ground in terms of male authority and rules governing sexual behavior, though the degree of their convergence would have varied by time and place.

The aspects of honor described above resonated with gendered relationships within marriage in late colonial Guatemala. In her study of the Guatemalan capital, Komisaruk (2013, 197) discussed idealized spousal norms found in court litigation. Expectations dictated that husbands were to provide for their families financially, demonstrate kindness and fidelity to their wives, and avoid drinking and gambling to excess. For their part, wives were to obey their husbands, put the needs of their husbands and children before their own, maintain sexual fidelity and modesty in public, and provide domestic services such a food preparation and laundry. These ideals theoretically gave men the right to punish their wives if they failed to fulfill them. Significantly, Komisaruk (2013, 224) found that honor in terms of female virginity and reclusion was not essential to courtship and marriage in the Guatemalan capital, especially among non-elites. Indeed, reclusion was unrealistic for women working in the city.

With its emphasis on patriarchal authority and control over female sexuality, the culture of honor naturally contributed to an environment in which women and girls were at risk of sexual and incestuous violence. In the Guatemalan case sample, incestuous crime was associated with a suggestion of force or intimidation on the part of the male approximately 27 percent of the time.[12] Father-types—fathers, stepfathers, and fathers-in-law—were responsible for 65 percent of incidents of incestuous rape (17 of 26 records) (see Table 2.1).[13] This is consistent with findings for other regions. For example, Lee M. Penyak's (2016, 165, Table 11) data for Central Mexico showed that fathers and stepfathers were to blame for 11 out of 16 cases of incestuous rape, or 69 percent. Carmen Castañeda's (1989, 100) sample of 31 cases of *violación* (sexual acts generally characterized by force or a lack of consent) from Nueva Galicia included 22 committed by relatives. Of these, fathers accounted for 8 cases, stepfathers for 6, and fathers-in-law for 1, or roughly 68 percent. Similarly, Eugenia Rodríguez Sáenz's (2005, 11, Table 3) data showed that fathers and stepfathers were responsible for 6 out of 9 sexual assaults committed by relatives in Costa Rica, or 67 percent. Thus, father-types regularly accounted for around two-thirds of incestuous rape in both the Mexican and Central American regions. Such percentages demonstrate the ability of father-types in particular to abuse their authority in an atmosphere that otherwise legitimated it and to impose their own incest codes on female kin.

While incest was among the grave crimes that theoretically nullified a father's rights over his children (see Premo 2005, 26), Guatemalan incest cases do not offer much information on this particular issue. There were occasions in which fathers and daughters were separated from one another (e.g. Case 66, Case 69). But perhaps the most explicit discussion of

Table 2.1 Incest and Sexual Violence

Case Number	Relationship	Approximate Age Difference
5	father/daughter	n/a
15	father/daughter	24 years
28	father/daughter	19 years
37	father/daughter	45–47 years
55	father/daughter	16–21 years
65b	father/daughter	22–24 years
66	father/daughter	13 years
10	stepfather/stepdaughter	25 years
19	stepfather/stepdaughter	26 years
49	stepfather/stepdaughter	n/a
58	stepfather/stepdaughter	21 years
63	stepfather/stepdaughter	25 years
64	stepfather/stepdaughter	n/a
2	father-in-law/daughter-in-law	37 years
2	father-in-law/daughter-in-law	40 years
61	father-in-law/daughter-in-law	21–22 years
65a	(future) father-in-law/daughter-in-law	25–26 years
9	political uncle/political niece	10–11 years
18	political uncle/political niece	3–4 years
64	political uncle/political niece	17 years
21	brother-in-law/sister-in-law	13 years
26	brother-in-law/sister-in-law	5–6 years
53	man/daughter of mother-daughter pair	37 years
45	man/sister 2 of 2	1–2 years
22	political first cousins	≤12 years
38	stepmother/stepson	6–8 years (stepmother is senior)

The term "political" indicates a relationship through marriage.

encroaching on a father's rights by removing a child from the household comes from a section of Case 37 that was incomplete, crossed out, and ultimately made void. In response to the suggested sentence of the *asesor* (legal advisor), which included the temporary removal of Francisca de León from her father's house, the *fiscal* (crown attorney) expressed hesitation about the actuality of the crime given the state of the evidence. He then began to express his apparent disapproval of depriving a father of "the prime gifts and services of his children that are owed him by nature."[14] Thus, it's possible that ideas about a father's rights factored into such separations. However, separation of illicit sexual partners was common practice in the colonial period regardless of whether incest was involved. (Typical penalties for incestuous crime will be discussed further in the following chapter.)

The generational differences within incestuous rape were reflected in the age discrepancies between the males and females involved. The median age difference between men and women was 21 years (with men senior) when age difference could be determined. This compares with a six-year median age difference (with men senior) for cases in which force was not apparent. The only incident of incestuous violence in which a woman was older than her rapist was in Case 38, which involved a stepmother and stepson. This compares with six cases in which women were senior to their male partner in apparently consensual unions.[15] Penyak (2016, 176) found a similar age range in his incestuous rape cases from Mexico. While rapists averaged 34.8 years in age, rape victims averaged 13.4 years of age, making for a gap of 21.4 years between them. For consensual unions, Penyak found only a four-year average age difference (with men senior). Thus, larger age discrepancies in favor of men were also conducive to incestuous violence.

Of course, it would be a mistake to think women always stood idly by during such excesses. As Stern (1995) noted for colonial Mexico, female kin and lovers created a world of "contested patriarchal pacts" in which the everyday operational meanings of patriarchal first principles were challenged. Various weapons were available to women for dealing with problems with the men in their lives. Some women used what Stern termed a "pluralization-of-patriarchs" strategy. This tactic essentially established rivalries and hierarchies between men with respective claims on the fate and well-being of a particular woman or girl to check the power of the most immediate patriarch. For example, a woman might seek help from her parental family to deal with her husband's family or alert local authorities who functioned as "superior patriarchs." Another strategy available to women was the "mobilization-of-female-alliances"—that is, going to female kin, friends, and neighbors for discussion of and intervention in troubles with men.[16] But Stern is careful to point out that female allies did not share the same institutional and cultural legitimacy as mobilized patriarchs (Stern 1995, 97, 100–6, 299).

These types of strategies surfaced in colonial Guatemalan incest cases as well. The 1749 incest case against Narciso Gonzales, a *mulato libre* ("free *mulato*") farmer living in Mixco, is demonstrative of the ways in which the coexistence of multiple patriarchs could benefit women in their dealings with violent male kin while simultaneously increasing their risk of (sexual) violence due to male-male competition (Case 5). On April 26, 1749, Gregoria Antonia Gonzales appeared before a local magistrate and denounced her father for violently taking her virginity and for repeated sexual acts with her over the course of three years.[17] She recounted how the acts were ongoing until Teodoro Ramírez and Josef Mansilla requested her marriage to Nicolás Ramírez, brother of Teodoro. The proposal was accepted under the condition that Gregoria (and Nicolás) would continue to reside with Narciso.

Sure enough, Narciso continued to have sexual relations with Gregoria after her marriage to Nicolás. Gregoria maintained that Narciso quarreled with her husband out of jealousy, even though he used the pretext that Nicolás had left Narciso's wife, Petrona Quintanilla, unaccompanied in Quetzaltenango. The quarreling lasted day in and day out, with Narciso swearing to kill Nicolás and his brother, and the fights continued even after the return of Petrona. Eventually, Teodoro and Nicolás approached the *provisor* (an ecclesiastical official)[18] to request Gregoria's placement in Teodoro's power, which was granted, and Narciso continued with his threats and affronts to the Ramírez brothers. The placement of Gregoria under the authority of Teodoro (as opposed to Nicolás) clarifies that Teodoro was functioning as the head patriarch within the Ramírez family.

One day, Narciso sent for Gregoria because he needed her to record some things for him, not knowing how to write himself. Accompanied by various youths from both Narciso's farm and Teodoro's home, Gregoria went by horse in that direction, but Narciso intercepted them. Succeeding in separating his daughter from the others, he eventually made her get off her own horse, transfer to his, and "sit like a man" in front of him as they rode off together. Once they stopped and dismounted, Narciso proceeded to undress her. He tied her hands to her feet and whipped her from the waist down, placing his foot on her face so she could not scream and acting jealous of various individuals with whom she was unfamiliar including an Indian farmhand named Juan. He then untied her and had a sexual act with her. He again wanted to know whether she had engaged in sexual relations with another man, which she denied, and he subsequently tied her up and whipped her some more. After seeing the lashes Narciso had given Gregoria, Petrona returned her to Teodoro. Gregoria ended her account by telling the magistrate that she came forward because of "fear, shame, and dread," her knowledge of the sin her father committed, and concern over the detrimental effects of her husband's return and discovery of the lash marks.

The proceedings also revealed that Narciso had severely lashed the aforementioned farmhand named Juan and delivered him bound to Teodoro. Asked regarding the motivation, Teodoro said that when Narciso brought Juan to him he told him that Juan was responsible for the loss of Gregoria's virginity and not him as had been rumored. Narciso proceeded to untie Juan and instructed Teodoro's brother and wife to kiss his feet (presumably as a sign of gratitude for delivery of the offending culprit).

With regard to Gregoria's return following the whipping by her father, Teodoro reported that Petrona told him that Narciso punished his daughter because he was upset that she was no longer under his authority, but that he had done so in her presence and only gave her six lashes over her clothes. In her own testimony, Petrona said that she told Teodoro the lashes were given in her presence so that Gregoria's husband would not be offended. Thus, Narciso acting alone in the punishment of his daughter would have contravened a right owed to a woman's husband. Even though the case was ultimately inconclusive since Narciso was never obtained, it highlights the ways in which a patriarchal family structure and struggles over authority and sexual possession could result in (sexual) violence against female kin. But we should also not forget Juan, whose alleged relationship with Gregoria had resulted in his own severe beating.

Cuckolded Men and Female Kin

Preoccupations with sexual possession were apparently at the root of two cases of father-daughter incest that followed episodes of marital infidelity. One of these cases involved Marcos de la Cruz Maquín (or Maquís), an Indian farmer living in Canales, who was tried for incest with his approximately twelve-year-old daughter Aquilina in 1807 (Case 55). The news of his sexual relations with Aquilina came from his wife and Aquilina's mother, Catalina Samayoa. When the magistrate asked Aquilina about her mother's statement (which is missing from the case file), she confirmed its accuracy regarding the night in question, as her father had come to her bed and done with her what he had done before. Following Aquilina's account (which is incomplete due to document damage), it appears her father may not have succeeded in consummating a sexual act with her on that particular night. However, her father did have numerous sexual encounters with her in the past, which had caused her pain, though her discomfort did not ever seem to deter him. She had not wanted to tell her mother about the situation because he had told her, "If you say something, you will make things worse for me, as they will put me in prison and you in the Casa Nueva [women's detention center]."[19] Thus, Marcos was able to guilt and scare Aquilina into silence.

In response to the magistrate's inquiry into her sexual history, Aquilina stated that her father was the first man with whom she had been sexually involved. However, after news got out about her father following his arrest, her uncle León solicited her and had sex with her three or four times, which also caused her pain. The fact that her uncle only approached her after learning that her father had been successful with his own advances shows how incestuous offenders could embolden others. Perhaps Marcos's absence provided further encouragement, since women without male kin around, even if only for a short period, were often regarded as ownerless property that a man was free to stake his claim on (Socolow 2015, 163).

After some delay, Marcos was taken from the prison where he was being held to testify. As was custom, he was asked the cause of his arrest. He stated that he did not know the reason, but had heard it was at the request of his wife Catalina. Questioned about the whereabouts of Aquilina, he said her mother had placed her in the house of the *comisionado* (or *comisario*, a royal official),[20] Juan Lorenzo Ferrera, as a domestic servant. Asked to explain why Catalina sent Aquilina to serve there, he began by telling the magistrate that this occurred around the time that he had learned that Catalina was involved with various other men. He had admonished her for it, though he apparently did so without getting ugly or violent towards her. It was in those days that Catalina accused him of getting up one night to seduce Aquilina. However, Marcos claimed he had only been at her bed because he was feverish (in the emotional sense). Later asked whether he customarily slept apart from his wife whenever they fought, Marcos answered in the affirmative and said that it was on one of those nights when she thought he was seducing Aquilina and sent her to sleep elsewhere. Upset by Catalina's misconception, he scolded and threatened her, yet did not get up. Hence, upon questioning, Marcos immediately positioned Catalina as the wrongdoer and himself as an intolerant yet merciful husband. He then explained away his presence in his daughter's bed and made himself the victim of an unfaithful spouse's ill judgment. In other words, Marcos was upholding patriarchal ideals while his wife and accuser was of suspect character and judgment.

One of the men Catalina was reportedly involved with was the *comisionado* of Las Tunas named Matías Roldán. According to Matías, Catalina came to him one night claiming that her husband wanted to kill her. Asking her why, she said that it was because Marcos had *su tropezón* ("his stumble") with their daughter Aquilina. Despite having Aquilina in her bed, Marcos got up to seduce her, and a fight began after Catalina rebuked him for it. Matías inquired with Aquilina, and she confirmed that her father had been involved with her in the past. Accordingly, Matías went to arrest Marcos for the alleged incest. In response to his admonishments, Marcos told him that

> he had sinned with his daughter because his wife gave him cause for regret, as he knew that she had illicit commerce with [him], with José and Manuel de Pinula, and others he does not remember, and that he could prove it.[21]

Matías stated that these were false justifications on Marcos's part. But such excuses, regardless of whether they were false, provide insight into what might justify incest in the minds of particular men—a wife's sexual infidelity. Matías arrested Marcos, though he managed to escape his custody, and left Catalina and the children in the house of Comisionado Ferrera.

In later testimony, Marcos continued to deny the incest with his daughter. He admitted that he told Matías he sinned with his daughter because of his wife's behavior. However, "it was not because he had actually committed such sin but rather because he was *apasionado* ('impassioned') by what they had told him about the *ilícita amistad* of the *comisario* and his wife."[22] Hence, even in the absence of a confession, Marcos's statements still indicate that some men viewed marital infidelity as justification for (forced) sexual relations with a daughter. Such claims may have also been a way to save face to some degree, considering the man on the receiving end of Marcos's assertion was not only a law enforcement official but also one of Catalina's alleged lovers.

Marcos maintained his innocence throughout the proceedings, and like Marcos, his legal representative (don Juan Josef del Castillo) portrayed Catalina as the real offender. He deduced that she wanted to clear her own name by accusing Marcos of "the most horrendous crime, and, in order to substantiate it, asked her daughter to damage the honor of her father, which is as far as malice can go."[23] Beyond this, Aquilina was never examined by midwives for evidence of the crime. The *procurador de pobres* (attorney assigned to aid the poor) also discredited Catalina's accusation, viewing her sex, *calidad* (Indian), relationship to Marcos, and suspicion regarding her extramarital affair as all marks against her. In the end, and after multiple delays in the proceedings, Marcos was sentenced to one hundred lashes and two years of public works in addition to the "habilitation" of his marriage. Aquilina did not incur any penalty, and it appears that her uncle was never tried for incest.

Similar themes surfaced in the 1815 case against José Silverio Ampérez, a forty-year-old Indian man and sugar miller residing near Chol (Case 65b). He was accused of incest with his daughter María Leandra, who was around seventeen years old at the time. Following Leandra's trial statements, José had taken her virginity four years beforehand in his banana grove. Even though she did not realize the act was morally wrong at the time, she protested, and he hit her with a switch three times for her resistance. The sexual acts continued for some time until she realized that it was wrong and fled to tell the priest of Chol what was going on. Once the two confessed, the priest had her taken from the side of her father and placed in *depósito* (temporary custody) for about a year. Shortly after she returned home from Chol, José began to repeat the sexual acts with her, which occurred about every eight-to-fifteen days over the course of a five-to-six-month period. Leandra informed her mother, María Manuela López, who indicated that they would inform the priest of the issue the next time they were in Chol. Manuela tried to prevent Leandra from being alone with José, but these efforts were unsuccessful since she was afraid of him. Eventually, Leandra and her mother reported what was happening to the priest in Chol "behind her father's back because of the fear [her] mother has of him because he is a very vicious man and would hit her for it."[24]

That these incidents came to light is impressive considering that José, like many other incestuous rapists, tried to keep Leandra silent about them over the course of their sexual encounters. Leandra related how he had instructed her to swear that nothing had happened between them if her priest were to ask, and to identify Manuel Cornel as the man responsible for her loss of virginity instead of him. Even after their involvement came to light and their priest told them to discontinue their sexual activity, José continued to pursue her. And she ultimately gave in to the petitions of her father, who was telling her God would forgive it all.

In contrast to Marcos in Case 55, José did not deny the incest with his daughter. When questioned about the cause of his arrest, he identified Leandra. Asked to elaborate, he said that "in revenge for Manuel Cornel's involvement with [Leandra] and then with [his] wife, María Manuela López, he had sexual relations with his daughter María Leandra, and, because of this, the justice [don Antonio Córdoba] imprisoned him."[25] In other words, José had sex with his own daughter to get back at Manuel for having had sex with both her and his wife. In defense of his actions, José stated that he did not understand the gravity of the crime despite the admonishments by his priest, blaming the devil for deceiving him and his daughter for returning home instead of taking any responsibility himself. Further, while Jose's rendition of events was consistent with his daughter's in various ways, unlike Leandra, he maintained that sex between them had been consensual and that she was not a virgin at the time because of her previous sexual activities with Manuel Cornel.

Vengeance also surfaced in the testimony of Manuel Cornel. Asked about José's testimony, he said that "having been accused by José that [he] had *ilícita amistad* with his daughter, María Leandra Ampérez, when this was not actually the case, he got angry and did it for real."[26] That is, he began a sexual relationship with Leandra because he was irritated by José's false accusation regarding the matter. Having discovered that she was not a virgin during their first encounter, he asked her who had taken her virginity, but she refused to tell him, saying he was the only man with whom she had been sexually involved. He contended that his relationship with Leandra was also spurred by events that transpired two years prior—Manuel had caught José having sexual relations with his wife, María Juliana Tobar, on two occasions, and she had confessed to them, telling him that they were against her will. Then,

> in revenge for what [José] Ampérez did with his wife, he was set on pursuing Ampérez's wife [Manuela]. As he could not achieve his goal and [his] wife [Juliana] learned about it, remembering what Ampérez had done with her, [Juliana] tried to persuade his wife to sin with [him]. She ultimately succeeded, and through her he was illicitly involved with María Manuela López ... about eight times.[27]

Hence, Manuel used sexual relations with two of José's kin—his daughter and his wife—to punish José for his sexual engagement with his own wife, never going after José himself. This contrasted with José, who evidently beat Manuel with a switch (in addition to having sex with his own daughter). What Manuel neglected to realize was that sex with a mother and her daughter constituted incest. He said he understood that sex with another man's wife was wrong, but he did not know whether it was more serious to do so when one was married or to have sex with a daughter and then with her mother.

In contrast to Leandra, Manuela testified that her daughter was never more specific than telling her that she no longer wanted to be at the side of her father (a fact Leandra attributed to her mother's fear of her father). She also identified Manuel as the author of Leandra's deflowerment. Asked about the timing of her own involvement with Manuel, Manuela said that a year after Manuel's relationship with Leandra, his wife began to solicit her for him. Juliana's petitions were so numerous that she finally agreed, and she was in *mala amistad* ("bad friendship") with Manuel for more than two years. Juliana helped them the entire time, once even keeping watch for José when Manuel was inside with Manuela. Manuela claimed to be unaware of José's involvement with Juliana when she started to see Manuel. However, it is apparent from the case that she knew her daughter had already been involved with Manuel, which made her party to incest. Ultimately, in response to the charges against her, she claimed that she was unaware of the gravity of her crimes, repented for them, and would not commit them again.

For her part, Juliana reported that she was unaware of any involvement between Manuel and Leandra (though this contradicted other testimony). However, she was aware of the relationship between Manuel and Manuela because she had facilitated it, being "irritated that [José] Ampérez, having been involved with [her], told her husband about it, with whom, because of this, and because of having caught her in the act with Ampérez, she had difficulties."[28] That is, Juliana had her own reasons for cultivating a sexual union between her husband and Manuela— she wanted to hurt José too. In later testimony, Juliana elaborated on her motivations to act as a mediator for the pair. She said that after her husband had caught her with José,

> he wanted to kill him, because of which, her husband gave her *mala vida* [i.e. some form of mistreatment or neglect]. Because he would calm down, and to get revenge, she committed this crime, not being aware of its gravity....[29]

In other words, Manuel was taking his frustrations out on his wife in lieu of confronting José directly. And, in order to alleviate the situation she found herself in, and to exact her own revenge on José, Juliana helped organize the liaison between Manuela and her husband. Thus, both Juliana and her husband used José's kin to avenge themselves. Notably, Juliana's stated ignorance regarding Manuel and Leandra's involvement would have freed her from being complicit to incest. Unfortunately, the only penalty information available for this case is with regard to Juliana, who was released. The others escaped from their respective detentions prior to sentencing.

The displacement in time and space of these cases suggests that Marcos and José were not alone in using marital infidelity to justify (forcible) sexual relations with a daughter. Why would this have been the case? Wounded manhood seems to be the easiest explanation. In her study of women and crime in Buenos Aires, Susan Socolow (1980, 44) noted how lower-class men might take out their frustrations with their social and economic roles on their wives, who occupied a subordinate position in relation to them. Perhaps daughters played a similar role, finding themselves on the receiving end of misdirected masculine fervor motivated by a challenge to a man's sexual monopoly on his wife. In a world where a wife was apparently out of one's control, daughters—disadvantaged not only by gender but also by generation—would make an easy target in a man's attempt to reassert his authority over his sexual property. That is, failure to fully possess one female dependent left another (more subordinate) one susceptible to sexual violence. In Case 65b, there was the additional circumstance of Leandra's involvement with the man who cuckolded her father, which would have made her a typical target in male sexual rivalries had she not been José's own daughter.

Blaming a wife's infidelity for incest may have also been strategic from a legal standpoint. A woman's misconduct could excuse harsh physical punishment, and even murder, at the hands of a spouse (see Terraciano 1998, 726; Socolow 2015, 71, 160, 165). Though the victims in the cases of Marcos and José were their daughters—not the offending spouses themselves—the use of a wife's infidelity to justify a man's (violent) behavior was certainly not without precedent.

There is also the question of the degree to which Marcos and José might have intended to injure their wives through sexual relations with their daughters. We know from modern studies related to father-daughter incest that men will sometimes flaunt a special relationship with a particular daughter to avenge themselves for perceived wrongs on the part of their wife and to keep their wives competing for their attention (Herman 2000, 115). There is no shortage of reports of female jealousy in the colonial record, and there are accounts of wives who were jealous of the affection their husbands had for a daughter.[30] Regardless of whether wives were key targets in these particular episodes, the idea that a man could justify such occasions with female adultery would surely impact women's lives and the mother-daughter bond. For instance, would women in marital or quasi-marital relationships feel more restricted in their sexual lives knowing a daughter could be subjected to incestuous violence upon discovery of their infidelity? And would daughters have an interest in the sexual lives of their mothers knowing how their fathers might react to an unfaithful partner? These are questions to which the documents do not yet yield answers.

As we saw in the case of Manuel Cornel, male sexual rivalries could also lead to three-party incest when vengeful sexual relations were not restricted to one female member of a rival's kin. This problem would have been exacerbated by any degree of shame that might accompany going to court for sexual offenses involving female relatives in lieu of personal retribution.[31] Thus, the same culture that equated honor with sexual dominance and cuckoldry with injured manhood also created social worlds in which formal incest codes were bound to be broken in one way or another. Women performed various roles in these scenarios, taking part as willing (though perhaps ignorant) participants in incestuous sexual relations, facilitators for such relations, or victims of incestuous violence. There is one final irony in the cases above—in trying to live up to a code of honor in many ways consistent with Hispanic traditions, Marcos, José, and Manuel (all of whom were Indian actors) would have ultimately reinforced colonial discourse linking incest and Indianness, which will be discussed in Chapter 6.

Alternatives to Living with Predatory Relatives

From the above, it is easy to see how many cases of incest would have never come to the attention of authorities. Predatory men often tried to scare their victims into silence, and the latter had reason to fear other kin in the household besides their rapists. For example, when Claudia Hernández learned that her husband lay down with her mute daughter while she was away, she came home and lashed the girl, who signed to her that she was not at fault because her stepfather had locked himself in with her (Case 64). Likewise, when a young girl named Ciriaca (no surname) was asked why she did not immediately tell her mother that her uncle raped her during her absence, she said "out of fear of how much she dreaded she would punish her"[32] (Case 9). Indeed, women were often blamed for their own rape, and parents were within their rights to carry out correctional measures. Further, Ciriaca's mother feared for her own safety. After she reported the crime to the authorities, she reportedly begged that her husband not find out about what happened because he would blame her for it and want to kill her. Unfortunately, Ciriaca's mother was not alone—many women had good reason to fear their husbands. In Case 2, for instance, Isabel Matul, an Indian woman from San Francisco el Alto who likely spoke K'iche',[33] stated through interpreters that her mother-in-law came to her one day tearful and asked, "If your father-in-law wanted to whip me, would you defend me?"[34] Asking her the reason, her mother-in-law said she had caught him and another daughter-in-law in *el pecado* ("the sin").[35] Circumstances such as these, not to mention any economic considerations, gave many women and girls little option but to remain in a dangerous situation.

In 1810 San Martín Cuchumatán, one woman felt so desperate after a misunderstanding about her father-in-law's intentions with her that she attempted to take her own life (AGCA A1.15 Leg. 3029 Exp. 29293). Following court records, Matea Escalante became intoxicated one evening with her father- and brother-in-law—Manuel and Pablo Paz. Via an interpreter, Manuel (presumably a speaker of Mam) stated that he returned to see how Matea was doing the following morning. When no one answered his calls at the door, he entered the house, awaking Matea in the process. She told those present to get a light and identify who had entered. Hearing this, Manuel said, "It's me, Child, I only came to see how you were this morning,"[36] and was bringing her some alcohol. However, Matea, who was drunk, "still wanted to set the house on fire, blabbering nonsense."[37]

Matea (also through an interpreter) described similar events. She reported how she had ordered her servants to grab a light and determine the identity of the individual who had come in. Following her cries, she heard her father-in-law identify himself and explain how he slept there because he had gotten drunk. Disturbed by this,

> thinking ill of her father-in-law and hopeless, among the other foolish things that she would do, as she was out of her senses, she took a machete from the field and cut her throat with the intent of killing herself.[38]

Ultimately, Matea admitted she had acted stupidly in injuring herself and that she was wrong about her father-in-law's intentions.

Matea's misconception of Manuel was corroborated by the (translated) testimony of María Rosaria, one of Matea's servants. She stated that Matea had only thought her father-in-law said he slept at her house with ill intent. In fact, "he spoke to her with love, telling her that it was him, that he had come to see how she was that morning."[39] After finding Matea with her throat cut, she and another servant named Tomasa tried to convince her that she had misjudged her father-in-law and that they would have observed any ill intent on his part. However, Matea was not persuaded until she returned to her senses and reflected upon the situation. While Matea's state of mind was clearly compromised when she decided to take her life, this case does suggest that some women may have viewed suicide as the only means to evade the prerogatives of male kin (or at least any repercussions that might result from them).[40]

Despite difficult circumstances, however, some individuals did report incestuous activities, and authorities regularly required new living arrangements. Further, the degree to which women were subject to patriarchal authority and any dangers it might entail varied. Komisaruk (2013) noted various challenges to normative marriage and patriarchy in late colonial Guatemala. For example, while survival in the countryside was often dependent on male subsistence agriculture complemented by female productive and reproductive roles, in the urban environment and on rural estates, the cash-based economy lessened the need for spouses. Also, female-headed households were not uncommon in Nueva Guatemala, where women constituted the majority of the population (Komisaruk 2013, 117, 241–2). Similarly, Stern (1995, 258) noted that gendered life among plebeians in Mexico City apparently transformed "the strains of contested patriarchal pacts into a crisis of their existence."

Conclusion

Overall, both *calidad* and the culture of honor played major roles in defining social worlds and possibilities in Spanish America. These factors seeped into interpersonal relationships in a variety of ways, contributing to marriages between relatives, incestuous sexual unions, and even sexual violence against female kin. An environment ripe for incestuous unions required measures for its regulation, and it is to law and criminal process that we now turn.

Notes

1 See van Deusen (2015) for a discussion of the breadth of people to whom the term *indio* could refer.
2 Though use of the terms *casta* and *calidad* to refer to this system has been found anachronistic or inappropriate for early Spanish America, they are relevant for the seventeenth and eighteenth centuries (see Schwaller 2016). In late colonial Guatemalan criminal records, when individuals were asked to provide their *calidad*, they responded with a socioracial term, making *calidad* the most appropriate terminology for the study at hand.
3 Information regarding the system of two-republics can be found in Borah (1983), Lutz (1994), and Schwaller (2016). See Hill, II (2002, 124–7) for a discussion of the Indian *cabildo* as a barrier/broker institution and Hill, II (2012) for an analysis of how Indian aristocrats utilized the introduced cabildo to maintain their status.
4 The enslavement of women and children under the age of fourteen was outlawed in 1534 (van Deusen 2015, 8), and women were declared exempt from tribute payments in 1756 (Hill, II and Monaghan 1987, 57). For a history of religious colonialism in Guatemala, see van Oss (1986). Sherman (1979) provides a comprehensive treatment of forced native labor in Central America. Information on the *laborío* and non-Indian tribute can be found in Lokken (2001) and Milton and Vinson, III (2002).
5 It was not until after Independence that Guatemala became conceptually divided between *ladinos* and *indios*, the former being associated with Western values and some degree of Spanish heritage, while the latter was viewed as racially and culturally distinctive (Taracena Arriola 1982, 99–100). This division was characterized by prejudicial notions of Indian inferiority, which has continued to have an impact on race relations in Guatemala to this day (see, for example, Hale 2006).
6 ...*la poca union que guardan entre si Yndios, y Ladinos*... AGCA A1.15 Leg. 5426 Exp. 46305.

7 Bernardo's surname was also spelled Cuachita, Quachito, and Cuachito.

8 ...*la muger q.e se mescla con otro q.e no sea de los de su casta p.r la mas perdida, y despreciable*...f. 14.

9 Notably, in 1803 royal officials determined that subsequent marriage between relatives who had produced incestuous offspring was sufficient to legitimate them (Gacto Fernández 1969, 104 in Twinam 1999, 130).

10 Works that discuss the culture of honor include Socolow (1980), Stern (1995), and the various contributions to Johnson and Lipsett-Rivera (1998b).

11 For discussion of the impact of colonialism on indigenous women's status, see Clendinnen (1982), Kellogg (1995), Restall (1997), and the various contributions to Schroeder et al. (1997). Works that consider social organization and descent reckoning include McCaa (2003) for the Nahua, Restall (1997) for the Yucatec Maya, and Sanchiz Ochoa (1980), Luján Muñoz (1983), and Hill, II (2002, 2012) for the Guatemalan region. Comments on adultery include Sanchiz Ochoa (1980, 190) and Terraciano (1998, 724, 729–30). Burkhart (2001, 92) mentioned that stoning, which many sources claim was the pre-Hispanic punishment for adultery, is found in the Bible as well. She also provided general commentary on the potential problems of using colonial texts to reconstruct pre-Hispanic cultural norms.

12 The relationship between Andrés Victorio and María Anastacia Vásquez was only counted once here, even though they were tried in 1794 and 1797 (Case 17).

13 Relationship types reflect accusations or the type of relationship being scrutinized.

14 ...*los primeros obsequios, y servicios de sus hijos, que le son debidos por naturaleza*... ACGA A1.15 Leg. 5475 Exp. 47050 f. 12v.

15 Cases 11, 29, 33, 45, 48, and 59.

16 Scandal and magic were the other two weapons discussed by Stern (1995, 108–10).

17 The nature of the relationship between Narciso and Gregoria would be contested later in the trial with the claim that Narciso and his wife had raised Gregoria but were not her (biological) parents. This issue will be discussed in Chapter 5.

18 See Schwaller (2011) for a description of the various roles within the ecclesiastical bureaucracy. The provisor was the chief administrative officer of a New World diocese under the bishop. The provisor was often also the vicar-general, the superior ecclesiastical judge of a diocese and chief administrative officer under the bishop (Schwaller 2011, 78, 279).

19 *Si decis algo me ajondás pues me meten en la carcel y á vós en la Casa Nueva.* AGCA A1 Leg. 2959 Exp. 27997 f. 3v.

20 See Schwartzkopf (2013, 740) for a discussion of the evolving role of *comisionados*. In the late colonial period, these individuals lived in largely indigenous communities and were sources of information and surveillance for the *alcalde mayor*.

21 ...*q.e abia pecado con su dha hija por tener que sentir de su muger, pues sabia que tenia ilicito comercio con el declarante, con José y Man.l de Pinula, y otros que no se acuerda; y q.e lo podia acreditar.* AGCA A1 Leg. 2959 Exp. 27997 f. 6v.

22 ...*no fue porq.e hubiera sido verdad q.e habia cometido tal pecado sino apacionado de lo q.e le habian contado de la ilicita amis[tad de]l Comisario y su muger.* f. 9.

23 ...*el mas orrendo crimen y p.a apoyarlo sugerir a la hija a q.e bulnerase el honor de su Padre, que es hasta donde puede llegar la malicia.* f. 15.

24 *...á escondidas de su Padre por el temor q.e le tiene á este la Madre de la Confesante por q.e es muy bravo, y luego la golpea.* AGCA A2.2 Leg. 237 Exp. 5068 f. 24.

25 *...haviendo tenido q.e ver con esta Manuel Cornel, y despues con la muger del q.e declara Maria Manuela Lopes; en venganza se enredó el con la referida su hija María Leandra, y q.e por esto lo puso preso el citado Jues.* f. 6v.

26 *...haviendosele imputado por este q.e el q.e declara tenia ilicita Amistad con Maria Leandra Amperes su hija, no siendo asi, le dio corage, y lo hiso de veras...* f. 8.

27 *...en venganza de lo q.e Amperes hiso con su muger, se empeño en perseguir á la de Amperes, y como no pudó conseguir su intento, y la muger del q.e habla lo trascendio, acordandose de lo q.e havia hecho con ella Amperes, trató de persuader á la muger de este á q.e pecase con el q.e declara, y q.e ultimamente lo consiguio, y por su medio tubo q.e ver ilicitamente con Maria Manuela Lopes...como unas ocho ocasiones.* f. 8v.

28 *...picada de q.e haviendo tenido q.e ver Josef Silverio Amperes con la q.e declara, se lo dijo el mismo á su Marido, con q.n por esto, y por haver la pillado en el acto con Amperes paso trabajos.* f. 14-v.

29 *...quiso aquel matar á este, por cuya causa el referido su marido la daba mala vida: q.e por q.e este se sosegara, y por vengarse cometio este pecado, no estando impuesta en la gravedad...* f. 18v.

30 See, for example, Rojas Flores (2007, 116). See also Case 15, where the defendant attributed the accusation of incest with his daughter to the crazy jealousies of his wife.

31 See Socolow (1980, 46, 51–2), Premo (2005, 125), and Komisaruk (2013, 238).

32 *...que de miedo de lo mucho q temio la avia de castigar.* f. 3v.

33 See Francisco de Solano (1969) for linguistic areas in late colonial Guatemala.

34 *...si tu suegro quisiere asotarme me defendereis...* f. 3v.

35 However, her mother-in-law denied having said this in her own testimony.

36 *Yo soy hija solo vengo á ver como haz am[aneci]do...*

37 *...quiso aun darle fuego á la casa hablando desatinos.*

38 *...juzgando mal de su suegro, y desesperada entre otros desatinos que iba á executar como que estaba fuera de si, tomó un machete del campo, y se hirio con el la garganta con animo de matarse...*

39 *...la habló con amor diciendola que el era que avia ido á ver como avia amanedido...*

40 See Ochoa Sanchiz (1980, 190) regarding reports of indigenous women who ran away to the wilderness to prevent Spaniards from forcing them to commit adultery.

Bibliography

Borah, Woodrow. 1983. *Justice by Insurance: The General Indian Court of Colonial Mexico and the Legal Aides of the Half-Real.* Berkeley, Los Angeles, London: University of California Press.

Burkhart, Louise M. 2001. "Gender in Nahuatl Texts of the Early Colonial Period: Native 'Tradition' and the Dialogue with Christianity." In *Gender in Pre-Hispanic America*, edited by Cecelia F. Klein, 87–107. Washington, DC: Dumbarton Oaks.

Castañeda, Carmen. 1989. *Violación, estupro, y sexualidad: Nueva Galicia, 1790–1821.* Guadalajara: Hexágano.

Clendinnen, Inga. 1982. "Yucatec Maya Women and the Spanish Conquest: Role and Ritual in Historical Reconstruction." *Journal of Social History* 15 (3): 427–42.

Gacto Fernández, Enrique. 1969. *La filiación no legítima en el derecho histórico español*. Seville: Universidad de Sevilla.

González S., Leticia, and Ann Jefferson. 1995. "Sexualidad femenina en el oriente de Guatemala, vista a través de las dispensas matrimoniales, siglo XIX." In *Memoria del Segundo Encuentro Nacional de Historiadores del 4 al 6 del diciembre de 1995*, 91–110. Guatemala: Universidad del Valle de Guatemala.

Hale, Charles R. 2006. *Más Que Un Indio: Racial Ambivalence and Neoliberal Multiculturalism in Guatemala*. Santa Fe: School of American Research Press.

Haskett, Robert. 1991. *Indigenous Rulers: An Ethnohistory of Town Government in Colonial Cuernavaca*. Albuquerque: University of New Mexico Press.

Herman, Judith Lewis. 2000. *Father-Daughter Incest*. Cambridge and London: Harvard University Press.

Herrera, Robinson A. 2003. *Natives, Europeans, and Africans in Sixteenth-Century Santiago de Guatemala*. Austin: University of Texas Press.

———. 2007. "Concubines and Wives: Re-Interpreting Native-Spanish Intimate Unions in Sixteenth-Century Guatemala." In *Indian Conquistadors: Indigenous Allies in the Conquest of Mesoamerica*, edited by Michel Oudijk and Laura Matthew, 127–44. Norman: University of Oklahoma Press.

Hill, II, Robert M. 2002. *Colonial Cakchiquels: Highland Maya Adaptation to Spanish Rule, 1600–1700*. Belmont, CA: Thomson Wadsworth.

———. 2012. "Three Families: Genealogies and Processes among the Sixteenth-Century Kaqchikel Maya." *Ethnohistory* 59 (3): 469–596.

Hill, II, Robert M., and John Monaghan. 1987. *Continuities in Highland Maya Social Organization: Ethnohistory in Sacapulas, Guatemala*. Philadelphia: University of Pennsylvania Press.

Jaffary, Nora E. 2007. "Incest, Sexual Virtue, and Mobility in Late Colonial Mexico." In *Gender, Race, and Religion in the Colonization of the Americas*, edited by Nora E. Jaffary, 95–107. Hampshire: Ashgate.

Johnson, Lyman L., and Sonya Lipsett-Rivera. 1998a. "Introduction." In *The Faces of Honor: Sex, Shame, and Violence in Colonial Latin America*, edited by Lyman L. Johnson and Sonya Lipsett-Rivera, 1–17. Albuquerque: University of New Mexico Press.

———, eds. 1998b. *The Faces of Honor: Sex, Shame, and Violence in Colonial Latin America*. Albuquerque: University of New Mexico Press.

Kellogg, Susan. 1995. *Law and the Transformation of Aztec Culture, 1500–1700*. Norman: University of Oklahoma Press.

Komisaruk, Catherine. 2013. *Labor and Love in Guatemala: The Eve of Independence*. Stanford, CA: Stanford University Press.

Kuznesof, Elizabeth A. 1995. "Ethnic and Gender Influences on 'Spanish' Creole Society in Colonial Spanish America." *Colonial Latin American Historical Review* 4 (1): 153–76.

Lokken, Paul. 2001. "Marriage as Slave Emancipation in 17th Century Guatemala." *The Americas* 58 (2): 175–200.

Luján Muñoz, Jorge. 1976. "Fundaciones de villas de ladinos en Guatemala en el último tercio del siglo XVIII." *Revista de Indias* 36 (145–146): 51–81.

————. 1983. "Changes in the Family Structure of the Pokomam of Petapa, Guatemala in the First Half of the 16th Century." *Journal of Comparative Family Studies* 14 (2): 215–27.

Lutz, Christopher H. 1994. *Santiago de Guatemala, 1541–1773: City, Caste, and the Colonial Experience*. Norman and London: University of Oklahoma Press.

Lutz, Christopher H., and W. George Lovell. 1990. "Core and Periphery in Colonial Guatemala." In *Guatemalan Indians and the State, 1540–1988*, edited by Carol A. Smith, 35–51. Austin: University of Texas Press.

MacLeod, Murdo J. 1973. *Spanish Central America: A Socioeconomic History, 1520–1720*. Berkeley: University of California Press.

McCaa, Robert. 2003. "The Nahua *calli* of Ancient Mexico: Household, Family, and Gender." *Continuity and Change* 18 (1): 23–48.

Milton, Cynthia E., and Vinson, III, Ben. 2002. "Counting Heads: Race and Non-Native Tribute Policy in Colonial Spanish America." *Journal of Colonialism and Colonial History* 3 (3): 1–18.

Offutt, Leslie S. 1997. "Women's Voices from the Frontier: San Esteban de Nueva Tlaxcala in the Late Eighteenth Century." In *Indian Women of Early Mexico*, edited by Susan Schroeder, Stephanie Wood, and Robert Haskett, 273–89. Norman and London: University of Oklahoma.

Penyak, Lee M. 2016. "Incestuous Natures: Consensual and Forced Relations in Mexico, 1740–1854." In *Sexuality and the Unnatural in Colonial Latin America*, edited by Zeb Tortorici, 162–87. Oakland: University of California Press.

Premo, Bianca. 2005. *Children of the Father King: Youth, Authority, and Legal Minority in Colonial Lima*. Chapel Hill: University of North Carolina Press.

Restall, Matthew. 1997. *The Maya World: Yucatec Culture and Society, 1550–1850*. Stanford, CA: Stanford University Press.

Rípodas Ardanaz, Daisy. 1977. *El matrimonio en Indias: realidad social y regulación jurídica*. Buenos Aires, Argentina: Fundación para la Educación, la Ciencia, y la Cultura.

Rodríguez Jiménez, Pablo. 1988. "Matrimonio incestuoso en el Medellín colonial 1700–1810." *Revista Extensión Cultural* 24–25: 52–8.

Rodríguez-Sáenz, Eugenia. 2005. "'Tiyita bea lo que me han hecho': estupro y incesto en Costa Rica (1800–1850)." In *El paso del cometa: estado, política social y culturas populares en Costa Rica (1800–1950)*, edited by Iván Molina Jiménez and Steven Palmer, 1–47. San José, Costa Rica: EUNED.

Rojas Flores, Jorge. 2007. "Ursula: The Life and Times of an Aristocratic Girl in Santiago, Chile (1666–1678)." In *Raising an Empire: Children in Early Modern Iberia and Colonial Latin America*, edited by Ondina E González and Bianca Premo, 107–36. Albuquerque: University of New Mexico Press.

Sanchiz Ochoa, Pilar. 1980. "Cambio en la estructura familiar indígena: Influencias de la Iglesia y la Encomienda en Guatemala." *Revista de la Universidad Complutense* 28: 169–91.

Schroeder, Susan, Stephanie Wood, and Robert Haskett, eds. 1997. *Indian Women of Early Mexico*. Norman and London: University of Oklahoma Press.

Schwaller, John Frederick. 2011. *The History of the Catholic Church in Latin America: From Conquest to Revolution and Beyond*. New York and London: New York University Press.

Schwaller, Robert C. 2016. *Géneros de Gente in Early Colonial Mexico: Defining Racial Difference*. Norman: University of Oklahoma Press.

Schwartzkopf, Stacey. 2013. "Rural Castas, State Projects, and Ethnic Transformation in Western Guatemala, 1800–1821." *Ethnohistory* 60 (4): 721–47.

Sherman, William L. 1979. *Forced Native Labor in Sixteenth-Century Central America*. Lincoln and London: University of Nebraska Press.

Socolow, Susan Migden. 1980. "Women and Crime: Buenos Aires, 1757–97." *Journal of Latin American Studies* 12 (1): 39–54.

———. 2015. *The Women of Colonial Latin America*. 2nd ed. New York: Cambridge University Press.

Solano, Francisco de. 1969. "Areas lingüísticas y población de habla indígena de Guatemala en 1772." *Revista Española de Antropología Americana* 4: 145–200.

Stern, Steve J. 1995. *The Secret History of Gender: Women, Men, and Power in Late Colonial Mexico*. Chapel Hill and London: University of North Carolina Press.

Taracena Arriola, Arturo. 1982. "Contribución al estudio del vocablo 'ladino' en Guatemala (S. XVI–XIX)." In *Historia y antropología de guatemala: ensayos en honor de J. Daniel Contreras R.*, edited by Jorge Luján Muñoz, 89–104. Guatemala: Universidad de San Carlos de Guatemala.

Taylor, William B. 1979. *Drinking, Homicide, and Rebellion in Colonial Mexican Villages*. Stanford, CA: Stanford University Press.

Terraciano, Kevin. 1998. "Crime and Culture in Colonial Mexico: The Case of the Mixtec Murder Note." *Ethnohistory* 45 (4): 709–45.

Twinam, Ann. 1999. *Public Lives, Private Secrets: Gender, Honor, Sexuality, and Illegitimacy in Colonial Spanish America*. Stanford, CA: Stanford University Press.

———. 2007. "The Church, the State, and the Abandoned: Expósitos in Late Eighteenth-Century Havana." In *Raising an Empire: Children in Early Modern Iberia and Colonial Latin America*, edited by Ondina E. González and Bianca Premo, 163–86. Albuquerque: University of New Mexico Press.

van Deusen, Nancy E. 2015. *Global Indios: The Indigenous Struggle for Justice in Sixteenth-Century Spain*. Durham, NC and London: Duke University Press.

van Oss, Adriaan C. 1986. *Catholic Colonialism: A Parish History of Guatemala, 1524–1821*. Cambridge: Cambridge University Press.

Waldron, Kathy. 1989. "The Sinners and the Bishop in Colonial Venezuela: The Visita of Bishop Mariano Martí, 1771–1784." In *Sexuality and Marriage in Colonial Latin America*, edited by Asunción Lavrin, 156–77. Lincoln and London: University of Nebraska Press.

3   Incest and the Law

Introduction

Exploration of incestuous crime in colonial Guatemala warrants review of the formal legal definition of incest and key features of the legal system in colonial Spanish America. Law in Spanish America was based on Castilian law, which, in turn, took many influences from Roman and canon law in both its procedural aspects and interpretation of incest. Though multiple jurisdictions operated simultaneously in Spanish America, the records of the incest cases in this study were produced in the Spanish secular courts. Accordingly, the focus will be on Spanish legal precedent and judicial procedure associated with *justicia real ordinaria* ("ordinary royal jurisdiction"). Early colonial observations of sexual and marital proscriptions among Mesoamerican groups will also be briefly examined since indigenous peoples made up the majority of inhabitants in the area. The typical penalties for incestuous crime in colonial Guatemala are considered as well to demonstrate what was potentially at stake for incestuous offenders and how sentences could vary based on personal characteristics and the circumstances of the crime.

Legal Culture and Precedent

By the late fifteenth and early sixteenth centuries, Latin Christianity held that there were three main bodies of law. The first was natural law (*ius naturale*), a body of law inherent to the universe and man, meaning all humans were subject to it (e.g. all humans are born and die). The second was human law (*ius gentium*). This was a common body of law and custom that might be found in the practices of all peoples (e.g. polygyny). The boundaries between these two bodies of law were debated, and behavior that contradicted these laws was deemed illicit whether carried out by Christians or non-Christians. Christian law and custom, on the other hand, was specifically reserved for, and expected to be observed by, Christians and their converts. For example, while polygyny did not go against natural and human law, it was incompatible with Christian law, meaning that those who professed the faith could not practice it.

A non-Christian, however, could engage in polygyny without causing scandal. This type of legal thinking would come to influence *derecho indiano*, the body of law governing colonial Spanish America, including its policies towards indigenous populations (Borah 1982, 266–7, 1983, 6–7, 28–30). Consequently, it surfaced in Guatemalan incest cases in a variety of ways, as will be seen throughout this study.

The definition of incest and the repercussions of incestuous activity articulated in Spanish law were primarily rooted in Roman and canon law. *Las Siete Partidas* (or "Seven-Part Code"), a thirteenth-century Castilian law code attributed to Alfonso X of Castile, was one product of the commingling of Roman and canon law. This code played a significant role in both Spanish and Spanish American law. Despite changes in legal codes in Spain and its colonies after its production, *Las Siete Partidas* continued to be cited by Latin American courts and judges even into the late nineteenth century (Aguirre and Salvatore 2001, 3).

Las Siete Partidas (1807 v. 3, 33–7) described the rules of consanguinity and affinity, defined the crime of incest, and outlined how incestuous persons were to be punished. Part IV, Title VI discussed the two ways of understanding degrees of relatedness: (1) In secular law, degrees of relatedness were based on the rules of inheritance when someone died intestate. (2) In canon law, degrees of relatedness took into consideration impediments to marriage.[1] The concept of incest was relevant to the latter system. In terms of consanguinity, canon law held that each generation above and below ego in the ascending and descending line constituted one degree. That is, parents were first-degree relatives, grandparents were second-degree relatives, and so on. Within the collateral lines, siblings equated to first-degree relatives, the children of one's siblings to second-degree relatives, and so on. Affinity, on the other hand, stemmed from sexual intercourse between a man and a woman (regardless of whether or not they were married). All of his relatives became connected to her through affinity of the same degree that they were related to him and vice versa. For example, a brother- or sister-in-law would be considered a first-degree affinal relative.

Following this process of degree reckoning, Part IV, Title II (which concerned marriage) held that a man committed *incestus* ("incest") when "knowingly lying with his female relative, or with a female relative of his wife or of another [woman] with whom he had lain to the fourth [canonical] degree."[2] Part VII, Title XVIII, Law I added that a man committed the sin of *incestus* when he knowingly lay with the wife of his male relative to the fourth degree. The same rules applied to women. Consanguinity and affinity to the fourth degree inhibited marriage and annulled it if it had already been contracted. Such marriage prohibitions remained even after the death of a spouse. In terms of adoption, this text decreed that a man should not marry his adopted daughter, nor should his sons marry her, while the adoption lasts. This also applied to a woman (and her daughters) with regard to an adopted son. However, sexual relations between individuals connected through adoption were not included in the definition of incest (*Las Siete Partidas* 1807 v. 3, 18–9, 36–7, 659). This is not wholly surprising because incest rules are not always synonymous with marriage proscriptions, even though they do tend to overlap (Goody 1956, 302; Fox 1980, 2, 161).

Las Siete Partidas (1807 v. 3, 18–9, 37–8) also made clear that spiritual kinship, or *parentesco espiritual,* was incompatible with marriage and sexual relations. As noted by Joseph H. Lynch (1986, 261, 281) in his discussion of early medieval Europe, spiritual kinship (and the sexual proscriptions that came with it) had become an essential component of Christianity by the eighth century. He explained that the incest taboo within spiritual kinship arose in the context of a negative view of human sexuality and the idea that baptism created a spiritual family that needed to be protected from the contaminating nature of sexuality. That is, incest taboos surrounding spiritual kin were one of the results of a general concern that sexual matters and holy matters needed to be kept separate.

According to *Las Siete Partidas* (1807 v. 3, 18–9, 37–8), spiritual kinship was *compadradgo*[sic] created through the sacraments of the Church—specifically the rites of baptism and confirmation—and it took various forms.[3] One form of spiritual kinship existed between *padres espirituales* ("spiritual parents") and the baptized or confirmed child (the *hijo espiritual,* or "spiritual child"). Spiritual parents in this sense were not equivalent to modern notions of godparents. The individual conferring baptism or confirmation and the individuals taking the infant from the baptismal font or accompanying the child at confirmation were all considered spiritual parents.[4] There also existed spiritual kinship between spiritual parents and the mother and father of the baptized or confirmed child—they were *compadres* (masc.) and *comadres* (fem.) of one another. In addition, spiritual ties arose between the *hijos espirituales* and the *hijos carnales* ("carnal children," or biological children) of an individual, who became each other's *hermanos espirituales* ("spiritual siblings"). Sexual relations between spiritual kin of the first two types were explicitly identified as incestuous in this text.

Las Siete Partidas (1807 v. 3, 19) classed sexual relations with a woman or man of a religious order as incestuous as well. Elizabeth Archibald (2001, 39) suggested that consideration of a breach of religious vows of chastity as incest in medieval Europe may have been influenced by Roman use of the term *incestum* in reference to sexual intercourse with a Vestal virgin. Of course, it would have also played into the general concern over maintaining a division between sexual and holy things noted by Lynch (1986).

Las Siete Partidas (1807 v. 3, 19, 659–60) provided guidelines for denouncing and penalizing incest. Following Part VII, Title XVIII, Law II, anyone could bring forward an accusation of incest within five years of its commission (thirty years if it had involved rape), and anyone could be accused of incest unless they were a boy under fourteen years of age or a girl under the age of twelve. According to Part IV, Title II, Law XIII, if someone committed incest, ideally, they would not marry unless they received a dispensation from the Church because they had been "so young that they were unable to maintain chastity."[5] If an incestuous person had married anyway, the marriage was still considered valid, though subject to restrictions on sexual intercourse between the couple. The repercussions of incest were more severe in Part VII, where Title XVII, Law III decreed that if a man was convicted of incest (at least in its consanguineous or affinal versions) with a woman to whom he was not married, he was to suffer the penalty for adultery—death.[6] Except in cases where one received a papal dispensation, men who knowingly married a relative would be subject to banishment. Other penalties included the loss of one's position in society for a man of high rank and public scourging for a man of low rank.

The Council of Trent (1545–1563), convened in response to the Protestant Reformation, reconfirmed incest prohibitions within the fourth degree. However, Jutta Sperling (2004, 74, 100) noted a greater tolerance for cousin marriages in Europe after Trent, when dispensations were readily granted for individuals related in the third and fourth degrees. Impediments to marriage deriving from affinity through fornication (as opposed to marriage) were limited to the second degree. Impediments stemming from "public honesty," which referred to a previous public engagement to a relative of one's intended, were limited to the first degree. Spiritual kinship was also narrowed, existing only between sponsors[7] (and the executioner) of baptism or confirmation and the baptized or confirmed individual and their parents (Buckley 2014, Session XXIV, Chapters II–IV). The tenets of the Council of Trent were accepted in Spain in 1564 and adopted in New Spain in 1585 (Castañeda 1989, 57).

Incest as defined in sixteenth- and nineteenth-century Castilian law reflected such precedents. Both the *Nueva Recopilación* (1567) and *Novísima Recopilación* (1805) stated that a man committed incest when he was sexually involved with a relative to the fourth degree, a *comadre*, a *cuñada* (in the broader sense of any female affinal relative),[8] or a woman in a religious order. (Note that sexual relations with a godchild were not specifically mentioned here.) The crime of incest also included sexual relations between a woman and an *hombre de otra ley* (i.e. a non-Christian) (*Segunda Parte* 1567, 193v; *Novísima Recopilación* [1805] 2011, 426).

The definition of incest in the *Nueva Recopilación* and *Novísima Recopilación* would have applied to both men and women with the exception of the matter of sexual relations with a non-Christian, which was apparently gender-specific. Precedents for this discrepancy existed in medieval Iberia during the Reconquest of Christian Spain. Heath Dillard (1976, 85–6) found that in both the *Fuero Sepúlveda* and the *Fuero Cuenca*,

Christian men did not commit any offense when they had sexual relations with a Muslim or Jewish woman. However, Christian women and their Muslim or Jewish lovers were to be executed if caught in the act. He posited that one reason for this asymmetry lay in notions of a Christian crusade against infidels. While Christian men who slept with non-Christian women were demonstrating their superiority over their inferiors, Christian women who slept with non-Christian men were sullied through such contact and brought disgrace upon the Christian community.

Notably, the dictionary definition of incest differed from its formal legal definition. Sebastián de Covarrubias (1611, 502) defined *incesto* simply as *el ayuntamiento con la que es parienta* ("sexual intercourse with she who is a relative") in his *Tesoro de la lengua castellana, o española.* Following the *Diccionario de Autoridades* (1726–1739 v. 4), *incesto* referred to "copulation or carnal access with a female relative through consanguinity or affinity."[9] This could explain why the only instances of sexual relations in the criminal records consulted for this study that were explicitly termed "incest" were those involving consanguineous and affinal kin. It appears intimacy between women and male religious was more appropriately classed as *sacrilegio* ("sacrilege") (see AGCA A2.2 Leg. 177 Exp. 3519). These definitional discrepancies suggest that prototypical "incest" involved consanguineous or affinal relatives, which is more in line with Western notions of incest today.

Even though marriage prohibitions to the fourth degree of kinship were reinforced at Trent, these prohibitions did not apply to the entire population of Spanish America. Impelled by reports of Indian marriages between relatives that would have been prohibited to Christians without a marital dispensation, Pope Paul III issued a papal bull in 1537 that allowed Indians to marry relatives within the third and fourth degrees of consanguinity and affinity without need for a dispensation. This privilege lasted throughout the colonial period. In 1585, *mestizos* were granted the same exemption. Still, there was fluctuation in who qualified as *mestizo* and how *mestizos* were treated when it came to dispensations. The Sixth Council of Lima (1772), for instance, decided that it was necessary for *mestizos* to seek dispensations for marriages in the third and fourth degrees of consanguinity. Individuals of African descent were also given special concessions, including the exemption in the 1537 bull. Though, here again, issues arose about the percentage of African blood required of an individual, and the Sixth Council of Lima obliged *mulatos* (like *mestizos*) to seek dispensations for marriages involving third- and fourth-degree consanguines (Rípodas Ardanaz 1977, 170–1, 185–7). Such precedents may have contributed to the fact that there were not any incest cases in the Guatemalan sample that exceeded the second degree.

One way in which the Church was able to instruct individuals in, and monitor relationships that fit within, its definition of incest was through the sacrament of confession. In a 1662 ecclesiastical manual written in Spanish and Kaqchikel, there is a section devoted to the sacrament of confession (Newberry Library Ayer MS 1508, 146–8). Regarding the Sixth and Ninth Commandments, which, respectively, refer to proscriptions on adultery and coveting a neighbor's wife, priests were instructed to ask male penitents if they had desired or had sex with a woman. Those who answered in the affirmative were then to clarify, first, if the woman was married, and second, if the woman was by chance a kinswoman or a kinswoman of their wife. If they answered positively to the latter, they were to indicate the degree of the kinswoman and whether she was a *comadre*. Similarly, if a woman confirmed she had desired a man, the first question the priest was to ask her was whether this man was a kinsman. If she said he was, then they were to ask to what degree and whether he was her *compadre*. Then, she was to be questioned regarding whether she had "known" a man. If she confirmed she had, the priest was to ask whether he was married and about any "degrees of *parentesco* ['kinship'], of consanguinity, and affinity, and *compadrazgo*."[10] It is unclear to what extent religious instruction in incest prohibitions was carried out much less successful in indigenous communities. It surely would have been uneven, and Guatemalan incest cases make evident that there was room for confusion among Indians and non-Indians alike.

Mesoamerican Antecedents

Early colonial sources provide some information on sexual and marriage proscriptions among Mesoamerican groups. For instance, Fray Toribio de Benavente Motolinía, a sixteenth-century Franciscan missionary, recorded how incest was perceived and punished in Central Mexico. In Chapter XVI of his *Memoriales*, he said that if a man lay with his stepmother, stepdaughter, or whole- or half-sister both were subject to the death penalty. Speaking more generally, Motolinía reported that death was the consequence for anyone who committed incest in the first degree of consanguinity or affinity, except for brothers- and sisters-in-law. In fact, it was custom for a brother (or brothers) to marry the wife (or wives) of their deceased brother, even if the latter had already fathered children (Motolinía 1903, 307–8). This suggests the Nahuas and Spaniards were largely in agreement that first-degree relatives were sexually off-limits, though, contrary to Spanish law, the Nahuas permitted a man's brother to marry his widow.

Fray Diego de Landa (also of the Franciscan order) gave some insight into marriage prohibitions among the Maya of the Yucatán. In Section XXIV of his *Relación de las cosas de Yucatán*, in which he discussed genealogies, he reported,

> Sons and daughters were always called by the name of their father and their mother ... in this way the child of Chel and Chan was

called Nachanchel, which is to say, children of so-and-so, and this is the reason ... the Indians say that those of the same name are relatives and they treat one another as such.... And, like so, no woman or man married another of the same name because in them there would be great infamy (Landa [1566] 2015, 50).[11]

Additionally, Landa said in Section XXV that marriage to a relative on one's father's side of the family was to be avoided, as was marriage to a sister-in-law (a brother's wife or wife's sister), stepmother, or maternal aunt. Marriage to any other maternal kin was considered legitimate (Landa [1566] 2015, 52). This indicates that restrictions on marriage were looser between maternal kin than paternal kin, which would have contrasted with Spanish marriage law, yet been consistent with a bias towards patrilineal descent reckoning noted for the area (Restall 1997, 123).

Fray Bartolomé de las Casas, a sixteenth-century Dominican friar, noted in his *Apologética historia sumaria* that Indians in the province of Guatemala were not allowed to marry anyone in their tribe or family. However, this did not include the children of a woman of one's tribe or family who had married into another one. That is, when it came to marriage, kinship impediments were skewed towards the male line. In accordance with this system, marriage to a maternal half-sister (as opposed to a paternal half-sister) sometimes occurred (Las Casas 1967, 517). Likewise, during a gathering of religious at Cobán in 1570, it was ordered that with regard to the sacrament of marriage, Indians should always be asked about "...kinship, both carnal and spiritual, through the grandmother, on the mother's side..." (Remesal [1619] 1988 v. 2, 346).[12] In other words, connections through women were not as strongly considered in marriage arrangements as those through men and so required special interrogation. Hence, as in Yucatán, and in contrast to Spanish law, maternal kin constituted more appropriate marriage partners than paternal kin. This discrepancy is again congruent with patrilineal descent reckoning, which was apparently observed among indigenous groups in the area (Sanchiz Ochoa 1980, 171).

In-laws were acceptable marriage partners in the Guatemalan region, at least under certain circumstances. Like Motolinía for the Nahuas, Las Casas (1967, 503, 517) noted that it was customary for Indian women in Guatemala to marry a relative of their deceased spouse, typically their husband's brother. On rare occasions, an individual might marry his stepmother (Las Casas 1967, 503, 517).[13] Another example of in-law marriage comes from the Xajil Chronicle. According to this text, a brother- and sister-in-law married one another in 1590 in Santa Lucía. However, when Father Fray Cristóbal de Olivera discovered the union, he had them punished. The man, witnesses to the marriage, and *fiscal* (assistant to a priest)[14] were lashed and put to work in the vegetable garden and the woman was imprisoned for six months. Her witnesses also served some time in jail (Maxwell and Hill, II 2006, 386–7).

The earliest criminal record from the case sample of this study, Case 1, similarly documents a marriage between in-laws. In 1682 San Juan Atitán, the *corregidor* (Spanish official in charge of a jurisdictional area termed a *corregimiento*) of Totonicapán was informed that Pedro Cardona, a *regidor* (town councilman), was *amancebado* with his step-daughter, Madalena Velasco. He had allegedly fathered two children with her, which he killed (when they were yet to be baptized) and buried in an unknown location. Madalena, presumably a Mam speaker, testified through an interpreter. She admitted to having sexual relations with Pedro in his *milpa* (cornfield) and said she did not think it was a sin. After she gave birth to a child, Pedro told her he wanted to marry her and that "it would not be good to go with a child in her arms."[15] Madalena reported that she did in fact marry him and that she did not know where he left the infant. The other child was born dead. Despite denying any involvement with his stepdaughter, Pedro did not escape punishment. His sentence included public shaming, one hundred lashes, banishment from within twenty leagues of his town, and placement in a home with a shackle on his foot "like a slave" for two years. His tribute obligations, clothing expenses, and court fees would be taken from his monthly salary.

The extent to which the principles articulated in these colonial period texts reflected pre-Hispanic traditions, or even colonial practice, is difficult to determine. Beyond the potential bias and errors of the sources themselves, there would have been considerable cultural heterogeneity through time and space. Nevertheless, we are left with the impression that sexual and marital proscriptions in Mesoamerica occasionally intersected with, but also diverged from, the ideal ones in Spain. Some groups apparently viewed maternal relatives differently than paternal ones when it came to marriage, and leviratic-like practices may have been customary in some places.

Legal Jurisdictions and Protections in Colonial Society

Shortly after the wars of conquest in the Americas, the Crown took measures to gain control over its new territories, which had been more or less left in the hands of the conquistadors. One method was to establish *audiencias* (high courts of justice with additional administrative and executive functions) in important colonial cities, the first of which was founded in Santo Domingo in 1526. Responsibilities of the *audiencias* included the enforcement of royal laws and supervision of colonial officials, holding them accountable for any misconduct. Accordingly, judges went on occasional inspection tours within their jurisdictions. An *audiencia* also exercised power in the ecclesiastical sphere through royal patronage, which granted temporal and spiritual jurisdiction to the Crown, and as a court of justice, whose jurisdiction extended into ecclesiastical matters. The Council of the Indies supervised administrative matters in the colonies and served as the high court of appeal for the colonial *audiencias* (Cunningham 1919; Burkholder and Chandler 1977).

Central America received its first *audiencia* following the New Laws of 1542. The Audiencia de los Confines, as it was termed, was first established in Honduras and formally convened in 1544. Under the advice of Alonso López de Cerrato, the president (or chief justice) of the *audiencia*, the seat of the *audiencia* was moved to Antigua Guatemala in 1549, where it became known as the Audiencia de Guatemala. Beginning with four *oidores* (judges),[16] by 1687 the Audiencia of Guatemala had five in addition to its *fiscal* (crown attorney). The seat of the *audiencia* was relocated to Nueva Guatemala following a destructive earthquake in Antigua Guatemala in 1773. Individuals occupying the office of the regent, a position created in 1776, would eventually come to act as the chief justices of their respective *audiencias* (Cunningham 1919, 211; Burkholder and Chandler 1977, 2, 230–1; Sherman 1979, 129, 151).

Whereas the viceregal *audiencias* in Mexico and Lima had both a criminal and civil *sala* ("chamber") with their own respective magistrates and *fiscales*, smaller *audiencias* like that in Guatemala only had one (Cunningham 1919, 18, 21 n. 32). The Real Sala del Crimen was a junior chamber of the Spanish *audiencias* with civil and criminal jurisdiction in first instance within a five-league radius of the seat of the *audiencia* (Borah 1983, 273, 444). The *audiencia* functioned as court of appeal for cases originating in lower tribunals within its jurisdiction (Cutter 1995, 53). Indeed, many cases were first tried under the direction of an *alcalde ordinario* (town magistrate) or an *alcalde mayor*, the head of a larger geographical area referred to as the *alcaldía mayor*.

The majority of incest cases analyzed here were forwarded to the Real Sala del Crimen following sentencing by a lower magistrate for its approval or reform regardless of whether an appeal had been made. There were various reasons for this. For example, in 1799 there was a royal order for lower magistrates to consult the Real Sala del Crimen prior to releasing a criminal when severe criminal cases resulted in absolutory sentences (see Case 25). In an incest case from 1804, reference was made to another order that required the Real Sala del Crimen to be informed of certain criminal persons in order to fill the fixed armed regiments at the border ports of the kingdom (see Case 43).

Parallel jurisdictions operated simultaneously in colonial Spanish America. In addition to ordinary royal jurisdiction, military and ecclesiastical jurisdictions had their own prerogatives (Cutter 1995, 6–7). Postal workers were also exempt from prosecution in the ordinary civil and criminal courts, falling instead under the jurisdiction of the mail administration (Sellers-García 2014, 105, 117). Criminal cases involving soldiers were carried out in military tribunals, with appeals made to the viceroy or governor (in their role as captain-general) (Cunningham 1919, 231). Sometimes conflicts over jurisdiction resulted in the need for one accused party to be tried in a military court, while another remained subject to an ordinary court (e.g. Case 67). However, if a crime was committed prior to enlistment in the military, ordinary jurisdiction would apply (e.g. Case 45).

Ecclesiastical jurisdiction was restricted to breaches of canon law (Borah 1983, 92). In fact, because the *audiencia* held jurisdiction over the secular church courts, it could intervene, if, for example, an ecclesiastical judge overstepped and assumed jurisdiction in temporal matters. Significantly, the *audiencia* did not have such authority in matters of the Holy Office of the Inquisition, an ecclesiastical tribunal with special royal protection until the late eighteenth century (Cunningham 1919, 411 n. 3, 420, 428–9).

The Holy Office of the Inquisition did not establish a tribunal in colonial Guatemala. Indians made up the vast majority of the Guatemalan population, and they had been removed from its jurisdiction in 1571 (see Jones 1994, 65–6; Few 2000, 166). As new converts to Christianity, Indians fell under the domain of a parallel institution active until 1820—sometimes termed the Indian Inquisition, the Office of the Provisor of Natives, or the Tribunal of the Faith of the Indians—that addressed issues related to religious orthodoxy among the indigenous population (Wiesner-Hanks 2010, 194). Spaniards and individuals of mixed race, on the other hand, were subject to the inquisitional tribunal based in Mexico City beginning in 1572. Still, inquisitional activity in Guatemala was relatively low when compared to other places in Spanish America. When active, it focused on issues such as blasphemy, witchcraft, bigamy, adultery, and solicitation during confession. Its authority was briefly suppressed from 1813 to 1817 following the liberal Spanish Constitution of 1812 (abolished in 1814) (see Jones 1994, 65–6, 232).

The crime of incest fell under *fuero mixto* ("mixed jurisdiction"), which meant that it could be tried in both the secular and ecclesiastical courts (see Case 3; Escriche 1874–1876 v. 2, 1104). Still, in line with the Church's subordinate position to the civil government and *audiencia*, the Church did not have the power to remove a criminal case that began in the secular courts from that jurisdiction or to change the sentences pronounced by secular authorities (Margadant 2001, 90). Further, the Mexican Inquisition was specifically warned by Rome in 1580 that it did not have the right to try incest (or sodomy) cases (Wiesner-Hanks 2010, 194).

As previously mentioned, the records from the Guatemalan case sample stemmed from the Spanish secular courts. However, sometimes these cases had been tried in the ecclesiastical courts beforehand. An injured party might take a case to secular magistrates following an ecclesiastical trial if they felt that religious authorities had not been effective (e.g. Case 62). One woman first went to ecclesiastical authorities regarding her husband's incestuous behavior with their daughter. However, while the case was still pending, she decided to take her complaint to royal authorities because she feared her husband (who had already threatened to kill her) would cause her injury (Case 15). Sometimes priests even sent individuals who came to them with a complaint to secular authorities (see Case 47).

It was not uncommon for both ecclesiastical and secular officials to be involved in Guatemalan incest cases, even when a trial was carried out in the secular courts. In cases of incestuous adultery, a guilty party might be sent to ecclesiastical authorities following the conclusion of the case for "habilitation of the marriage." According to the Church, incestuous activity rendered a spouse incapable of sexual union with their partner until this process was undergone and the created impediment removed. Ecclesiastical divorce was also an option after a spouse committed incest (see Case 56 and AGCA A1.15 Leg. 5387 Exp. 45660).

Like their Spanish counterparts, Indian towns had their own *cabildos*. Spanish law granted these *cabildos* the authority to resolve petty disputes at the local level (Hill, II 2002, 127). Even though the Spanish judiciary technically held authority in more serious offenses, indigenous leaders often held de facto jurisdiction. In fact, Robert M. Hill, II (1989, 180) found that criminal procedures were being carried out even at the sub-level of the *parcialidad*[17] through the mid eighteenth century in Tecpán. Here, *parcialidad* leaders heard disputes and administered corporal punishments to their members in their own houses. Because indigenous authority figures often had the ability to govern and enact justice on their own terms, not all criminal cases involving indigenous people made it to the Spanish courts.

When Indians did engage with the Spanish legal system, they were theoretically granted special privileges and protections. In Roman and medieval European jurisprudential thinking, *miserabiles* were the poor, ignorant, and wretched folk in need of special protections. The status of Indians in the Americas became more and more likened to that of this class, and therefore, they were arguably deserving of a reduction or elimination of legal fees and simplification of the legal process (Borah 1983, 5, 13, 80, 83). Further, the *fiscal* acted simultaneously as the *protector de indios* ("protector of the Indians") and was responsible for reviewing all *audiencia* decisions related to Indian matters (Hill, II 2002, 136).

Such privileges were referenced in Guatemalan incest cases involving Indians. For example, legal advisors proposed exemption from court fees for Indian defendants "because of their *calidad*" (e.g. Case 47). In Case 2, the magistrate ordered the trial to be carried out briefly and summarily since it was *cosa de Indios* ("an Indian matter"; i.e. involved Indians). Further, legal counsel regularly used the issue of *calidad* when formulating a defense for the criminal actions of Indian clients, as did Indian actors themselves. The role of *calidad* in defensive strategies will be discussed further in Chapter 6.

Colonial law also granted Indians the right to use the *audiencia* as a court of first instance, a court of appeal, or together with lower level indigenous authorities (Kellogg 1995, 7). Simón Hernández, an Indian man arrested for suspected incest with his daughter in 1802, exercised this privilege (Case 31). The circumstances of the alleged incest were being investigated by the *alcalde mayor* of Escuintla, who supposedly had ill will against Simón. This led the latter to demand to be tried in first instance by the tribunal of the *audiencia* of Guatemala.

Indians had particular rights in relation to ecclesiastical authorities as well. In fact, secular authorities had to intercede after Miguel de Velasco, priest of Jutiapan, took charge of a case of stepfather-stepdaughter incest involving Miguel Vásquez, an Indian man from the town of Comapa (Case 6). According to Velasco, the *provisor* had left the punishment of Miguel at his discretion. Thus,

> following the footsteps of the Apostle—that those who publicly sin, be publicly corrected—...I decided to give said public incestuous person fifty public lashes. Upon being summoned for said penitence, he clamored, asking that they not dishonor him and for a pecuniary penitence of one hundred [pesos] which could be applied to this church instead, simultaneously promising correction.[18]

Velasco accepted the offer of pesos from Miguel.

The *alcalde mayor* of Escuintla, Juan de Rivera y Pérez, wrote to the *fiscal* regarding the matter. He reported that Velasco, acting as ecclesiastical judge, had ordered Miguel apprehended and imprisoned in Jutiapan. This went against royal law, as the initial investigative phase of the trial should have occurred in Miguel's hometown of Comapa. Rivera y Pérez ordered for it to be carried out accordingly, but this apparently did not occur. He learned that Miguel was not released until after he had become gravely ill in prison and gave the one hundred pesos to Velasco and a mule to the notary. Thus, Rivera y Pérez demanded that Velasco return the pesos and mule to Miguel.

Miguel later told Rivera y Pérez that he had suffered further material losses at the hands of Velasco. Velasco had told Miguel's wife that he had an order from his superior to give Miguel two hundred lashes. Fearing the dishonor that would come from this, she went to a man who was the *compadre* of the priest so that he would intercede and have the penalty converted into a pecuniary one. Velasco originally wanted two hundred pesos for the church, but since she did not have it, she gave him sixty-two pesos and a large pot (for the processing of sugarcane) instead. Rivera y Pérez ordered Velasco to return these items as well. Yet, at the time of his report, Miguel had not yet received the pesos, pot, or mule that had been taken. Beyond this, there had been an attempt to confiscate the sugarcane Miguel had been left by his deceased brother, though it had not been actualized.

Upon receipt of this report, the *fiscal* discussed Velasco's various legal errors. They included his infraction with regard to Book I, Title XIII, Law VI of the *Recopilación de leyes de los reynos de las Indias* (1680), which prohibited priests from apprehending, sentencing, lashing, or cutting the hair of the Indians. He also pointed out his violation of Book I, Title XX, Law VI that barred priests from sentencing Indians to pecuniary penalties. The laws prohibited such penalties because of it "being so easy, especially for priests, to impose a penalty of lashes on them for whatever crime, and after, in the name of compassion, to convert it into a monetary one, obliging them to this under threat [of lashes]."[19] Ultimately, the *fiscal* felt it would be appropriate to have the *provisor* facilitate the return of the one hundred pesos to Miguel and penalize Velasco for his offenses to both the royal authorities and Miguel. He also believed the *provisor* should investigate the matter of the sixty-two pesos, pot, and mule and have Velasco return them if they were in fact taken. Further, any confiscation of Miguel's sugarcane needed to be suspended until request for assistance was made to the *audiencia* as dictated by law. The *audiencia* judges agreed with the *fiscal*, and notice was sent to the *provisor*. Eventually, a new order was sent to the more recently appointed *provisor* because the former one apparently did not comply.

In sum, crime and punishment were complex issues in colonial Spanish America. Spanish courts were subject to various jurisdictional divisions, and indigenous *cabildos* and leaders exercised a great deal of autonomy in criminal matters. Crimes like incest could be tried in royal and ecclesiastical courts, but royal authorities retained the right to intercede when ecclesiastical authorities disregarded royal law as it pertained to the indigenous population or otherwise.

Procedural Aspects of Ordinary Royal Courts

Criminal procedure in colonial Spanish America was based on a Castilian legal procedure inspired by *Las Siete Partidas* and the *ius commune* tradition.[20] Charles R. Cutter (1995) described the three main phases of this procedure—the *sumaria*, the *plenario*, and the *sentencia*. The *sumaria* was a preliminary investigative phase involving a magistrate and his assistants attempting to establish the facts surrounding a crime. A defendant was presumed guilty and remained ignorant of the charges during this phase. If injuries had occurred, a physical examination of the injured person by a medical expert might be ordered (Cutter 1995, 109, 113–6). Midwives or surgeons could also establish the actuality of a pregnancy when relevant (e.g. Case 26). Next, witnesses of the crime were questioned, all of whom were qualified to speak at this point in a trial, even though they might later be disqualified for being a relative or otherwise interested party (Cutter 1995, 116, 126). Statements were recorded by a notary or, in their absence, a magistrate accompanied by *testigos de asistencia* (witnesses). A witness would then affirm its accuracy, signing it if they were literate.

An accused person could be arrested at various points of the *sumaria* (Cutter 1995, 120). Some individuals were held in prison during the course of the trial (which could last for years). However, prison was not the only option for detention. For example, a pregnant woman might be placed in the care of a relative to prevent any danger to the fetus (e.g. Case 58; see also Case 28). Once in custody, accused persons would provide a *confesión* ("confession"), a statement in response to the accusation, which oftentimes took the form of a denial despite its name.

Individuals on trial could choose their own defense counsel or have a legal advocate appointed by the court. Generally speaking, a *defensor* represented adults and a *curador* acted for minors and Indians (as juridical minors). While Cutter (1995, 126) found that defense counsel was assigned following the *confesión*, colonial Guatemalan cases indicate that *curadores* were assigned prior to the *confesión*. In fact, if someone was sworn in without a *curador* present, their *confesión* could be made null, at least when that individual was Indian (see Case 47). Still, defense counsel for all accused persons was only present when a client was sworn in and when the *confesión* was read back to a client for affirmation. In other words, an accused person was questioned without their attorney present. Interpreters were also required for individuals who did not speak Spanish adequately, and legally, two interpreters should have been present, though this was not always the case (see Case 61).

The next major phase of a criminal trial was the *plenario*, the period in which trial participants tried to prove their respective positions. During the *plenario*, a defendant was formally charged with a crime. Plaintiffs presented formal complaints when asked by the court, and defendants ratified (or amended) their *confesión*. This phase could also include requests for witnesses to reaffirm their testimonies, summons of new witnesses, and disqualifications of others because of their relation to the parties involved. Often, a magistrate would form an *interrogatorio*, a set of questions for the various witnesses to answer. If any inconsistences surfaced among testimonies, a magistrate could form a *careo*, a process in which different parties were brought together to confront one another. (*Careos* could be utilized during the *sumaria* as well.) The *plenario* also included a formal defense of the defendant, carried out either by the accused themselves or by a legal representative (Cutter 1995, 126–8).

The last phase of criminal proceedings was the *sentencia*. During this stage, a magistrate used his discretion (*arbitrio judicial*) to formulate a punishment. Magistrates were not allowed to explain their reasoning for a sentence. However, legal opinions and references to specific laws or legal doctrine do appear in case records, such as in the commentaries presented by *fiscals* and legal representatives prior to sentencing. Ultimately, colonial magistrates drew from a variety of sources to come to their conclusions, utilizing not only written law but also *doctrina* (opinions of jurists), custom, and *equidad* (a sense of fairness). This casuistic approach meant judicial decisions were inconsistent across cases. Further, an accused person could be released on account of an empire-wide pardon (*indulto*) that accompanied a celebration such as a royal wedding (Cutter 1995, 34, 130–1, 141–2). Given this background, we can now turn the typical penalties associated with incestuous crime in colonial Guatemala.

Criminals and Penalties in Guatemalan Incestuous Crime

Examination of penalties (or their absence) within the Guatemalan case sample provides some insight into how legal authorities responded to individuals allegedly involved in incestuous crime. Because incestuous crime so often coincided with other crimes such as adultery, and considering that sample size is limited by the historical record, it is difficult to confidently determine one-to-one correlations between incestuous crime and particular penalties.[21] Nonetheless, sentencing data is revealing in terms of gender, *calidad*, and marital status.

It was not uncommon for individuals in the case sample to escape (major) punishment.[22] When sentencing was recorded, individuals were released, considered as time served, and/or received no (major) penalty approximately 37 percent of the time (49 out of 134 records). Women were more likely than men to fall into this "acquittal" group, with women accounting for 61 percent of acquitted individuals (30 of 49 records) and men for only 39 percent (19 of 49 records). This is consistent with a general pattern in colonial Latin America in which women tended to be punished more leniently than men (Socolow 2015, 158). Such discrepancies make sense considering Iberian law codes characterized women as *imbecillitas sexus* (i.e. an imbecile by her nature), and Castilian law grouped them with children, invalids, and delinquents (see Pescatello 1976, 141–2).

While the gender of a defendant was always evident in criminal cases, *calidad* and marital status were not. Out of 167 records of penalty data, only 89 contained *calidad* information. When *calidad* was recorded, individuals of mixed race accounted for 36 percent (32 of 89 records). Yet, they constituted 58 percent of acquittals (14 of 24 records). Indians, on the other hand, accounted for 55 percent of the total (49 of 89 records), but for only 38 percent of acquittals (9 of 24 records). Spaniards made up 9 percent of the total (8 of 89 records) and only 4 percent of acquittals (1 of 24 records). Thus, individuals of mixed race were the most likely to escape (major) punishment, and Indians were the least likely. Individuals who were *not* married (single or widowed) were more than 2.5 times as likely to be acquitted as individuals who were married (32 versus 12), perhaps because of the coinciding crime of adultery (cf. Castañeda 1983, 114).

While Komisaruk (2008, 371) concluded that sexual violence was largely disregarded in colonial Guatemala, the incest data suggests that the presence or absence of coercion impacted sentencing. When rape was *not* an apparent factor, men accounted for 42 percent of acquittals (13 of 31 records). This decreased to 33 percent when rape was allegedly involved (6 of 18 records). Correspondingly, women constituted 58 percent of acquittals in the absence of rape (18 of 31 records), which increased to 67 percent when rape was allegedly involved (12 of 18 records). This suggests that men were slightly less and women were slightly more likely to be acquitted when coercion formed part of an accusation. The treatment of rape as an aggravating circumstance is also evidenced by discourse. For example, Vicente Fuentes in Case 61 (also in Chapter 1) was told that his crime of sexual relations with his daughter-in-law was magnified because they had been *a la lucha* (i.e. against her will). The apparent concern with coercion in incestuous crime corresponds with Penyak's (2016, 162) findings for Mexico, where ecclesiastical and civil officials likewise considered incest more troubling when it involved violence.

Individuals who did not escape penalty were subjected to four principal categories of punishment—corporal punishment, various forms of forced labor, confinement, and/or orders for physical separation between or a cease (or limit) of communication with at least one of the incestuous parties. Orders intended to prevent communication between parties affected approximately 62 percent of penalized individuals (53 of 85 records).[23] These individuals were almost equally distributed by gender—25 out of 53 records for men, and 28 out of 53 records for women. For individuals whose *calidad* was reported, Indians accounted for 55 percent (16 of 29 records), individuals of mixed race for 31 percent (9 of 29 records), and Spaniards for 14 percent (4 of 29 records).

Two penalties tended to be associated with men, particularly Indian men—forced labor and lashes. Thirty-one percent of penalized individuals were sentenced to forced labor (26 of 85 records), which included armed service, public works projects, and other forms of service. Men accounted for 77 percent of such sentences (20 of 26 records). When controlled for individuals of known *calidad*, Indians accounted for 70 percent (14 of 20 records). Of these, 10 were indigenous men and 4 were indigenous women. Individuals of mixed race accounted for 25 percent (5 of 20 records) and Spaniards for 5 percent (1 of 20 records).

Lashes only affected 13 percent of penalized individuals (11 of 85 records). Ninety-one percent of individuals who received lashes were men

(10 of 11 records). Indians made up 80 percent of individuals of known *calidad* sentenced to lashes (8 of 10 records). Seven were men, and the Indian woman was the only woman in the sample to be sentenced to lashes. Individuals of mixed race accounted for the remaining 20 percent (2 of 10 records). Indeed, Spaniards were rarely subjected to corporal punishment for their crimes. Lashes do not appear in the case sample after 1810, the year in which the Governor and Captain General of Guatemala abolished the practice of whipping commoners and Indians charged with crimes (Salazar 1928 in Jones 1994, 238).

Thirteen percent of penalized individuals were sentenced to confinement (11 of 85 records). This penalty was also gendered—women outnumbered men 9 to 2. Seven of these women were not married (one did not have her marital status listed), suggesting sentences of confinement were more appropriate for single or widowed women. This likely reflects the general concern among colonial authorities to maintain marital units whenever possible. For individuals of known *calidad*, Indians accounted for close to 72 percent (5 of 7 records), individuals of mixed race for 14 percent (1 of 7 records), and Spaniards for 14 percent (1 of 7 records).

Overall, women had a greater tendency to be acquitted than men in incestuous crime, and this tendency increased when sexual violence was involved. When penalties did result, orders aimed at impeding communication between parties were the most common. Lashes and forced labor tended to be a male punishment, whereas confinement was largely a female one. While Indians constituted approximately 55 percent of individuals of known *calidad* in the case sample, they were underrepresented in terms of acquittals and overrepresented when it came to the penalties of forced labor, lashes, and confinement. These discrepancies are particularly striking when juxtaposed to the special considerations Indians were theoretically granted within the court room.

Conclusion

The legal definition of incest in colonial Spanish America was one that was largely inherited from Roman and canon law. Colonial sources suggest that this definition of incest would have resonated in some ways with Mesoamerican incest codes, though the degree of convergence would have varied through time and space, and there were certainly significant differences. The full legal definition of incest was quite extensive, but not all individuals were required to abide by it. In addition, dictionary definitions of incest and the types of cases termed "incest" in colonial Guatemala suggest a working definition of incest that was narrower in scope than its legal counterpart. Even within these tighter parameters, colonial actors continued to commit incestuous offenses, whether they were aware of their illegality or not, finding themselves pleading before any number of individuals within the complex legal terrain of the period.

Women fared better than men when it came to acquittals, especially when rape was involved, and Indians and married individuals were less likely to be acquitted than their non-Indian and single/widowed counterparts. Still, these were not the only issues that factored into judicial response. Colonial authorities were also often concerned with the type of incest that occurred.

Notes

1 Following Jack Goody (1983, 136), the Church had used two systems for determining degrees of consanguinity—the Roman and the Germanic—with a formal shift to the Germanic system in the eleventh century. The Roman system counted degrees by the number of acts of generation between two individuals such that an uncle and niece, for example, were related in the third degree. That is, ego to ego's parent equaled one degree, ego's parent to ego's grandparent equaled one degree, and ego's grandparent to ego's uncle equaled one degree, totaling three degrees. In the Germanic system, sibling groups formed a generation, and degrees were counted by determining the number of generations from a common ancestor. In this system, an uncle and niece would be related in the second degree.

2 ...*yaciendo á sabiendas con su parienta, ó con parienta de su muger ó de otra con quien hobiese yacido fasta el quarto grado....* This is in accordance with the dictates of the Fourth Lateran Council of 1215, which narrowed incest prohibitions from the seventh to the fourth canonical degree of consanguinity and affinity.

3 *Compadradgo* (or *compadrazgo*) would come to refer specifically to the connection between a godparent and the parents of a child. See *Diccionario de Autoridades* (1726–1739 v. 2). This text defines this term in the context of baptism, though presumably it would also apply to confirmation.

4 Spouses of spiritual parents were also included in this category, at least for the rite of baptism.

5 ...*tan mancebos que non podiesen mantener castidat....*

6 It is unclear from the wording whether a woman would also be put to death for committing incest or whether she would be subject to the penalty for adultery specific to women.

7 Only one person was to act as a sponsor for baptism. At most, one man and one woman were permitted. The number of sponsors was not specified for confirmation. However, it was spoken of in the singular.

8 Following the *Diccionario de Autoridades* (1726–1739 v. 2), *cuñado(a)* referred to any relative through affinity regardless of degree. However, its authors noted that in contemporary common usage it denoted a husband or wife of a sibling or the brother or sister of one's spouse.

9 *Cópula o accesso carnal con parienta por consanguinidad o afinidad.*

10 ...*grados de parentesco, de conSaguinidad, y aFinidad, y compadrazgo....* Newberry Library Ayer MS 1508, 147v-8.

11 *A sus hijos e hijas los llamaban siempre por el nombre del padre y de la madre...de esta manera, el hijo de Chel y Chan llamaban Nachanchel, que quiere decir hijos de fulanos y esta es la causa...dicen los indios que los de un nombre son deudos y se tratan por tales...Y asi ninguna mujer u hombre se casaba con otro del mismo nombre porque en ellos era gran infamia.*

12 ...*parentesco, así carnal como espiritual de la abuela, de parte de la madre....*

13 See also Fuentes y Guzmán ([1690] 1882 v. 11, 32).

14 The responsibilities of a *fiscal* included ensuring that all residents attended Mass, teaching children the catechism, and recording matters such as the rite of baptism (Burkhart and Gasco 2007, 212). See, for example, Case 1. This type of *fiscal* differed from the crown attorney referred to by the same title.

15 ...*no era bien fuese co[n] Una criatura en los brazos*... f. 1v-2.

16 *Oidores* were judges with civil *and* criminal functions in Guatemala and other non-viceregal audiencias.

17 *Parcialidad* was the Spanish term for a pre-Hispanic Maya unit of social organization, several of which might have technically fallen under the jurisdiction of a colonial town.

18 ...*siguiendo las huellas del Apostol que los que publicam.te pecan, publicam.te sean corregidos...determiné darle a dho insestuoso publico sincuenta asotes publicos, y siendo requerido para dha penitencia clamó disiendo que pedia no lo desonrrasen y que ofrecia la penitencia pecuniaria de sien para que se aplicasen a esta Yglec.a y Juntam.te prometiendo emmienda...* f. 1, f. 20v.

19 ...*siendo tan facil, especialm.te á los Curas, imponerles por qualquier delito pena de asotes, y despues con titulo de piedad, compensarla en dinero, obligandolos á esta con amenaza...* f. 12.

20 The *ius commune* tradition generally refers to a culture of legal thought formed by a combination of canon and Roman law.

21 In fact, in Case 22, the magistrate explicitly stated that Eusebia Escalante's sentence of reclusion stemmed from perjury.

22 Penalty information was taken from records of 167 individuals in which Josef Silverio Ampérez (Case 65), Andrés Victorio (Case 17), and María Anastacia Vásquez (Case 17) were counted twice because they were each tried on two separate occasions. Punishments such as spiritual exercises, the habilitation of marriage, or court fees were not included as major penalties in the quantitative data. However, all penalty information, including these minor sentences, can be found in the Incest Case Log in the Appendix.

23 If a cease of communication was ordered of one party, all parties whom the order would affect were included in the total number of those subjected to this penalty.

Bibliography

Aguirre, Carlos, and Ricardo D. Salvatore. 2001. "Writing the History of Law, Crime, and Punishment in Latin America." In *Crime and Punishment in Latin America: Law and Society Since Late Colonial Times*, edited by Ricardo D. Salvatore, Carlos Aguirre, and Gilbert M. Joseph, 1–32. Durham, NC and London: Duke University Press.

Archibald, Elizabeth. 2001. *Incest and the Medieval Imagination*. Oxford: Clarendon Press.

Borah, Woodrow. 1982. "The Spanish and Indian Law: New Spain." In *The Inca and Aztec States, 1400–1800: Anthropology and History*, edited by George A. Collier, Renato I. Rosaldo, and John D. Wirth, 265–88. New York and London: Academic Press.

———. 1983. *Justice by Insurance: The General Indian Court of Colonial Mexico and the Legal Aides of the Half-Real*. Berkeley, Los Angeles, London: University of California Press.

Buckley, Theodore Alois. 2014. *The Canons and Decrees of the Council of Trent*. London: Aeterna Press. Kindle.

Burkhart, Louise M., and Janine Gasco. 2007. "The Colonial Period in Mesoamerica." In *The Legacy of Mesoamerica: History and Culture of a Native American Civilization*, edited by Robert M. Carmack, Janine Gasco, and Gary H. Gossen, 2nd ed., 182–221. Upper Saddle River, NJ: Pearson Prentice Hall.

Burkholder, Mark A., and D. S. Chandler. 1977. *From Impotence to Authority: The Spanish Crown and the American Audiencias, 1687–1808*. Columbia: University of Missouri Press.

Castañeda, Carmen. 1983. "La memoria y las niñas violadas." In *La memoria y el olvido: Segundo Simposio de Historia de las Mentalidades*, 107–15. Mexico City: UNAM.

———. 1989. *Violación, estupro, y sexualidad: Nueva Galicia, 1790–1821*. Guadalajara: Hexágano.

Covarrubias Orozco, Sebastián de. 1611. *Tesoro de la lengua castellana, o española*. Madrid: Luis Sánchez. Google Books.

Cunningham, Charles Henry. 1919. *The Audiencia in the Spanish Colonies: As Illustrated by the Audiencia of Manila (1583–1800)*. Berkeley: University of California Press.

Cutter, Charles R. 1995. *The Legal Culture of Northern New Spain, 1700–1810*. Albuquerque: University of New Mexico Press.

Diccionario de Autoridades. 1726–1739. 6 vols. Madrid: Real Academia Española. http://web.frl.es/DA.html.

Dillard, Heath. 1976. "Women in Reconquest Castile: The Fueros of Sepúlveda and Cuenca." In *Women in Medieval Society*, edited by S. M. Stuard, 71–94. Philadelphia: University of Pennsylvania Press.

Escriche, Joaquín. 1874–1876. *Diccionario razonado de legislación y jurisprudencia*. 4 vols. Madrid: Eduardo Cuesta. https://catalog.hathitrust.org/Record/009264676

Few, Martha. 2000. "On Her Deathbed, María de la Candelaria Accuses Michaela de Molina of Casting Spells." In *Colonial Lives: Documents on Latin American History, 1550–1850*, edited by Richard Boyer and Geoffrey Spurling, 166–77. New York and Oxford: Oxford University Press.

Fox, Robin. 1980. *The Red Lamp of Incest*. New York: E. P. Dutton.

Fuentes y Guzmán, Francisco Antonio de. (1690) 1882. *Historia de Guatemala: ó Recordación Florida*, edited by Justo Zaragoza. Madrid: Luis Navarro.

Goody, Jack. 1956. "A Comparative Approach to Incest and Adultery." *The British Journal of Sociology* 7 (4): 286–305.

———. 1983. *The Development of the Family and Marriage in Europe*. Cambridge: Cambridge University Press.

Hill, II, Robert M. 1989. "Social Organization by Decree in Colonial Highland Guatemala." *Ethnohistory* 36 (2): 170–98.

———. 2002. *Colonial Cakchiquels: Highland Maya Adaptation to Spanish Rule, 1600–1700*. Belmont, CA: Thomson Wadsworth.

Jones, Jr., Oakah L. 1994. *Guatemala in the Spanish Colonial Period*. Norman and London: University of Oklahoma Press.

Kellogg, Susan. 1995. *Law and the Transformation of Aztec Culture, 1500–1700*. Norman: University of Oklahoma Press.

Komisaruk, Catherine. 2008. "Rape Narratives, Rape Silences: Sexual Violence and Judicial Testimony in Colonial Guatemala." *Biography* 31 (3): 369–96.

Landa, Fray Diego de. (1566) 2015. *Relación de las cosas de Yucatán*. Madrid: Ediciones Q.

Las Casas, Fray Bartolomé de. 1967. *Apologética historia sumaria*. 3 ed. Vol. 2. Mexico: UNAM.

Las Siete Partidas. 1807. 3 vols. Madrid: Imprenta Real.

Lynch, Joseph H. 1986. *Godparents and Kinship in Early Medieval Europe*. Princeton, NJ: Princeton University Press.

Margadant, Guillermo Floris. 2001. "El concepto de incesto aplicado por la justicia eclesiástica en la Nueva España y en el México independiente preliberal." In *La sexofobia del clero y cuatro ensayos histórico-jurídicos sobre sexualidad*, edited by Guillermo Floris Margadant, 61–95. México: Miguel Ángel Porrúa.

Maxwell, Judith M., and Robert M. Hill, II. 2006. *Kaqchikel Chronicles: The Definitive Edition*. Austin: University of Texas Press.

Motolinía, Fray Toribio de Benavente. 1903. *Memoriales de Fray Toribio de Motolinía*, edited by Luís García Pimentel. México: En casa del editor.

Novísima recopilación de las leyes en España. (1805) 2011. Charleston, SC: Nabu Press.

Penyak, Lee M. 2016. "Incestuous Natures: Consensual and Forced Relations in Mexico, 1740–1854." In *Sexuality and the Unnatural in Colonial Latin America*, edited by Zeb Tortorici, 162–87. Oakland: University of California Press.

Pescatello, Ann M. 1976. *Power and Pawn: The Female in Iberian Families, Societies, and Cultures*. Westport and London: Greenwood Press.

Recopilación de leyes de los reynos de las Indias. 1680. Madrid: Julián de Paredes.

Remesal, Fray Antonio de. (1619) 1988. *Historia general de las Indias Occidentales y particular de la gobernación de Chiapa y Guatemala*. 2 vols. México: Editorial Porrúa.

Restall, Matthew. 1997. *The Maya World: Yucatec Culture and Society, 1550–1850*. Stanford, CA: Stanford University Press.

Rípodas Ardanaz, Daisy. 1977. *El matrimonio en Indias: realidad social y regulación jurídica*. Buenos Aires: Fundación para la Educación, la Ciencia, y la Cultura.

Salazar, Ramón A. 1928. *Historia de veintiún años: la independencia de Guatemala*. Guatemala City: Tipografía Nacional.

Sanchiz Ochoa, Pilar. 1980. "Cambio en la estructura familiar indígena: Influencias de la Iglesia y la Encomienda en Guatemala." *Revista de la Universidad Complutense* 28: 169–91.

Segunda Parte de las Leyes del Reyno: Libro Sexto. 1567. Alcalá de Henares: Casa de Andrés de Angulo. https://catalog.hathitrust.org/Record/009264129

Sellers-García, Sylvia. 2014. *Distance and Documents at the Spanish Empire's Periphery*. Stanford, CA: Stanford University Press.

Sherman, William L. 1979. *Forced Native Labor in Sixteenth-Century Central America*. Lincoln and London: University of Nebraska Press.

Socolow, Susan Migden. 2015. *The Women of Colonial Latin America*. 2nd ed. New York: Cambridge University Press.

Sperling, Jutta. 2004. "Marriage at the Time of the Council of Trent (1560–1570): Clandestine Marriages, Kinship Prohibitions, and Dowry Exchange in European Comparison." *Journal of Early Modern History* 8 (1): 67–108.

Wiesner-Hanks, Merry. 2010. *Christianity and Sexuality in the Early Modern World: Regulating Desire, Reforming Practice.* London and New York: Routledge.

4 Blood Is Thicker than Water

Introduction

Criminal records provide insight into the culture of kinship in colonial Guatemala and its impact on the ways incestuous crime took shape. Debate among legal advisors and defense counsel, statements from defendants and witnesses, and patterns within incestuous crime itself are all indicative of a cultural context in which people tended to value consanguineous kin more highly than affinal kin and kin-like individuals. What also becomes clear from these records is how the nature of a kin tie factored into sexual relations and the legal process, contributing not only to the realization of sexual relations between kin but also to the interpretation of evidence, testimony, and criminality.[1]

Valuations of Incest in Its Various Forms

As we have seen, the term "incest" in its legal definition referred to sexual relations between a variety of individuals. Using "incest" as an umbrella term for sexual intercourse between individuals of such differing connections implies that incest was equally deviant regardless of the particular form it took. However, the greater willingness of the Church to grant dispensations for marriages between third- and fourth-degree relatives following the Council of Trent and the exemption of many non-Spaniards from charges of incest beyond the second degree suggests otherwise (see Chapter 3). Indeed, Penyak (2016, 162) found that ecclesiastical and civil officials in Mexico held a nuanced view of incest, generally considering it nefarious and unnatural when it involved close kin (or violence), but reasonable and natural when cousins desired marriage to a social equal. In colonial Guatemalan incest cases, some individuals distinguished between types of incest, whereas others did not.

It was not uncommon for Guatemalan criminal proceedings to note the degree of incest committed. In fact, some records only include the degree of relatedness between the parties, neglecting to mention the type of relationship between them (e.g. Case 23, Case 57). Only a handful of incest cases in the case sample clearly exceeded first-degree incest.

However, first-degree incest cases occasionally show how degrees of relatedness could impact judicial response. For example, in a 1784 case of stepfather-stepdaughter incest, the *asesor* of the case cited the *Tractatus de Poenis Delictorum* (1603) when stating that incestuous crime could be punished with the death penalty when committed in the closer degrees (Case 10). Similarly, in an 1801 case against Josef Eustaquio García for incest with his daughter, the *fiscal* mentioned in passing "the difference and greater gravity of nefarious copulation between father and daughter compared to incest in general"[2] (Case 28).

Accordingly, some viewed incest between certain consanguines as more criminal than that between others. This discrepancy appeared in a 1785 case of mother-son incest from Nueva Guatemala (Case 11). Don Manuel Hernández Córdova, defense counsel for the son, believed the pair to be innocent, using the mother-son relationship in his justification. He wrote,

> Indecent coitus between an aunt and nephew or between cousins—not to mention that between a mother and son—causes natural horror. Nature itself completely resists it, for nature would run rampant otherwise. And for much greater reason, it resists the manifestation of the coitus of which my party is accused because it's his sixty-year-old mother. It would have been impossible for them to overcome this natural resistance in one fell swoop (and age also happens to be a factor). A continuation of prior affectionate actions would have been necessary for it, with which, even though with much difficulty, the natural horror could perhaps be overcome, but there has been no previous crime.[3]

In other words, first-degree incest between a mother and son is less likely to manifest than second-degree incest such as that between cousins because it is more unnatural, especially when the mother's age is taken into consideration. The fact that mother-son incest involved relatives through the direct line of descent—as opposed to collateral ones—may have also factored into his reasoning here, as will be discussed below.

The gender of a parent was not a major contributor to deviance discourse surrounding parent-child incest as has been found in other contexts.[4] There is certainly an asymmetry in terms of frequency of occurrence in the colonial Guatemalan sample, with father-daughter incest accounting for thirteen cases and mother-son incest for only one (see Table 4.1). This is consistent not only with an environment infused with patriarchal values but also with the apparently universal tendency to avoid sexual relations between mother and child.[5] Though the *alcalde ordinario* in Case 11 referred to mother-son incest as *el más abominable incesto* ("the most abominable incest") and as *tan execrable delito* ("such execrable crime"),

Table 4.1 Incidents of Incest by Kinship Type

Kinship Type		N	Total
Affinity			57
	stepfather/stepdaughter	15	
	brother-in-law/sister-in-law	15	
	man/mother-daughter pair	9	
	man/sister pair	5	
	political uncle/political niece	4	
	father-in-law/daughter-in-law	4	
	stepmother/stepson	1	
	woman/brother pair	1	
	woman/father-son pair	1	
	political first cousins	1	
	n/a, but affinal	1	
Consanguinity			17
	father/daughter	13	
	mother/son	1	
	brother/sister	1	
	uncle/niece	1	
	first cousins	1	
N/A			8

adjectives like "abominable" and "execrable" surfaced in cases of father-daughter incest as well (Case 41, Case 55, Case 66). Further, commentators could be quite explicit regarding the abnormality of father-offenders. The trial of Patricio de León, a farmhand accused of attempted *estupro* (loss of virginity) of his daughter, provides one example (Case 37). According to Asesor Eusebio de Silva,

> the crime of which [these proceedings] deal is atrocious and in such degree that in neither canon nor civil law is there found explicit text that deals (in the matter of incest and its penalties) with that executed between father and daughter. [Incest] is a truly unforeseeable crime, and its repugnance was specified for us since the beginning of written law. Even when Seneca the Elder, a Gentile, happened to touch on the deformity of coitus between immediate relatives, he considered it extremely criminal. And effectively, in common law, the culprits of this crime were punished with the penalty of death, having force of law, for example, sexual relations with a stepdaughter, stepmother, niece, etc. Therefore, being of superior gravity that which Patricio

de León is said to have had with his young daughter Francisca, the only option would be (following the merit of the trial) to order him hanged.[6]

Silva then went on to state the elements of the case that were in Patricio's favor, including the need for greater evidence in incest of the first degree than in common crimes of the flesh, where *presunción vehemente* ("strong presumption") plays a greater role than *prueba positiva* ("definitive proof"). (This particular issue will be discussed further below.) In the end, Patricio received twenty-five lashes and six months of public works. Thus, despite the presence of various forms of gender inequality in colonial society, there is no clear evidence from colonial Guatemala that mother-son incest was more wholly condemned than father-daughter incest.

Some individuals placed greater weight on incest between consanguines than between affines. This distinction appeared in the criminal records associated with Esteban Quiñones, who was tried for incest with his stepdaughter in 1784 (Case 10). According to his *defensor*, Marcelo de Rivera y Córdova, "the incest that he committed is not one of the most abhorred ones and which the laws punish with greater severity because the girl is not his relative through consanguinity but rather through affinity."[7] In contrast, the *fiscal* of the case argued that *Las Siete Partidas* did not differentiate between consanguineous incest and affinal incest in terms of penalties.

Looking at the case sample as a whole, incest cases involving individuals connected through affinity are better represented. In fact, cases of affinal incest are more than three times as common as those involving blood relatives (see Table 4.1).[8] The greater frequency of affinal incest compared to consanguineous incest could be indicative of a greater willingness on the part of residents of colonial Guatemala to participate in the former over the latter. At the least, it suggests an increased likelihood for affinal incest accusations to be brought forward. In terms of sentencing, individuals accused of affinal incest fared slightly better in terms of acquittals (about 40%, or 40 out of 99 records) than those accused of consanguineous incest (29%, or 7 out of 24 records).[9] Further, a greater proportion of incidents of consanguineous incest involved rape (41%, or 7 of 17 records) than their affinal counterparts (26%, or 19 of 72 records),[10] which implies that affinal incest was more likely to be consensual than consanguineous incest. Like the *defensor* for Esteban Quiñones, these tendencies suggest that affinal incest enjoyed a greater level of cultural acceptability than consanguineous incest. With an increased tolerance for affinal incest, one would also expect to find a larger absolute number of female affinal kin among rape victims than female blood kin. This pattern did, in fact, obtain, with female affinal kin representing nearly 75 percent of the total number of rape victims (19 versus 7) (see Table 2.1).

There was not any apparent association between incest type (affinal versus consanguineous) and socioracial group. Jaffary (2007, 99) found that in Mexico, Indians tended to submit dispensation applications to remove affinity impediments to marriage, whereas Spaniards were more likely to submit applications for consanguinity impediments. In colonial Guatemala, cases of affinal incest outnumbered cases of consanguineous incest 3 to 1 when one or more Indians were involved and 3.8 to 1 when one or more individuals of mixed race were involved. Spaniards only accounted for four cases of incest—two were affinal and two were consanguineous (see Table 4.2). Hence, tendencies towards affinal incest prevailed for both Indians and those of mixed race, while Spaniards demonstrated no clear tendency.

Whether or not affinity had been formally contracted through marriage or informally through sexual intercourse also had the potential to influence legal opinion. In 1801, Manuel Canales was accused of incest with a woman whose relationship to him was not specified and the carrying of arms (Case 27), a privilege typically reserved for Spaniards barring special circumstances (see Burkholder 1998, 23; Schwaller 2016, 104). During the trial, Fiscal Piloña indicated he was not opposed to converting the punishment of Manuel from two years of imprisonment to two years of public works, "considering the *parentesco* between the two originated from illicit copulation"[11] (cf. Waldron 1989, 159) and the carrying of arms in public had not been proven.

Overall, legal professionals seem to have agreed that incest in general was criminal, but some perceived certain forms of incest as more criminal, unnatural, etc. Variation in this regard is not surprising since multiple cultural and legal resources were available for use when it came to formulating arguments. But the greater representation of criminal records pertaining to first-degree and affinal incest is suggestive that

Table 4.2 Incidents of Incest and *Calidad*

Calidad	Kinship Type	N	Total
Indian			26
	Affinity	18	
	Consanguinity	6	
	N/A	2	
Mixed Race			24
	Affinity	19	
	Consanguinity	5	
Spanish			4
	Affinity	2	
	Consanguinity	2	

sexual relations between first-degree and affinal relatives were more likely to manifest than sexual relations between relatives of greater degrees and through blood ties. To be sure, relatives of the first and second degrees were more likely to interact with one another on a regular basis, making consensual and forced sexual relations between them a greater possibility. Further, knowledge of extended kin may have been limited, and many individuals in the case sample would have been exempt from accusations of incest beyond the second degree due to their socioracial classification. The tendency towards affinal incest appears to speak to a greater level of cultural acceptability of incestuous relations of this type, especially when comments to the same effect are taken into consideration.

Sharing a Bed: Assumptions Regarding Kin and Sexual Relations

In his highly influential *Summa Theologica*, St. Thomas Aquinas commented on the danger of blood relatives living in close proximity to one another. He stated plainly that prohibitions on sexual unions between relatives were needed because opportunities for them would be frequent otherwise, thereby allowing lust to enervate the minds of men (Aquinas 1265–1274, Q. 154, Art. 9, Part 2). Echoes of such concerns reached colonial Latin America and had implications for the sleeping arrangements of kin since sleeping areas were associated with sexual intimacy. For example, Bishop Mariano Martí of Venezuela warned heads of households against allowing members of the opposite sex to share beds and sleeping quarters (see Waldron 1989, 169–70). In colonial Guatemalan criminal records, individuals who shared a bed were often suspected of sexual involvement by both authority figures and laymen alike. However, finding relatives together in a bed proved to be more complicated when it came to interpreting motive.

This issue of bedsharing surfaced in an 1803 incest case against Domingo Morales and his sister-in-law, María Dolores Gaitán (Case 39). In making his arguments, the *procurador de pobres* (attorney assigned to aid the poor) representing Dolores referenced the *doctrina* of Antonio Gómez, author of *Comentarios a las Leyes de Toro* (1552), which was written with respect to the Laws of Toro promulgated in Spain in 1505. He argued that following this text,

> to find relatives naked in the same bed does not establish presumption nor evidence of copulation between them because, even though it would be sufficient with respect to *extraños* ["strangers," i.e. non-relatives], relatives have in their favor a stronger and more vehement presumption of honesty born from shared *parentesco*.[12]

That is, unlike non-relatives, relatives can share a bed without causing suspicion. However, he went on to say that Gómez included in this text his own contrary opinion that

> to find consanguines naked in the same bed is sufficient evidence of the incest, but he [Gómez] also says that this should only be understood when these *collateral* [emphasis added] relatives lie in the bed secretly and occultly, and not in public, because in this case such evidence would not be sufficient.[13]

In other words, relatives who share a direct line of descent have a greater presumption of honesty than collateral relatives do, but if the latter are open about sleeping in the same bed, then it is likely they are not trying to conceal any illicit sexual activity. Because the attorney proceeded to apply the *doctrina* of Gómez to a case involving a brother-and sister-in-law, collateral relatives through affinity also benefited from the presumption of honesty to a certain degree as long as they did not keep their sleeping arrangements secret. In fact, Gómez himself spoke in terms of *parientes* and *parientas* (male and female relatives through consanguinity or affinity) (Nolasco de Llano 1785, 355), as opposed to *consanguineos* ("consanguines"). Of course, opinions regarding the presumption of honesty clearly varied.

Sleeping arrangements between parents and children were theoretically subject to regulation. For instance, during their inspections of Indian dwellings in Jacaltenango, *corregidores* "checked to see that each house had beds above floor level, that each contained only one family, that children's beds were separate from those of their parents, and that male and female children had separate beds" (Collins 1980, 117–8).[14] Attempts such as these to keep parents and children from sleeping together could have been inspired by contemporary anxieties that children who witnessed their parents having sex would be encouraged to do the same (see Lavrin 1989, 77). However, prevention of parent-child incest likely played a part as well. This is evident from the account of Pedro Cortés y Larraz, Archbishop of Guatemala, who toured and interviewed priests throughout the Archdiocese in the late eighteenth century. He recorded that the priest of the parish of San Cristóbal Totonicapán, a largely K'iche' area, told him that "the dominant vices there are inebriation and lasciviousness, abandoning themselves to horrible incests between parents and children ... the immediate risk being that everyone sleeps together"[15] (Cortés y Larraz 1958, 105). Allusions to such risk were not limited to interactions between colonial authorities and indigenous populations. In Case 11 above, Josef María Santa Cruz (a *mestizo*) was asked whether he ever slept "in the same bed under the same cover as his mother, and if he has ever experienced from her a particular action or affection that might denote some lewd request."[16] He answered in the negative, and both he and his (*mestiza*) mother indicated that they had slept separately since he was young.

Indeed, testimonies suggest that age factored into the presumption of honesty when parents and children shared a bed. This sentiment was alluded to in an 1801 case of father-daughter incest involving Josef Eustaquio García, an Indian bricklayer residing in Nueva Guatemala (Case 28). According to his sixteen-year-old daughter María Josefa, her father came home drunk one night and eventually got on top of her when she was well asleep. She told him, "Tata ['Dad' or 'Daddy'], I'll tell Nana ['Mom' or 'Mommy']," and called to her mother several times. But her mother did not hear her, and she ceased calling her because she feared her father would hit her. María Josefa tolerated him for a little less than a half hour before she again told him she would tell her mother. At that point, he let her be. She did not tell anyone about what happened because she feared what would happen to her. This incident marked María Josefa's loss of virginity, and she was now pregnant.

Interrogated about the matter, Josef Eustaquio similarly stated that some acquaintances brought him home drunk one night. He said he lay down in the first bed he came across without distinguishing between them. He was upset when he woke up the following day with his daughter next to him and remonstrated his wife for allowing him to sleep in her bed. Evidently, Josef Eustaquio considered this behavior inappropriate. Apparently, his wife did too, telling him that they left him there because they were unable to move him.

Both María Josefa and her mother, Gorgonia Valensuela, were questioned about whether the girl's father ever slept in her bed. Gorgonia said her daughter was given a separate bed once she started getting older. However, it was in the same room as the parents' bed because they were poor. María Josefa said she and her father only shared a bed the night of the incident. Like her mother, she said that "ever since she was young, or 'reason entered her,' her mother put her in a separate bed such that she never made use of her father's bed, even though they were in the same room."[17] Thus, while it may have been acceptable for young children to share a bed with their parents, sleeping arrangements needed to be altered once they reached a certain age (cf. Case 11).

The association between age and permissible sleeping arrangements also appeared in the proceedings carried out against an Indian family in San Miguel Totonicapán (Case 19). In 1797, suspicion arose that Miguel Caixon[18] committed incest with his stepdaughter. During a search of the home, the *comisionado* encountered Miguel's wife, Antonia Chaclan (or Sic),[19] lying down with a small child of about three years of age. Following his statement, Antonia asked him what he was looking for and told him that only she and her husband were there, sleeping on the floor. However, the *comisionado* reportedly found a large naked woman stretched out and face down beneath the sleeping mat. When he asked who she was, Antonia claimed she was a *criatura* ("infant" or "young child"). Obviously not believing her, the *comisionado* slapped the woman and said, "Get up *criatura*!" The report of the *comisionado* insinuates that Antonia thought a *criatura* sleeping alongside her and Miguel did not constitute a criminal matter. She not only used the term *criatura* to describe an older individual, but also failed to acknowledge the child she was holding when telling the *comisionado* that only she and her husband were there.

The issue of the bed came up in the testimonies of Antonia and Miguel, which were taken with the aid of an interpreter and likely originally given in K'iche'. At this point in the proceedings, it was known that Juana Velasco (Antonia's daughter and Miguel's stepdaughter) was about twenty-five years old. For her part, Antonia claimed that her daughter hid underneath the straw flooring of the dwelling, not under the sleeping mat. In so doing, she distanced her daughter from the controversial sleeping area altogether. In contrast, Miguel did not deny that his stepdaughter was in his bed. Instead, he said that even though the authorities found her there, she was sleeping next to her mother so they could share a blanket because they only had two. His explanation implies that the presence of Antonia (and a need to stay warm) would add a licit hue to an otherwise damning discovery. Thus, a female parent sharing a bed with an adult daughter was not as scandalous as a male stepparent doing the same, and Miguel may have been drawing from assumptions related to blood kin *and* a heteronormative environment in making his point, considering parents were not necessarily free from suspicion when it came to bedsharing.

In sum, testimony related to sleeping arrangements could constitute a significant piece of evidence in trials dealing with "crimes of the flesh," but in the context of incest, the issue of bedsharing reveals mixed messages regarding assumptions about kin. On the one hand, kin (or at least certain kin) were assumed to naturally avoid sexual engagement with one another in a space otherwise associated with sexual intimacy. On the other, kin (and colonial authorities) needed to be diligent about maintaining boundaries in such spaces, at least once children were beyond a certain age.

(Dis)Respecting Kin

As in many realms of kin relations, the issue of *respeto* ("respect") sometimes emerged in colonial Guatemalan incest trials. In his work on late colonial Mexico, Stern (1995, 213) discussed how the various meanings of *respeto* "incorporated a core idea of restraint, a deference to order, place, and legitimacy that restrained destructive inner impulses— whether the impulse to challenge authority or to abuse it." In Guatemala, sexual relations with one's kin could be framed as a lack of respect.

Disrespect in these terms surfaced in Case 11 against Manuela Antonia Hernández and Josef María Santa Cruz for mother-son incest. When Josef María was informed of the charge, he claimed that he "has never, at any time, nor through ill thought, had with his mother the slightest insolence regarding the matter, as in addition to being an older woman, he has always kept a mother's due respect."[20] In other words, respect towards and sexual relations with one's mother was incompatible in his eyes. Such sentiments were not without precedent. St. Thomas Aquinas pointed out the inconsistency between respect for one's parents (and other blood relatives) and the shamefulness of sexual intercourse (Aquinas 1265–1274, Q. 154, Art. 9, Part 2).

This aspect of respect was not limited to consanguineous kin or the parent-child tie in colonial Guatemala. Micaela Gerónima Catalán, a witness in an incest trial involving José María Díaz (alias Cantarillas) and his sister-in-law Agustina (no surname listed), demonstrated this in her statement (Case 68). Micaela said that she had lived with the pair for a period of time, and it was evident to her that they saw one another as brother- and sister-in-law. Agustina had taken care of *las cosas de la casa* ("the things of the house") since José María was widowed by her sister. Micaela claimed that she had never witnessed

> any action that might indicate wrongdoing, as Cantarillas treats Agustina with the *respeto de cuñada* ["a sister-in-law's respect"], sleeping each one in their bed, and they only receive one another when it is time to eat and drink...and when his wife died, she left Agustina, her sister, in charge of caring for her husband the same as she had.[21]

Hence, Micaela defended her housemates against the charge of incest by drawing on a discourse of respect and an emphasis on sleeping arrangements. Further, the remainder of the interactions between the two accused were largely the result of Agustina fulfilling her sister's wishes. If this was truly the case, Agustina would no longer be able to carry out this obligation, as she and her brother-in-law were ordered to separate their residences.

Despite the opposition between sexual relations and respect towards kin, concern over maintaining respect could actually contribute to their manifestation. In 1793, doña Micaela Sermenio denounced her husband, a Spanish man by the name of don Juan Manuel Dardón, for a long-term *concubinato* with their daughter María Josefa (Case 15). Though it had been going on for ten years, Micaela believed that for the first seven years, her husband only used María Josefa *en tactos* ("in touches"), not taking her virginity until later. She maintained that María Josefa was never agreeable to her father's indecencies, but she went along with them "possessed by fear, terror, and respect with regard to his quarrels and threats."[22] Her daughter always told her about what happened in the hope that she would rectify the situation, telling her when she was young to not leave her alone with her father, and once she was older, "to remedy her misfortune, as she was condemned and against her will would go to hell."[23] This latter statement speaks tragically to how the psychological trauma of incestuous rape could include concerns about the afterlife. According to Micaela, her husband intended to alternate whose bed he slept in, sleeping with her some nights and with their daughter on others. After he slept in their daughter's bed for five consecutive nights, Micaela made a formal accusation to a priest, and María Josefa was put in *depósito*.

María Josefa's statement was thematically similar to that of her mother. She reported that nine years prior her father, "taking advantage of *halagos de padre* ['affectionate displays of a father'] and [her] innocence, had *polución* with her; that is, he used her legs and area external to her uterus for rubbing and ejaculation."[24] These episodes continued with frequency, even taking place when her mother was nearby. (Her mention of the presence of her mother seems to have been a means to highlight the gall of her father.) After many years, he took her virginity by force, "and even though he maintains that she gave her body to him, she was possessed by terror and respect."[25] He continued in *concubinato* with her for the next year, and there were so many acts she could not number them, "but he did not consummate any of them *intra vas* ['inside the vessel'] because he had particular diligence in *extravasación* [i.e. ejaculation outside of the vagina]."[26] Recently, her father had been sleeping with her in the same room as her mother, who slept alone with the other children in her bed. Asked what measures she took to avoid the persecution by her father, she said that she always told her mother what happened (despite her father warning her against it) and asked her to rectify it. However, her mother, "not having greater freedom than her, nor better reach, wanted to remedy it quietly and with the complaints"[27] she made to ecclesiastical and royal authorities. Micaela's relative inability to help her daughter without the aid of male authorities underlines the inferior position of female allies compared to mobilized patriarchs (see Stern 1995, 98–108).

From the statements of María Josefa and her mother, it is clear that violent intimidation was not the only factor contributing to María Josefa's continued sexual abuse by her father. Kin norms that demanded respect towards one's father also played a part. Both women used the concept of respect in their attempt to alleviate culpability on the part of María Josefa. As a daughter, she was in a subordinate position relative to her father, making resistance that much more untenable. In fact, María Josefa argued he even used fatherly affection to take advantage of her as a young girl, implicitly suggesting another man would not have been so successful. Initially blinded to the crime by youth and trust in a father's love, she was later obliged to participate out of respect and fear. Respect, then, could be a double-edged sword.

This dual nature of respect also appeared in a case of alleged incest between a stepfather and stepdaughter. In 1810, Felipe Gil, resident of Santa Cruz del Quiché, was accused of mistreating his wife because of his relationship with her daughter, Petrona Alvarado, who was nineteen years old and pregnant (Case 58). When giving her statement, Petrona was asked how she could have had sex with Felipe, given that he was the husband of her mother, "committing such repugnant excesses." She replied that

> as she was a girl and had a reverential respect towards him, she would always obey him in whatever he ordered of her, leaving the house with him on trips or to their farm. As soon as they were alone, he caressed her, she attributing these affections to an honest love, until he purposely started pushing the boundaries with her little by little on the occasions, without words nor awareness intervening. Once there was time to reflect, Felipe Gil had already consummated the act with her. [She] did not have sexual relations with any other person than him, and she always gave in, even though with repugnance, because she did not dare to tell him no.[28]

In other words, being young and undesirous of disrespecting or offending her stepfather in some way, Petrona obliged him when he wished to have sexual relations with her, and she continued to do so even after she understood their impropriety. For Petrona, respect demanded consent even in matters she (and others) deemed inappropriate.

Ironically, Petrona was scolded during questioning that she should have viewed Felipe with *respetos de padre* ("a father's respect") since he was married to her mother and refused to comply with his sexual advances. Here, the two competing narratives of respect emerged side by side. In one, respect demanded compliance in sexual matters, whereas, in the other, respect was wholly opposed to such matters. Because Petrona leaned towards the former, while the magistrate was partial to the latter, Petrona's defense was compromised. She was instead portrayed as breaching kin norms. Ultimately, Felipe and Petrona were released due to a general royal pardon. Felipe needed to cover the fees of the trial and carry out measures for the habilitation of his marriage. Petrona was instructed to move in with her grandfather.

In Cases 15 and 58, both María Josefa and Petrona had been reared by their persecutors and their abuse had started when they were young, undoubtedly making the power these father-offenders wielded over them particularly strong. But *respetos de padre* could contribute to incestuous violence against women outside their natal homes as well. Recall Rosalía Surqueah, whose story opened this book (Case 61). She and her husband lived with his parents, and she was sexually assaulted by her father-in-law on two occasions. Among the arguments made in her defense was the idea that, even if Rosalía had not refused sex with her father-in-law, one could assume that respect for her father and fear of raising a hand to him would have prevented her from defending herself.

Overall, these cases demonstrate an intimate link between notions of familial respect and incest. While respect towards kin theoretically presented an impediment to sexual relations between them, this same respect could contribute to sexual violence against female relatives. This kind of environment would no doubt lead to feelings of ambivalence within the realm of kin relations, an essentially universal feature of kinship systems (see Peletz 2001).

Kin and the Justice System

Guatemalan incest cases reveal not only expectations of kin in terms of sexual relations but also assumptions about how kin would behave in the courtroom. Indeed, family members played a major role in criminal proceedings involving incestuous crime. In cases in which a plaintiff was identified (48 of 75 records),[29] relatives (through blood or marriage; one was a godparent) of one or more parties were responsible for bringing the accusation forward approximately 71 percent of the time (34 of 48 records) (see Tables 4.3 and 4.4).

Significantly, women outnumbered men nearly 2 to 1 as plaintiffs in these cases when authority figures are excluded (see Tables 4.5 and 4.6).[30] The discrepancy between male and female plaintiffs demonstrates how women in particular relied on the courts for the correction of perceived wrongs within the familial and marital realm, a pattern that was likely in response to a lack of authority within the home itself.

Plaintiffs gave various reasons for coming forward. According to Manuel Valencia, he went to authorities to clear his conscience and "because he was a Christian and eager for the honor of God" (Case 7).[31] When Ana Alvarado (mother of the aforementioned Petrona Alvarado) was asked her intention in denouncing her husband, she said "only the ability to live with him licitly should he be excused"[32] and that she would forgive him for his injury to her (Case 58). Of course, accusations that plaintiffs went to the authorities out of revenge or ill will towards the defendants were not uncommon, and plaintiffs and witnesses alike could find themselves swearing under oath that they did not testify for such reasons.

Table 4.3 Plaintiff(s) Type in Incest Cases

Relative(s)	Self	Other	N/A	Total
34	2	12	27	75

Table 4.4 Case Numbers by Plaintiff(s) Type

Relatives	Self	Other	N/A
2, 6, 7, 8, 9, 10, 12, 15, 16, 18, 21, 22, 25, 26, 28, 29, 32, 35, 44, 45, 47, 48, 55, 56, 58, 60, 61, 62, 63, 64, 65a, 65b, 66, 73	5, 59	4, 11, 14, 20, 24, 30, 31, 37, 39, 46, 53, 69	1, 3, 13, 17a, 17b, 19, 23, 27, 33, 34, 36, 38, 40, 41,42, 43, 49, 50, 51, 52, 54, 57, 67, 68, 70, 71, 72

Table 4.5 Plaintiffs by Gender

Women	Men	Authorities	N/A	Total
34	19	3	26	82

Table 4.6 Case Numbers of Plaintiffs by Gender

Women	Men	Authorities	N/A
5, 6, 8, 9, 10, 15, 16, 17a, 18, 21, 22, 25,28, 29, 30, 35, 39, 45, 47, 48, 53, 55, 56, 58, 59, 60, 62, 63, 64, 65a, 65b, 66, 73	2, 4, 7, 11, 12, 24, 26, 31, 32, 37, 44, 46, 61, 65a, 73	14, 20, 69	1, 3, 13, 17b, 19, 23, 27, 33, 34, 36, 38, 40, 41, 42, 43, 49, 50, 51, 52, 54, 57,67, 68, 70, 71, 72

As discussed in Chapter 2, some women and girls were afraid to look for aid when they experienced abuse at the hands of male kin. Case 16 reflects these concerns and shows how the courtroom could be rigged in favor of a patriarch even when plaintiffs decided to come forward. In 1794 Nueva Guatemala, Valentina and Sabina Castellanos reported their widowed father, Tomás Castellanos, to the *alcalde de barrio* (an official charged with law enforcement in a subdivision of a city) for physically mistreating them and kicking them out of the house because of a *mala amistad* he had with Ana María Turcios. Because their brother, Mariano Castellanos, had already been ordered to distance himself from a woman named Ana María, the magistrate asked if this was the same woman. The girls answered in the affirmative, which implied Ana María was in an incestuous relationship with a man and his son. According to the *alcalde de barrio*, Valentina and Sabina "begged me for their accusation to never be known because of the cruel punishment that they would experience."[33] Thus, he proceeded to carry out measures with the greatest secrecy to obtain the truth. Nonetheless, Tomás eventually appeared at court saying he knew about the accusation of his daughters and Ana María's arrest following it. Tomás claimed Ana María took care of his house and that the punishment of his daughters was the result of their misconduct—Sabina was pregnant from a married man.

When Valentina and Sabina were brought in to formally testify, the father-daughter relationship between them and Tomás worked against them. The magistrate asked Valentina "the reason she had to denounce her father, fathers being the people to whom children owe the most reverence and love across the land?"[34] Just by denouncing her father, then, Valentina was automatically put on the defensive. The magistrate questioned Sabina in like manner, and both of them referenced their father's mistreatment. But the ability to frame a denunciation against one's father as somehow disrespectful or disloyal surely would have contributed to an atmosphere in which children were hesitant to bring one forward.

Tomás, on the contrary, utilized the father-daughter relationship to his advantage. When he appeared at court a second time, he reiterated that, as a widower, he felt it was necessary to have someone care for the family when he was away earning a living, and that he looked upon his daughters with tenderness and kindness as he sought to protect their honor. Further, "Children are crows for picking out one's eyes. And, according to law, they should not dishonor their father except in capital cases, as so orders the Fourth Commandment of the Ten Commandments [i.e. 'Honor your mother and father.']."[35] In other words, Tomás was acting in the interest of his daughters in correcting them, but they were acting unlawfully in reporting him to the authorities. In a later statement, Tomás said that he presumed his older daughters were utilizing the false accusation to avenge his attempts to correct their excesses. Ultimately, the resolution of the case left Tomás with the court fees and Ana María with instructions to return to her husband's side.

Similar themes surfaced in Case 66 in which Juana Josefa Gómez, an Indian girl of about fourteen years of age, accused her father of being sexually involved with her sister María Baltazara. Fearing he would do the same with her, she reportedly asked the *alcalde* of Canales, "for the love of God, to find her a home where she can serve [as a domestic servant] because she did not want to be with her father."[36] Don Vicente Arrazola, *defensor* for her father, briefly noted "the oddity that it is for a child to accuse their father."[37] In like manner, the *curador* for María Baltazara referred to Juana Josefa as *la vil denunciante de su padre* ("the wicked denouncer of her father"). Further, he argued that María Baltazara admitted to the crime during a *careo* with her father (and after initially denying it) because, "as she would see her father José María confess to a crime that he had not committed, she, in order to not refute him, not knowing what he was doing, manifested her conviction."[38] Fear of punishment by the authorities was also a factor. Thus, this case not only points to an environment in which a child might fear going to the authorities with a problem but also to one in which they could be intimidated into changing their testimony after a trial began.

Yet, kin norms also had the potential to support denunciations by family members. After María Baltazara denied any sexual engagement with her father, the *comisionado* ordered her to not perjure herself, "as her own sister Juana Josefa accuses her, that she has not been pressured nor obligated to denounce them."[39] That is, no one would falsely accuse a sibling on their own. Still, for her part, María Baltazara retorted that "her sister is a liar. And, perhaps, they have counseled her."[40]

Likewise, in 1810 San Raymundo, doña Josefa Soto reported an alleged ongoing relationship between her sister and husband to the authorities (Case 62). She had denounced them many years before, and despite various complaints and measures taken to end the relationship, it continued. When her sister, doña Salomé Soto, was questioned about the accusation, she argued that her involvement with her brother-in-law ended eleven or twelve years prior and that her sister's recent claims were spurred by jealousy. Nonetheless, the magistrate reprimanded Salomé for being untruthful, "as, with [the accusation] coming from her sister, there must be definitive reasons for [Josefa] to complain of her illicit commerce with her husband—not jealousy alone."[41] In other words, a woman would not be so careless as to denounce her own sister to the authorities unless she was certain of her guilt.

Sometimes expectations of kin in the legal arena depended on whether an individual was a relative through consanguinity, affinity, or neither. In 1811, Pedro Calderón, a *mulato* tailor in Nueva Guatemala, was accused of physically and verbally abusing his wife and the *estupro* of his stepdaughter, Petrona Calderón (Case 63). The formal denunciation came from his sister-in-law (aunt of Petrona), but Petrona testified against him. During her testimony, Petrona recounted the violent rape by her stepfather. The marks he left on her face caught the attention of her aunt, who asked Petrona about them. Petrona responded, "I'm sorry that my little sister is growing up because otherwise she would not see the bad example of my father."[42]

Pedro denied the accusation and drew on the issue of relatedness to defend himself. He claimed that Petrona only testified against him at the advice of her aunt—with whom he had not gotten along—who went so far as to tell Petrona that she was not his daughter. He explained how his wife was pregnant with Petrona, a *hija de otro* ("daughter of another"), when they married, but as this was not known, Petrona was baptized under the assumption that she was a legitimate daughter. Told by the *alcalde ordinario* that

> it is unbelievable that the counsel of the aunt would make such a greater impression on Petrona than the natural impression of a father on a daughter that she would falsely accuse him, [Pedro] said

it's not surprising that the girl would give in to the advice of the aunt when the latter has impressed upon her that she is not his daughter.[43]

Thus, Pedro believed that Petrona's new awareness that he was not her (real) father contributed to her willingness to testify falsely against him. In other words, a (real) daughter, in this case one that shared a blood tie, would have behaved differently.

Don Joaquín Mariscal, the *procurador de número* (municipal lawyer) who assisted Pedro, spoke in a similar manner. Rhetorically asking why Petrona would *levantar el cuello* ("raise her head") against his client, he argued, "She would not have dared such disrespect if her aunt Antonia had not encouraged her insubordination, making her realize that she was not his daughter."[44] Mariscal's requests to the magistrate included the release of his client and an order for Petrona to *se sugete á su padrastro* ("respect her stepfather"). Thus, a daughter—as opposed to a stepdaughter—would not display contempt for her father, and a stepdaughter might require a reminder that a stepfather was due the same respect. Here again, it is apparent that the discourse of respect would discourage some children from going to the authorities. Indeed, Petrona's almost fatalistic attitude towards the sexual abuse from Pedro appears in her comment to her aunt about the future of her little sister.

The importance of consanguineous relatedness to truth telling also appeared in the aforementioned case against don Juan Manuel and María Josefa Dardón for father-daughter incest (Case 15). Even though María Josefa testified to her father's use of her "outside the vessel" and his responsibility for her deflowerment, don Juan Manuel completely denied the accusation. In a written document, he even proceeded to disown his family because of their behavior, including his daughter's testimony against him. In a section of this rather lengthy text, he wrote,

...I am not a married man nor do I have any children because a woman that I had in my company, who was caring for me for some time, left and took her children as soon as she got bored of caring for me.... The girl that accuses me of such enormous crimes is the daughter of the woman that cared for me and is named María Josefa. She is not my daughter because, if she were, she would not dishonor her father with such lack of restraint.... If I were her father—like she says—*le tirara la sangre* [i.e. blood would drive her] to come for her father upon seeing him in the calamity that he is and imprisoned for such great crimes of which she accuses him. Thus, I take as null her false statement. And though [María Josefa] considers herself the daughter of Micaela [Juan Manuel's wife], she is not because, if she were, she would not try—nor would she have tried—to separate her father from the side of her mother knowing that they were married. Therefore, she is not a daughter but rather a *pepe* [a non-biological child reared in the home].[45]

Following this document, don Juan Manuel believed that a biological daughter would not make a false accusation against her father that would result in his harm or the disunion of her parents. In fact, María Josefa became increasingly removed from consanguineous connections within the family as his argument evolved. In injuring her father, María Josefa became fatherless. Having jeopardized the marital bond between her parents, she could no longer claim either of them.[46]

Similar themes surfaced in a 1796 case in which Engracia Mangoche, resident of Nueva Guatemala, accused her husband of mistreatment and the violent *estupro* of her niece, Cecilia Mangoche (Case 18). Cecilia also testified to the *estupro*. But while her husband was in custody for the trial, Engracia decided to drop her complaint because her family was suffering in his absence. However, the case was continued *de oficio* (on the court's initiative) because of the gravity of the crime.

In later testimony, Engracia reported, "I have come to learn that Cecilia is not a blood relative of mine by any means."[47] Cecilia (and her sister) "are surnamed Mangoche, and they treated me as a relative. I ignorantly took them as such. This is why Cecilia says my husband is the person who took her virginity, even though this is false."[48] She then went on to say that if what Cecilia said was true, Cecilia was the one who incited it. Engracia's words make clear that accusations from non-relatives warranted a greater amount of suspicion than those from blood kin. Indeed, Engracia agreed with Cecilia when she believed she was her niece. However, when it turned out otherwise, Cecilia became a slanderer. Regardless of whether Engracia's revelation was new—or even truthful—Engracia clearly hoped it would resonate with authorities and prompt her husband's release. In the end, Engracia's husband was included in a general royal pardon, which resulted in his release from prison, though he was to neither reside nor communicate with Cecilia in the future. Engracia, on the other hand, was to be tried for perjury.

Yet, one could assume that consanguineous kin might lie in court if it meant that a blood relative would profit—rather than suffer—from it. In 1809 Nueva Guatemala, Isidora Caseros, a thirty-six-year-old *mulata* woman, was charged with injuring María Josefa Pineda, which ultimately resulted in the latter's death (AGCA A2.2 Leg. 230 Exp. 4899). The two were *hermanas de leche* ("milk sisters"). This theoretically meant that they breastfed from the same woman, though this term apparently described individuals who were raised together as well. Both María Josefa and Bartola Betancurt, mother of María Josefa and the woman who raised Isidora, presented Isidora as the instigator in the scuffle. Even though Bartola and Isidora referred to one another as "mother" and "daughter," Isidora allegedly called María Josefa an *hija de puta* ("daughter of a whore"). This slur was an insult to mother and daughter alike, suggesting that the relationship between Isidora and Bartola was distinctive. Further, Isidora discounted Bartola's testimony when she said, "one cannot presume that she [Bartola] would side with [her] over her own daughter [María Josefa]."[49] Like Isidora, Asesor Robles underlined how the agreement between María Josefa and Bartola that Isidora was the insulter in the incident should be suspect because, "in legal opinion, it is always assumed that a parent wants to help their child."[50] Thus, blood ties could actually lead someone to testify falsely for the sake of a relative. Both this case and Case 15 above indicate that ties between parents and non-biological children raised in the home could be construed as more fragile than those with other children.

The testimony of spouses could also be called into question, particularly in the case of women. One example comes from the 1798 case against Hipólito Cojulum,[51] an Indian man from Quetzaltenango accused of various crimes including the rape and deflowerment of his sister-in-law, spousal abuse, and causing his wife to miscarry on two occasions (Case 21). Hipólito's legal representative argued that wives, especially when offended, could make "an ant the size of an elephant" (i.e. they exaggerate). Thus, it was not surprising that Hipólito's wife and *los suyos* ("her people") would incriminate him to the degree that they did. Likewise, when Joaquín Mariscal, *procurador de pobres*, represented Marcos Maquín in Case 55 (see Chapter 2), he tried to debunk the accusation of incest by arguing that the statements of Marcos's wife were not creditworthy "due as much to her sex and *calidad* as to the inability to discover with what intention or what antecedents she, as his own wife, would be compelled to bear such scandalous witness against her husband."[52] And this was in addition to her husband's suspicions that she was in *ilícita amistad* with another man.

In similar fashion, Manuel Rodenas, a *mulato* hatter from Cuyotenango, claimed his wife falsely denounced him to the authorities for sexual involvement with his stepdaughter and political niece because she despised him, was in a relationship with another man, and wanted to be free of him (Case 64). Manuel maintained that "if he had committed such excesses, he would confess to it *como hombre* ['like a man']," and "if she was willing to bear witness against her daughter, what would stop her from bearing witness against [him]?"[53] That is, if his wife showed no restraint in slandering her daughter, she would be even less inclined to do so when it came to him—a spouse as opposed to a child. Countered with testimony from Alejandro Vidal that supported the accusation that Manuel's stepdaughter had become pregnant, Manuel argued that Alejandro was his contrary because of a past dispute between them over some beasts of burden, "and, as nephew of [his] wife, they took advantage of the occasion to form this calumny against [him]."[54] Thus, even though Alejandro was Manuel's nephew through marriage, he was more closely affiliated with Manuel's wife, and because of such (blood) ties and his own personal motives, Alejandro was willing to testify falsely against Manuel.

Thus, the nature of a kin tie (or its absence) played a significant role in the criminal process. It could influence whether a crime was reported and impact how denunciations and statements were received. Even legal outcomes would have been contingent upon the degree to which authority figures were swayed by expectations of how particular kin would behave, an issue of no small importance in incest cases, which were inherently a family matter.

Conclusion

Given the above, it is clear that the essence of kin ties factored into colonial Guatemalan incest cases in a variety of ways. It had the power to make some incestuous acts more deviant than others and could impact interpretations of evidence and testimony. It undoubtedly contributed to the realization of sexual relations between kin and prevented accusations of incest (and other crimes) from coming to formal trial. One concept that stands out among these various threads is an emphasis on consanguineous kinship, a *la sangre tira*, or "blood is thicker than water," ideology. What also begins to become apparent is the potential for individuals to use relatedness in strategic ways as they engaged in the legal process.

Notes

1 Similar to Buffington's (2000, xi) use of the term "criminality," its use here is intended to highlight the constructed nature of criminal matters.

2 *...la diferencia, y maior gravedad de la copula nefaria, entre padre, é hija, comparada con la de incesto en general...* AGCA A1.15 Leg. 4381 Exp. 35730.

3 *...no digo entre Madre, e hijo, pero entre tia, y sobrino, ó entre primos, causa natural horror el co[i]to inhonesto, se resiste por si enteram.te a la naturaleza por desvocada que sea, y con mucho mayor Razon se resiste el dar excensia al que se imputa a mi p.te por ser su Madre de sessenta años; y por q.e no era posible que de un golpe huvieran vensido esta natural resist.a y casual, por Razon de la hedad; havia p.a ello precisam.te de haver precedido continuaz.n de acciones cariñosas, con que aunq.e con mucha dificultad tal vez, se Huviera Ydo vensiendo el natural horror, pero nada delito ha precedido...*

4 See, for example, McKinnon (1995) on scientific discourse and Archibald (2001) on classical and medieval literature.

5 See, for example, Fox (1980, 48).

6 *...el delito de que tratan es atroz, y lo es en tanto grado, q.e ni por dro. Canonico, ni Civil, se encuentra texto expreso que trate (en materia de incestos y sus penas) del executado entre el Padre y la hija; delito verdaderam. te q.e ni aun se presume, y su repugnancia nos quedó detallada desde la ley escrita; y aun Seneca el mayor, siendo Gentil, quando á otro proposito tocó p.r insidencia la deformidad del coito habido entre los Parientes ó deudos immediatos, lo calificó por criminal criminalisimo; y efectivam.te p.r dro. comun, los reos deste delito eran castigados con pena de muerte, haviendo*

fuerza, como p.r exemplo, el acceso con la entenada, Madrasta, sobrina, &.a con q.e siendo de Sup.r gravedad el que se dice haver tenido Patricio de Leon con su tierna hija Fran.ca no havia otra cosa q.e hazer, sino p.r el merito de la causa mandarlo ahorcar... AGCA A1.15 Leg. 3028 Exp. 29261 f. 9v-10.

7 *...el incesto q.e cometio no es de los mas áborrecidos, y que castigan con mas severidad las Leyes, por que la Muchacha no es su Parienta por con-sanguinidad, sino por áfinidad.* f. 5v.

8 Note that incidents of incest outnumber incest cases because some cases included multiple accusations of incest.

9 These percentages derive from penalty data that was limited to individuals charged with single (as opposed to multiple) incestuous relationships/inci-dents and whose sentences were recorded.

10 These percentages come from data on eighty-nine two-person relationships where affinity and consanguinity could be determined. (Eight others did not have the relevant relationship information.) Three-party incest cases were broken into two data records (e.g. man/sister 1 of 2, man/sister 2 of 2).

11 *...mediante á que el parentesco, que entre los dos mediaba, provenia de copula ilicita...*

12 *...el hallarse desnudos en un mismo lecho los parientes no funda presun-cion, ni prueba de copula entre ellos; p.r q.e aunq.e bastaria respecto de los estraños, tienen los parientes a su favor mas fuerte y vehemente presuncion de honestidad, nascida del mismo parentesco.* AGCA A2.2 Leg. 205 Exp. 4188 f. 32v.

13 *...el hallarse los consanguineos desnudos en un mismo lecho prueba sufi-cientem.te el insesto: pero tambien dice q.e debe entenderse quando estos parientes colaterales yacieren en el lecho secreta, y ocultam.te, y no en pu-blico, p.r q.e en este caso no bastaria semejante prueba.* AGCA A2.2 Leg. 205 Exp. 4188 f. 33.

14 Collins cited a bound volume of *cabildo* records related to the management of the community fund of Jacaltenango dated from 1627 to 1756.

15 *...los vicios dominantes son la embriaguez y lascivia, abandonándose a in-cestos horribles entre padres y hijos...siendo el riesgo próximo el dormir todos juntos.*

16 *...en una propria cama, vajo de una misma cubierta con la referida su Madre, y si por parte de esta á experimentado alguna [vez], accion, ó cariño especial q.e denote algun requerimiento torpe...*

17 *...desde pequeña ó desde q.e le entro la razon le puso su Madre cama sepa-rada de suerte q.e nunca se sirbio de la de su Padre aunque estaban en una misma piesa...* AGCA A2.2 Leg. 199 Exp. 4085 f. 9v-10.

18 Miguel's surname was also written as Cayxon, Caxon, Caison, Cayson, Caychon, and Cahxon.

19 Antonia's surname was also written as Chacal, Chabalan, and Zic.

20 *...nunca, en ningun tiempo, ni por mal pensamiento ha tenido con la referida su Madre el mas leve descomedimiento sobre el particular, pues á mas de ser Muger mayor, siempre le ha guardado el respeto devido de Madre...*

21 *...accion alguna que indique maldad pues Cantarillas trata a la Agustina con el respeto de cuñada durmiendo cada uno en su cama y solo si se resiven a la hora de comer y beber...y quando murio la muger de aquel le dejó encar-gado a la Agustina su hermana q. cuidase el lo mismo que ella...*

22 *...poseida de miedo, terror, y respeto, á sus riñas y amenasas...* f. 4v.

23 *...remediasse su desgracia, pues se condenaba, y contra su voluntad se hiba al infierno...* f. 4v.

24 *...valiendose de los halagos de Padre y de la inocencia de la exponente, la primera vez tubo polucion con ella, esto es, q.e usaba de sus piernas, y lo externo del utero p.a la confricacion, y poluccion...* f. 6.

25 *...y aunque extorta le entregó su cuerpo, fue poseida del terror, y del respeto...* f. 6v.

26 *...pero ningo. consumó intra vas. p.r q.e tenia particular estudio, en la extravasacion...* f. 6v.

27 *...no teniendo mas livertad q.e ella ni mejores alcancez, queria remediarlo con disimulos y con las quejas...* f. 7v.

28 *...como ella hera muchacha y le tenia un respeto reberencial spre. le obedecia en cuanto le mandaba saliendo con el fuera de la casa á biajes y a su Labor, y q.e spre. q.e estaban solos, el la acariciaba atribuiendo ella estos cariños á un amor onesto, hasta q.e el poco, á poco se fué exediendo con ella en las ocaciones á proposito sin mediar palabras ni conosim.to y q.e cuando hubo lugar a la refleccion yá Felipe Gil havia consumado el acto con ella: q.e la q.e declara no tenia trato con ning.a otra persona mas q.e con el, y spre. sedia aunq.e con repugnancia p.r no atreberse á desirle q.e no...* f. 9v.

See Premo (2005, 61–8) for a discussion of the concept of "reverential fear" and debate about who had the capacity to inspire it.

29 Again, Cases 17 and 65 were broken into 17a/17b and 65a/65b.

30 Sometimes multiple plaintiffs who did not share a gender came forward to make an accusation. Thus, each plaintiff was considered individually in these tallies.

31 *...p.r ser cristiano, y desseoso de la honrra de Dios...*

32 *...solo el poder abitar con el lisitamente si se le dispensaba...* f. 5.

33 *...me rogaban no se supe ese nunca su delacion por el cruel castigo q.e experimentarian.* f. 1v.

34 *...el motibo q.e tuvo p.a denunsiar á su P.e siendo sobre la tierra los P.es las personas a qns mas reverensia y amor deben los hijos?* f. 5.

35 *...los hijos son cuerbos p.a sacar los ojos y que conforme a dro No deben tirar contra su Padre sino en cassos capitales por el capitulo Quarto del Decalogo Que hassi lo manda...* f. 6v.

36 *...por amor de Dios que le buscase una casa donde servir por que no queria estar con su Padre...*

37 *...lo estraño que es, el q.e un hijo acuse á su Padre...* f. 12.

38 *...como viese q. su P.e Jose M.a huviese echado sobre si un crimen q. no habia cometido, esta por no desmentirle, ignorando lo q. hasia, manifestó su convencimiento...* f. 14v.

39 *...pues su propria hermana Juana Josefa la acusa, que esta no há sido apremiada, ni obligada para que los denunciase...* f. 5.

40 *...es mentirosa su hermana, y tal ves la han aconsejado.* f. 5.

41 *...pues no pueden ser zelos solamente pues de su hermana; sino motivos positivos los que le asisten para querellarse de su ilicito comericio con su marido...* f. 16v.

42 *...siento q.e mi hermanita esté creciendo p.r q.e no viese el mal ejemplo de mi Padre.* f. 5v-6.

43 *...la sujestion de la tia no es creible que hiciese en la petrona maior imprecion que la natural de un[a] hija á un Padre para caluniarlo dijo que no es de estrañar el que se dejara la muchacha llevar del concejo de la tia quando esta le ha impuesto de que no es su hija.* f. 11v.

44 *Ella no se hubiera atrevido á semejante desacato, si su tia Antonia no la hubiera sugerido á la desovediencia manifesta[n]dola que no era hija suya.* f. 20.

45 *...no soy casado ni tengo hijos ningunos p.r que una muger q. tuve en mi compania esta me estubo cuidando p.r algun tpo. y asi q. se aburrio de cuidarme se mud[ó] y se yevó a sus hijos...una muchacha q. aparese acriminandome de unos tan enormes delitos, q.e esta es hija de la muger q. me cuidó, y se yama Maria Jososefa [sic] la q. no es hija mia p.r q. si lo fuera no tirara tan desenfrenadam.te en contra de su padre...si fuera su padre como eya dise le tirara la sangre a bolber p.r su padre viendolo en la calamidad q. se halla, y preso con tan grandes crimenes de q. lo acusa, y asi doy p.r nula su declarasion falza, y esta se tiene p.r hija de la dh.a Micaela, y no lo es p.r q si lo fuera no procurara ni ubiera procurado desunir a su padre del lado de su madre sabiendo q. eran casados luego no es hija sino pepe...* The term *pepe* is discussed further in the following chapter.

46 Don Juan Manuel would later deny authorship of this text.

47 *...me he enterado de que dha Secilia no es parienta por ningun termino en sanginidad mia...* f. 21.

48 *...se hapellidan Mangoches, y estas me tratab.n de pariente, Yo con la Ygnorancia dha por tal las conocia= Por lo que es, que la dha Secilia dise ser mi Marido quien la deve su onór, sin embargo de ser falso...* f. 21-v.

49 *...no es presumible que esta se abanderize mas á la que confiesa que á su misma hija.* f. 6v.

50 *...en el concepto legal siempre se presume q.e el padre quiere favorecer la causa de su hijo.* f. 18.

51 Hipólito's surname was also written as Cojulun, Cojulún, Coxulum, Coxulun, Cujulun, Cujulum, and Cuhulum.

52 *...tanto por su sexo y calidad, quanto por que siendo la muger propia, no puede descubrirse con que intension, y quales antecedentes la compelerian á deponer contra su marido un testimonio tan escandaloso...* f. 34v-5.

53 *...si huviera cometido tales exesos como hombre lo confesara...quando á su hija le levantó este testimonio como no se lo ha de levantar al confesante.* f. 18.

54 *...y como sobrino de la muger del declarante se valieron de la ocasion para formarle esta calumnia al confesante.* f. 18.

Bibliography

Aquinas, Thomas. 1265–1274. *Summa Theologica.* Translated by Fathers of the English Dominican Province. Claremont, CA: Coyote Canyon Press. Kindle.

Archibald, Elizabeth. 2001. *Incest and the Medieval Imagination.* Oxford: Clarendon Press.

Buffington, Robert. 2000. "Introduction: Conceptualizing Criminality in Latin America." In *Reconstructing Criminality in Latin America,* edited by Carlos Aguirre and Robert Buffington, xi–xix. Wilmington, DE: Scholarly Resources Inc.

Burkholder, Mark A. 1998. "Honor and Honors in Colonial Spanish America." In *The Faces of Honor: Sex, Shame, and Violence in Colonial Latin America,* edited by Lyman L. Johnson and Sonya Lipsett-Rivera, 18–44. Albuquerque: University of New Mexico Press.

Collins, Anne Cox. 1980. "Colonial Jacaltenango, Guatemala: The Formation of a Corporate Community." Ph.D. diss., Tulane University.

Cortés y Larraz, Pedro. 1958. *Descripción geográfico-moral de la diócesis de Goathemala.* Guatemala: Tipografía Nacional.

Fox, Robin. 1980. *The Red Lamp of Incest.* New York: E. P. Dutton.

Gómez, Antonio. 1552. *Comentarios a las Leyes de Toro*. Salamanca: Andreas a Portonarijs.

Jaffary, Nora E. 2007. "Incest, Sexual Virtue, and Mobility in Late Colonial Mexico." In *Gender, Race, and Religion in the Colonization of the Americas*, edited by Nora E. Jaffary, 95–107. Hampshire: Ashgate.

Lavrin, Asunción. 1989. "Sexuality in Colonial Mexico: A Church Dilemma." In *Sexuality and Marriage in Colonial Latin America*, edited by Asunción Lavrin, 47–95. Lincoln and London: University of Nebraska Press.

McKinnon, Susan. 1995. "American Kinship/American Incest: Asymmetries in a Scientific Discourse." In *Naturalizing Power Essays in Feminist Cultural Analysis*, edited by Sylvia Junko Yanagisako and Carol Delaney, 25–46. New York and London: Routledge.

Nolasco de Llano, Pedro. 1785. *Compendio de Los comentarios extendidos por el maestro Antonio Gómez*. Madrid: Imprenta de Don Joseph Doblado. Google Books.

Peletz, Michael G. 2001. "Ambivalence in Kinship since the 1940s." In *Relative Values Reconfiguring Kinship Studies*, edited by Sarah Franklin and Susan McKinnon, 413–44. Durham, NC and London: Duke University Press.

Penyak, Lee M. 2016. "Incestuous Natures: Consensual and Forced Relations in Mexico, 1740–1854." In *Sexuality and the Unnatural in Colonial Latin America*, edited by Zeb Tortorici, 162–87. Oakland: University of California Press.

Premo, Bianca. 2005. *Children of the Father King: Youth, Authority, and Legal Minority in Colonial Lima*. Chapel Hill: University of North Carolina Press.

Schwaller, Robert C. 2016. *Géneros de Gente in Early Colonial Mexico: Defining Racial Difference*. Norman: University of Oklahoma Press.

Stern, Steve J. 1995. *The Secret History of Gender: Women, Men, and Power in Late Colonial Mexico*. Chapel Hill and London: University of North Carolina Press.

Vela y Acuña, Juan. 1603. *Tractatus de Poenis Delictorum*. Salamanca: Martín Pérez.

Waldron, Kathy. 1989. "The Sinners and the Bishop in Colonial Venezuela: The Visita of Bishop Mariano Martí, 1771–1784." In *Sexuality and Marriage in Colonial Latin America*, edited by Asunción Lavrin, 156–77. Lincoln and London: University of Nebraska Press.

5   Relative and Strategic Kinship

Introduction

Models of kinship that emphasize the contextual nature of relatedness and strategic maneuvering within kin relations (e.g. Yan 2001) come to the fore in colonial Guatemalan criminal proceedings. Investigations into incestuous crime were particularly susceptible to conflict between malleable kinship practices and demands for precision in relatedness. Ultimately, sexual relations and the legal process forced individuals to distinguish between "real" kin and other types of individuals regardless of whether such distinctions were especially relevant in other contexts. Such nuance could be as liberating as it was limiting, and individuals in colonial Guatemala were adept at exploiting kinship and incest norms to suit what a particular situation demanded.[1]

"Real" Children and Pepes

As in other areas of Spanish America, residents of colonial Guatemala regularly incorporated non-biological children into their kin networks. Laura Shelton's (2007) study on the northwestern region of Mexico shed some light on the practice of circulating children and the nature of relationships between children and their guardians in colonial Latin America. She discussed how people often took children into the home under the assumption that they would provide household labor as they grew older. However, this did not involve a formal adoption process, and Shelton described these children as occupying an ambiguous status. For instance, they were occasionally listed as both servants and family members in census records. Significantly, guardians often described these relationships in terms of reciprocity, obligation, and charity, and they expected "adopted" children to show gratitude for their upbringing. Shelton (following Milanich 2002) suggested the abuse that such children could experience "was part of the subordination inherent in their ambiguous status as 'adopted children' and *criados* ['servants']" (Shelton 2007, 231). Colonial Guatemalan criminal cases reiterate some of the themes discussed by Shelton, but they also show how this form of kinship practice sat uneasily with incest codes, placing these types of children at increased risk for sexual violence in the process.

In colonial Guatemala, the term *pepe* (or *pepecito* in the diminutive) referred to non-biological children raised in the home. This term apparently derived from the verb *pepenar* ("to pick up"). For example, a woman from Ciudad Vieja used the verb *pepenar* to describe literally picking up an infant from the ground (AGCA A2.2 Leg. 237 Exp. 5055). Thus, this verb (and its linguistic derivatives) would surely provide an apt metaphor for bringing unwanted or otherwise orphaned children into one's home.

Kinship terminology often accompanied relationships between *pepes* (or their categorical equivalents) and the members of their foster homes, which could lead to confusion over the nature of relatedness. Potentially incestuous acts prompted the clarification of kin ties and discourses of "real" kin. For example, in 1798 Manuela de Oliva complained to the authorities in Nueva Guatemala that Manuel Matute, a *mulato* muleteer, had taken the virginity of her young granddaughter, the first cousin of his wife (Case 22). However, when asked how the girl was related to her, Manuela said she was not. Rather, "she raised the father of the girl as a *pepe*, for which reason, the children call her 'Grandmother.'"[2] Asked how Manuel's wife (Manuela's niece) was related to the girl, Manuela said she was not. Instead, "because of [Manuela] having raised her, she calls her 'Cousin,' but there is not any *parentesco*."[3] In accordance with the apparent lack of kin ties, Manuel escaped a formal charge of incest. And, eventually, it was revealed that another individual was responsible for the girl's deflowerment. The case of Manuela de Oliva and her "granddaughter" shows how concerns over incestuous crime forced individuals to distinguish between (real) relatives and *pepes* (and their families) and, in so doing, set limits on kinship's apparently malleable nature.

Such constraints placed "adopted" children at greater risk of sexual assault. The aforementioned trial involving Petrona Alvarado and her stepfather, Felipe Gil, provides one example (Case 58, also in Chapter 4; see also Case 15). During inquiries into the girl's parentage, one witness, Vicente Aguilar, mentioned debate regarding the matter. He contended that

> she is daughter of Ana Alvarado. [Ana] gave birth to her prior to her first marriage to Benito Berriondo, who treated this girl with the affection of a taken-in orphan. Some in the town believed her to be the daughter of Benito and Ana, others the daughter of [Ana] only, and some thought she was neither the daughter of Benito nor Ana but rather that she was what they call a "pepe."[4]

Here again, we see that the essence of kin ties was not always clear to outsiders. But neither was it always obvious within the family circle, as

Felipe himself stated that while some said Petrona was his wife's daughter, he (like others in town) believed she was a *"pepe*, or girl who his wife, Ana Alvarado, had taken into her house to raise out of charity."[5] It was with this understanding that he opted to court her. Charged with incest with the daughter of his wife, he excused himself "because of his ignorance and having believed that she was a girl his wife had raised because she was an orphan or for some other charitable reason."[6] In other words, Felipe found sexual relations with a *pepe* somewhat acceptable and assumed the court would be sympathetic to the position he now found himself in. Though stated ignorance of kin ties could have been sincere in this case, there is no doubt some might have chosen to exploit the potentially blurred nature of kin ties to defend themselves while on trial.

Similar themes surfaced in the 1749 incest case against Narciso Gonzales (Case 5, also in Chapter 2). His daughter Gregoria denounced him for the loss of her virginity and repeated sexual acts afterwards. She also reported a severe whipping at his hands. Despite Gregoria and various others referring to Narciso as her father, Francisco Orozco and María Victoria swore before a priest that they were her (real) parents, the record of which was brought to the court by Petrona Quintanilla, wife of Narciso. The pair asserted that *como frágiles* ("as fragile persons"), they begot Gregoria fifteen years beforehand. When the priest asked why they did not raise Gregoria if she was their daughter, they replied, *por no ser hija habida en matrimonio* ("because she was not a daughter begotten within marriage"). Asked how Narciso and Petrona came to have Gregoria, María Victoria said that

> because of the respect that she had for her mother, Magdalena de Estrada, and the great fear of her aunt, María Felipa, she allowed her aunt to give the child Gregoria Antonia—her daughter—to Narciso Gonzales and his wife, Petrona Quintanilla, so that out of charity they would raise her.[7]

A couple of days later, Petrona appealed to the magistrate. She claimed that Gregoria had sinisterly complained that

> I and my husband Narciso are her legitimate parents and that, as such, we raised and married her off after my husband Narciso violently took her virginity without bearing in mind that he was her father....From which complaint results not only the defamatory calumny against the upbringing that she owes us but also the dispossession of our small amount of assets that we currently suffer. And, as the complaint is sinister and the alleged gravity—that, as a father, he took the virginity of his daughter—does not attend, nor even being evident to me that he executed it in the absence of this relationship, I, therefore, turn to V. M. ["Your Mercy"]....[8]

Ultimately, Petrona requested the return of the sequestered assets because she had acquired them, not her husband. While it is impossible to know Gregoria's actual genealogical background, Petrona's statement again shows that sexual violence against an "adopted" child was not as criminal as that against a (real) child, leaving the former in a more vulnerable position for such violence.

The above cases indicate that when it came to sexual relations, kinlike *pepes* approximated outsiders in their homes, and any protection against sexual violence offered by incest codes did not necessarily extend to them. At the same time, their incorporation into the family could be so deep that confusion over the nature of relatedness could result, and sexual offenders and their allies could draw upon (and perhaps manipulate) such messiness to their own advantage.

Degrees of Sisterhood

The utility of kinship fluidity to incest trials is especially explicit in an 1803 case from Nueva Guatemala involving Domingo Morales, a *mulato* weaver, and his sister-in-law, María Dolores Gaitán (Case 39). Domingo denied the *amancebamiento*. In his testimony, he admitted to living with Dolores and explained that the priest don Tomás Zapata had left him and his now deceased wife, Ramona Josefa Gaitán, in charge of her. Domingo also reported how he went to visit Father don Julián Cos to tell him about the recent gossip surrounding the alleged involvement between him and Dolores. He asked him "if since Dolores and his deceased wife were not sisters but rather both daughters of unknown fathers, he would be able to marry Dolores so as to not leave her abandoned."[9] His motivation for the marriage was to put a stop to the gossip, and the priest allegedly told him it was acceptable and to carry it out as soon as possible. However, for lack of money, it was not realized.

As in the previous cases, the relationship between Dolores and Ramona was important to establish because it had implications for the relationship between Dolores and Domingo. If these two women were not sisters, Domingo and Dolores were not brother- and sister-in-law and an accusation of incest was moot. Initially, Domingo said that Dolores and Ramona shared a mother, which made them *hermanas uterinas* ("uterine sisters"), elsewhere termed *hermanas de madre* ("maternal half-sisters"). Because Domingo claimed that these women "were not sisters," yet still described them as *hermanas uterinas*, it is apparent that in his mind, they were not (real) sisters but rather shared a more qualified form of sisterhood. That is, (real) sisters were apparently the products of shared bilateral descent. Perhaps, Domingo would have even interpreted a shared paternal line differently than that of a shared maternal line considering Mesoamerican antecedents (discussed in Chapter 3) and a degree of patrilineal bias in Western kinship systems at this time.

Domingo's position on the relationship between him and Dolores emerged in a note (penned by another) that he sent to Dolores while both were being detained for the trial. It read,

> Dear *Prenda de mi Corazón* ["Token of my Heart"] and *Todo mi Consuelo* ["All my Solace"], María [Dolores] Gaitán...*Hija* ["Child"], this [note] merely serves to inform you that it will not be long before they take rocks and stone us. And because of all of this, and to reestablish your reputation and mine, I send this to you so that you know that the intention that I have at present is for us to get married. This being under your consideration, let me know if it is your desire to continue the matter. I do this as much for the desire that I have for you as to regain your honor and to put an end to so much gossip, for the term with which they label us is so vulgar—they call us "incestuous." And, so, I wait only for your response to write to the priest and execute the proceedings. I promise to behave like a good man and to care for you like you deserve. I assure you that it is fine—there is not any impediment—for they think that you are my sister-in-law and that we cannot marry each other. Thus, do not delay in responding to me as soon as you can... Domingo Morales.[10]

This letter makes clear that Domingo did not think that the form of sisterhood between the two Gaitán women was substantial enough to make Dolores his sister-in-law (cf. Case 17).

However, sexual relations with two maternal half-sisters did, in fact, equate to incest (see Case 17). This may be significant considering Domingo later changed his stance on the relationship between Dolores and Ramona. According to the magistrate, Domingo

> has verbally alleged that even though in public opinion they were regarded as, and reputed to be, such [maternal half-] sisters, they actually were not. Rather, they were only *de leche* ["milk sisters"] because his wife had merely been left at the doors of Manuela de León and her husband, Pantaleón Gaitán.... And María Dolores is the legitimate daughter of the named consorts.[11]

Therefore, the magistrate ordered the examination of the baptismal records of these women "in order to find out with certainty whether they are sisters or not."[12] Baptismal records listed María Saturnina Gaitán (presumably Dolores) as a legitimate daughter of Pantaleón and Manuela. The marital records of Domingo and Ramona identified Ramona as a legitimate daughter of the couple as well.

Domingo's new position on the relationship between Dolores and Ramona introduced another degree of sisterhood to the discussion—that of *hermanas de leche* ("milk sisters"). The use of the phrase "only *de leche*" makes apparent that this was an even lesser form of sisterhood than that of *hermanas de madre*, and the subsequent need to verify "whether they are sisters or not" demonstrates that *hermanas de leche* were again not (real) sisters. Elsewhere, Domingo stressed that Ramona only carried the surname Gaitán because she was raised as a *pepe* in the house of Pantaleón, and that this was the reason that people had mistakenly testified against him.

Don Mateo de la Canal, *defensor* of Domingo, reiterated the divide between "real" sisterhood and other sisterhood in his defense. Building on his client's statement that a priest placed Dolores in the care of him and his wife, he said it was entirely plausible that

> with the death of the legitimate parents of [Dolores] and the latter finding herself completely orphaned, Father Zapata, being invested in her safety, would have handed her over to her *hermana de leche* as Domingo has recently said in trying to disprove the public opinion that his wife Ramona and María Dolores were *hermanas en realidad* ["real sisters"].[13]

In other words, *hermanas de leche* were not actually sisters, even though they may have played similar roles.

In order to better defend his client, Canal requested that Father Zapata provide information regarding the case. In a note, Father Zapata recounted meeting Pantaleón and Manuela. While he was immediately made aware of their three children—Inés, Florencio, and María Dolores—several years passed before he learned about their daughter Ramona. A few years later, Ramona and Domingo came to visit him with Dolores in their company. When he asked Ramona how this came to be, she said that "with the death of her parents, the girl had come to look for her, and she, as an older sister, took her in and had her in her power."[14]

Initially, Canal admitted that this information did not seem to aid his client. However, he suggested that Father Zapata's understanding of Ramona as a legitimate child and her alleged self-description as an "older sister" did not necessarily indicate that they were in fact sisters. Indeed, "*expuestos* [or *expósitos*, 'foundlings']—just like legitimate children—address and revere as parents those who raise and maintain them."[15] Further, *expuestos* and legitimate children "view and treat each other like siblings in both public and private settings."[16] Canal eventually went on to say that it was *por metáfora* ("through metaphor") that Ramona said she took Dolores in *por hermana mayor* ("as an older sister"). Through these words, Canal created a divide between "real" and metaphoric kinship and highlighted the potential for individuals to be mistaken about the nature of a kin tie.

Canal used similar logic to dismiss the marital records that included a description of Ramona as a "legitimate daughter" of Pantaleón and

Manuela. He proposed a degree of indifference among those watching as to whether such identification was accurate for someone who could only be taken as such, especially since the couple did not have any children of their own at the time. Here again, Canal exploited the potential ambiguities arising out of the incorporation of non-biological children into the home to introduce doubt into the accusation of incest.

It will be recalled from Chapter 3 that *Las Siete Partidas* defined incest as sexual intercourse between individuals who *knew* they were relatives. The importance of knowledge of kin ties in incestuous crime also surfaced in the case against Domingo and Dolores. According to Canal, "The truth is that if [Domingo] Morales lived in doubt that he was truly María [Dolores's] brother-in-law...it certainly cannot be argued that Morales committed incest, even when convinced that he was sexually involved with María [Dolores],"[17] which both denied. As support, he cited the love note from Domingo, which demonstrated that he "effectively was not in the belief that she was his sister-in-law *en realidad*."[18] Similarly, don José Ballesteros, the *procurador de pobres* who represented Dolores, argued that "if they knew that they were relatives, they have in their favor the presumption of honesty. If they took themselves as *libres de parentesco* ['free of kinship'], there is no such incest, especially not having proved coitus."[19] The use of ignorance of kin ties as a defense in the courtroom speaks to a certain acknowledgment on the part of legal professionals that confusion about relatedness was indeed a real-world problem and, therefore, a viable excuse for incestuous acts and relationships that had already come to fruition. In the end, Domingo and Dolores were ordered to cease communication with one another.

Overall, the trial of Domingo and Dolores reveals the existence of varying degrees of sisterhood in which some sisters were considered more "real" than others. And, as in the cases above, "real" kin ties carried more weight than other ones when marriage and incest were on the line. Ignorance of such "facts," while unable to erase them, could free someone of a crime intimately linked to them, making kinship's nuanced and malleable nature a feature to be capitalized on, even when kin ties were known.

Kinship as Innocence in Incestuous Crime

While some people chose to argue for an absence of (real) kin ties to justify sexual relations or betrothal, others used their presence to cast doubt on the actuality of incestuous relations. For example, in defense of Marcos Maquín—accused of father-daughter incest—the *procurador de pobres* pointed out not only the *calidad* of his client (Indian) and his lengthy imprisonment during the trial but also the fact that this was a crime "whose perpetration one cannot wrap their head around as nature itself opposes it" (Case 55, also in Chapter 2).[20] Beyond this, there was not any evidence to prove it, nor an admission to the crime on the part of his client. Thus, the defense attorney's strategy was partially dependent on the apparent unlikelihood of this type of crime happening in the first place (cf. Case 11 in Chapter 4).

A similar strategy emerged in the 1802 incest case against Simón Hernández, an Indian man and *maestro de coro* (choirmaster) in the church of Chiquimulilla, who was accused of incest with his daughter (Case 31). Though the nature of the kin tie between Simón and Josefa de la Cruz would be contested during the trial, when Simón's wife came to his defense, she emphasized the parent-child relationship between the two. Speaking to the *alcalde mayor*, Simona Bautista stated that the accusation that her husband had *ilícita amistad* with her daughter was false and stemmed from the ill will of the *alcalde segundo* (a *cabildo* official) and his wife, María Grageda. Simona recounted one occasion when María, after

> seeing the love that my husband has towards his children—as a father, after all—told me that it seemed to her that my husband was, or dealt, illicitly with my daughter, I responding to her that it could not be, that he was always like that, that he was loving towards all his children.[21]

Clearly worried that María misunderstood her husband's affections towards their daughter, Simona intended to clarify that they were nothing out of the ordinary. Rather, Simón was behaving as would any normal father. In essence, his very identity as Josefa's father made his behavior towards her natural and undermined any accusation of incest.

María's alleged reaction to Simón is consistent with a wider tradition within Western Christendom in which affectionate displays between individuals—including parents and children—were curtailed to avoid sexual arousal or suspicion of sexual advances (see Brundage 1987, 8). And, in her own testimony, María suggested that Simón's behavior was anything but normal. She reported how Simona had shared with her evidence of Simón's special treatment of Josefa in relation to Simona and his other daughters (cf. Herman 2000). For example, Simona supposedly told her about how she had not eaten for several days because Simón made a key to the kitchen and gave it to Josefa, telling her, "You are who [fem.] rules here—not [Simona]."[22] When María asked Simona if she believed Simón was illicitly involved with Josefa, Simona confirmed she was suspicious because he frequently made Josefa's husband and another daughter of his (also named Simona) leave the house, and then, sitting in a hammock together, Simón would light a cigar and give it to Josefa, telling her, "This is Simona [the cigar], this is you [his middle finger]."[23] The *dedo de en medio* ("middle finger") was also commonly referred to as the *dedo del corazón* ("finger of the heart") because of its perceived intimate connection with the heart (see *Diccionario de Autoridades* 1726–1739 v. 3). In associating Josefa with this finger, Simón clarified that she had a special place in his heart compared to his other daughter. Further, Simón would tell Josefa that if it became necessary for someone to leave the house, it would be María Luisa (presumably another daughter) and not her. María Grageda's testimony complicated the image Simona Bautista presented of a man merely expressing fatherly love because it set his affection towards Josefa apart from that towards his other daughter(s) and positioned her as the (female) head of the household.

For their part, both Simón and Josefa denied being father and daughter and any sexual involvement between them. Testimony suggests that had Simón not been Josefa's father, he would have been her political uncle. According to Josefa, her (real) father was a man by the name of Sebastián Morales, and her mother gave birth to her out of wedlock, marrying another man afterwards. Still, within the same statement in which she maintained that Simón was not her father, she referred to him as "her Tata Simón" and, more simply, as "her Tata." The case ultimately culminated in the release of Simón, an order for the reunification of Josefa with her husband, and a mandated separation of Simón and Josefa's residences.

The above examples show opposing strategies for dealing with accusations of incest. Whereas some individuals chose to stress kin ties (and the norms surrounding them) to undermine denunciations of this sort, others highlighted an apparent abnormality in kin relations to make a case for them. The former seems paradoxical when the criminal category of incest alone suggests an acknowledgement of its potentiality, but, obviously, some hoped to benefit from assumptions of its rarity.

The (Dis)Appearance of Kinship in Sexual Relations

Guatemalan incest cases provide insight into how kinship might (dis) appear in sexual relations between relatives. This is especially true of rape cases such as that against Vicente Fuentes for the sexual violence he perpetrated on his daughter-in-law, Rosalía Surqueah (Case 61). During the trial, Rosalía recounted the moments surrounding one of the assaults. Vicente was telling her that "she was a bitch, that he was not her father, and she was telling him that it did not matter, that something would happen to him, and he responded to it all by telling her to not be afraid."[24] Thus, it is apparent that Rosalía hoped that referring to Vicente as a father would help protect her from the forced sexual act. It was a defensive strategy, but when he rejected such identification, he disarmed her. She then tried to convince him that there would be repercussions regardless but without success.

Taken together, Vicente's alleged statements and subsequent execution of the rape indicate that he believed the act was justified. Indeed, the *procurador de pobres*, one of Vicente's legal representatives, argued that Rosalía would have known what Vicente intended by calling her a "bitch" and claiming that he was not her father, and he contended that the incest would not have happened if she actually resisted. In other words, it was not rare for the rejection of (particular) kinship identification to imply subsequent sexual intercourse, and knowing this, Rosalía had plenty opportunity to refuse him had she so chosen.

Rosalía's second legal representative, Juan José de León, phrased the encounter in similar terms. He recalled how Rosalía reminded Vicente (during their *careo*) of "the words that she uttered to extinguish the ardor of passion that consumed him and the answers that he gave her to soften her persistence."[25] Hence, even though in different ways, both Rosalía and Vicente utilized their understandings of kinship and incest to support their aims during the violent conflict between them. Whereas Rosalía emphasized particular kin ties, Vicente tempered them. His refusal to accept identification as Rosalía's father implies that he did not find relatedness through first-degree affinity restrictive in terms of sexual relations in the same way as that through first-degree consanguinity. This again speaks to a greater tolerance for affinal incest over consanguineous incest, as discussed in Chapter 4.

Similar themes emerged in the trial against Miguel Caixon and his stepdaughter, Juana Velasco (Case 19, also in Chapter 4). Speaking through an interpreter, Miguel denied any sexual involvement with Juana. While Juana (also through an interpreter) initially testified in the same manner, she later verified the accusation. She recounted how one night about eight years prior Miguel came home tipsy while she was there alone. He lay down next to her and solicited her. He proceeded to beat and rape her, "even though she resisted, asking him, if he did not understand that they thought of him as a father? And, how could he want to do those things being married to her mother?"[26] When she scolded him about it the next morning, he told her that because he was drunk, he did not realize what he was doing, and for her to stay quiet about it and not tell her mother. However, he continued to pursue her (without her mother's knowledge). Juana's rendition of events makes clear that she anticipated that pointing out her stepfather's role as a father figure and his relationship with her mother might discourage him. But, like Rosalía, Juana failed to convince him. Ironically, the fatherly roles of Vicente and Miguel that these women chose to emphasize made them vulnerable to an abuse of authority in the first place.

It should also be briefly noted that Juana's mother, Antonia Chaclan (or Sic), found herself charged with being a *consentidora* ("consenter") to the crime, and as such, she was equally on trial. In her defense, her legal representative pointed out that Antonia had

> complete confidence in her husband because he had raised Juana since she was little, and for this reason, considered her a daughter,

as she reciprocally treated him, regardless of whether the mother was around. This faith was great enough to not suspect the slightest malice.[27]

In other words, Antonia's trust in her husband to behave in accordance with the norms governing father-daughter relations freed her of charges of complicity to the crime. This argument further highlights the value of kin norms to a legal defense and demonstrates how individuals who were otherwise able to aid female kin subject to sexual assault could be blinded to it.

References to kin ties were not exclusive to sexual encounters between father-types and daughter-types. Records from an 1803 incest case involving two Indians from Jocotenango, José Hernández and Anica Lantán, the former's stepmother, provide one example (Case 38). According to José, his relationship with his stepmother began after the death of his father and at her request. Anica disagreed, claiming that José solicited her—and even forced her—"to sin" with him. In fact, she had wanted to marry a man named José Simeón after her husband died, but her stepson asked her why she planned to marry this man and told her to marry him instead since *no era su madre* ("she was not his mother"). During a *careo*, Anica testified in a similar manner, stating that the first time they had sex, José had come home drunk, telling her that "she was not his mother, that they were quite able to sin."[28] The words of José in this version of the story suggest that while stepmothers and mothers may have been conceptually parallel, they remained distinctive from one another when it came to sexual intercourse. And like Vicente Fuentes above, José emphasized this difference in order to persuade Anica to submit to him sexually and even marry him.[29]

Allusions to affinity contracted outside of marriage apparently accompanied the sexual violence that ultimately led to the 1805 criminal proceedings against a Spanish man named don Apolinario Rivas. He stood accused of incestuous *amancebamiento* for his sexual involvement with doña Isidora (or Decidora) Bocanegra and her sister, doña Teodora Bocanegra (Case 45). Following trial records, Apolinario and Isidora had been involved with one another for quite some time. When Apolinario was first apprehended for this *ilícita amistad*, he explained that he was taking the necessary steps to marry Isidora. He was then ordered to marry her within the period of fifteen days. However, the aunt of the Bocanegra sisters informed the authorities that he could not actually marry Isidora because of the impediment stemming from his involvement with Teodora, a claim substantiated by the man who was to be in charge of Apolinario's custody until the execution of the marriage.

Teodora recounted the sexual encounter between her and Apolinario. During the year of 1803, she traveled with Apolinario to a fiesta.

Since they arrived late, Apolinario looked for accommodations. They slept in a room with various other people and separate from one another,

> but after they blew out the candle, [Apolinario] Rivas came to her to force [i.e. rape] her. And even though [she] resisted with the reflections that he had taken communion that day, that he had *amistad* with her sister, and, lastly, that it was not her desire, Rivas answered that he did not want to marry her sister. And even though she ultimately made clear to him that she found him to be a loathsome person, Rivas achieved his lewd desires, as she did not want to evade them by screaming because she feared she would scandalize the people who were sleeping there and that her honor would be damaged.[30]

Thus, Teodora used various observations to dissuade Apolinario from raping her, including his relationship with her sister (cf. Case 54). However, he rendered her defense ineffective by arguing that he did not aspire to marry Isidora anyway.

For his part, Apolinario denied the incident. He claimed he was so drunk that night that, to his knowledge, he did not even get undressed. He admitted that on one occasion when Isidora was pressuring him to effect their marriage he declined, telling her he had an impediment. However, during a *careo* with Isidora, Apolinario said he did not explain the nature of the impediment to her. Isidora, on the other hand, maintained that he told her about his sexual relations with her sister after she pressed him to clarify the matter.

Regardless of what actually happened and the motivations behind it, this case reveals the strategic use of kinship and incest in a couple of ways. First, as in some of the cases already mentioned, we find a woman trying to discourage a man from engaging with her sexually by referencing kin ties. Second, it becomes apparent that an individual could avoid an undesired marriage, or pestering to effect one, by creating (or feigning) impediments to marriage derived from sexual relations with a relative of a prospective partner. This latter form of strategizing has been noted by scholars of other areas as well. For example, Jaffary (2007, 104) suggested that reluctant grooms in the Archdiocese of Mexico might have actually encouraged denunciations of matrimonial impediments. Also, Rodríguez Jiménez (1988, 57) proposed that women in colonial Medellín may have used their knowledge of the dispensation system to remove themselves from an oppressive relationship.

Comments on kin ties during sexual assault reflect how women and girls could feel powerless on their own to defend themselves from male relatives. This is particularly clear in the case against Josef Teodoro Juárez Coronado (alias Masate) for the *estupro* of his wife's niece Cecilia (Case 18, also in Chapter 4). Engracia Mangoche, Cecilia's aunt and

Josef's wife, reported that she had suffered at the hands of her husband for a long time and hoped that with care she could curb her husband's behavior.

> But far, Señor [the *alcalde ordinario*], from observing in him Christian behavior, his infamy has gotten to the point that a few hours ago—without fearing God, the Law, nor me—he violently deflowered my young niece who lives under my care.[31]

Engracia described the incident in more detail in her statement the following day. She testified that her husband shut himself in the house with Cecilia while she was on the patio and a scream followed. She heard Cecilia

> telling her husband, "Let go of me!", "For Holy Mary's sake, don't be shameful!", "Know that I will tell your wife, as I am a *doncella* [virgin] and the niece of your wife!", to which he responded that even so, once he puts his foot in the mud, he knows how to get it out, and that if she told [Engracia], he would kill her [Engracia].[32]

Josef's previous desires to cause Engracia injury combined with these new threats prevented her from obstructing the *estupro*, "even though the door was open and her husband in the bed with her niece."[33] In her own statement, Cecilia similarly mentioned how she told Josef to let her go in the name of the Virgin Mary and threatened to tell her aunt about the attack. Cecilia also clarified that Josef had threatened to kill her—not her aunt—if she told her aunt about the deed.

Based on the above testimonies, Cecilia found it necessary to mention things beyond herself (e.g. the Virgin Mary, her aunt) to discourage her political uncle from continuing with his assault (cf. Case 28 in Chapter 4). This response is presumably the result of a power imbalance between them. Cecilia's use of the formal "you" form with Josef may also reflect a power imbalance between them, but it is unclear how he addressed her. Cecilia's defensive strategy resonates with Stern's (1995, 103–8) delineation of the mobilization-of-female-alliances strategy. It also adds another dimension to it—that of a perceived otherworldly female ally (and, in this case, Mother) rooted in Catholic doctrine to whom all practitioners of the faith, whether male or female, owed reverence. Despite Cecilia's attempts, her approach was ultimately unsuccessful due to her uncle's confidence in getting away with the crime and his threat of murder. Notably, Engracia later dropped her complaint, denied that Cecilia was her niece, and suggested the *estupro* was a false accusation (see Chapter 4).

In the previous cases, men tended to overlook and diminish relatedness with female kin with whom they wished to have sexual relations, whereas women exhibited a greater degree of hesitation and stressed kin ties to defend themselves from unwanted sexual engagement. This discrepancy makes sense in the context of gendered rape patterns in which these men represented the aggressors. Still, criminal records show that women, like their male counterparts, might also choose to conceal relatedness during (consensual) sexual relations between kin.

In 1806, Vicente González's wife, Juana Balladares, accused him of incest with his *hermana entera* ("whole sister") (Case 48). During her testimony, Juana shared some of the alleged dialogue between Vicente and his sister Manuela during their sexual activity together. Listening from outside the room, she heard Manuela say, "Hurry, before your mother and wife get here."[34] Vicente then told her to turn to one side, but she replied that "she did not want it that way and for him to get on top of her instead."[35] Since Vicente and Manuela apparently shared a father *and* mother in accordance with the "whole sister" designation, the choice of "your mother" as opposed to "our mother" is noteworthy. Such use glosses over their relationship to one another. Thus, positioning oneself as a kinsperson, as in the cases of sexual assault mentioned above, became unnecessary, and perhaps even undesirable, in consensual relations between kin. Of course, both Vicente and Manuela, who identified one another as "brother" and "sister" without any qualification, denied the accusation.

In sum, sexual relations between kin encouraged colonial actors to stress, qualify, or disregard relatedness. These dynamics reflected power imbalances between male and female relatives and the greater ability of men to impose their own interpretations of incest on the women in their lives. Such asymmetries often left female affinal kin particularly vulnerable to sexual violence.

Reclassifying Kin

Some colonial actors chose to reclassify kin or attribute kin ties to non-kin to obfuscate the sexual nature of a relationship or defend themselves during a trial. The 1815 incest case against José María Díaz (alias Cantarillas) and his sister-in-law Agustina represents one instance of this tactic (Case 68, also in Chapter 4). The pair shared a residence, and some people believed they were romantically involved. A witness named Pedro Sorzo recalled hearing José María fighting with a woman by the name of Manuela Villeda, about which Pedro spoke with her afterwards. Manuela told Pedro the fight with José María stemmed from jealousy. Clearly on Manuela's side, Pedro went to the home of José María and told him to leave her alone. Agustina jumped up agitated and said that "her father" had not been home when Pedro said he saw him. She then remonstrated José María, reminding him how she forbade him from visiting those houses and asking his reason for venturing there. Considering her suspicion and jealousy, Pedro promised

> to put her in the Casa Nueva [women's detention center] because [José María] was not her father but rather her brother-in-law, and it is absolutely evident to him that they live together like husband and wife and that their store is a Sodom because of the liquor and comingling that goes on there to the detriment of the Royal University.[36]

Manuela Villeda testified in similar terms, saying that "Agustina tells the public that Cantarillas is her father, and as he is an older man and she very young with respect to him, some people could believe it."[37]

The testimonies of Pedro Sorzo and Manuela Villeda imply that Agustina referred to José María as her father to hide the fact that they were actually brother- and sister-in-law and romantically involved. This cover-up indicates that a father and daughter living together was less likely to incite scandal than a brother- and sister-in-law doing the same. It also demonstrates how lovers could modify kin labels to dispel suspicion of an amorous relationship.

Suspicion that someone could hide a sexual relationship through the attribution of kin terms also surfaced in an 1815 report from Nueva Guatemala (AGCA A1.15 Leg. 4471 Exp. 37723). The *alcalde de barrio* apprehended several people when he was making his rounds, one of whom was Josefa Martínez. Josefa and a man she identified as her nephew Lucio were out riding horseback at the time with her seated in front of him. During questioning, she explained that she was uncertain about his surname. Asked if she was with him because of an *ilícita amistad* since she would surely know his surname if he were a relative, she denied it and said that "they are not actually relatives. Rather, he calls her 'Aunt' because of the affection that he has for her."[38] Thus, the potential for someone to disguise a sexual partner as a relative was a real concern for law enforcement, and such potentialities show how incest codes could come into play outside of kin relations.

Even members of religious orders used kinship terms for such ends. The records of a 1796 case carried out in response to the involvement of Roberta Estrada with Fray Joseph María Rodríguez included details about how the couple was able to conceal their relationship (AGCA A2.2 Leg. 177 Exp. 3519). One strategy involved dressing Roberta in men's clothing as they traveled together, which resulted in her arrest in the town of Todos Los Santos.[39] Also, the *alcalde mayor* of Totonicapán, who would organize Roberta's transport and custody following her arrest, reportedly told one of the witnesses in the trial that the friar had previously tricked him by telling him that Roberta was his child. Unfortunately, it is not clear whether Fray Rodríguez referred to Roberta as his *hija* ("daughter") or his *hijo* ("son")—considering her male dress around this time—because the final letter of the word that would indicate the gender of the child disappears into the margins of the document. This explanation does not seem like the most obvious choice for a friar considering the vows of chastity associated with the profession. (At other points in their travels, they apparently described Roberta as his servant.) Of course, offspring from sexual liaisons involving male religious were not unheard of, and some men fathered children prior to entering the religious life. Aware of this climate, Fray Rodríguez, like his lay contemporaries, chose to transform his lover into his child to avoid scrutiny and scandal.

Analogy was also used to cast a relationship in a different light. This approach appeared in an 1821 incest case against Rosalío Yescas and María Ramona Álvarez Román, brother- and sister-in-law (Case 73). Neither Rosalío nor Ramona admitted to a sexual relationship with the other. In dismissing the accusation, Rosalío said that "he has never had such *amistad*, as he has always treated Ramona and his other sisters-in-law the same—like sisters."[40] Hence, Rosalío attempted to erase any impression of an incestuous relationship with Ramona through comparison of his behavior towards sisters and sisters-in-law. In so doing, he drew from expectations that sexual relations between close consanguineous kin were less likely to occur than between close affinal kin.

Domingo Álvez, an Indian man from San Francisco el Alto, employed a similar use of analogy when he found himself accused of incest with his two daughters-in-law in 1710 (Case 2, also in Chapter 2). Through the aid of interpreters, Domingo initially contested the accusation. He argued that

> he is fearful of God and knows quite well the gravity of the sin of which he is accused, and he has never had, in neither words nor deeds, illicit dealings with either of his two daughters-in-law because he has always viewed and looked after them like his own daughters.[41]

Further, had he wanted to insolently engage in some indecency with one of them, he would have justly feared the possibility of them divulging it to their husbands, mother-in-law, or relatives. In the end, Domingo admitted to the crime with one of his daughters-in-law, and both were subjected to public shaming and lashes following the trial.

The above criminal records speak to the utility of kin labels and analogy when it came to obscuring illicit sexual activity. Such strategies drew from assumptions that kin were less likely to engage in illicit sexual activity than non-kin and relatives through blood were more likely to avoid sexual contact with one another than relatives through marriage.

Compadrazgo and Marital Fidelity

There were not any incest trials in the case sample that focused on incest between spiritual kin. Still, we do find individuals who used spiritual incest as a frame of reference in their attempts to modify particular behaviors of their own or others. For example, colonial actors sometimes repurposed the institution of *compadrazgo* to ensure marital fidelity.[42] On April 13, 1763, Manuel Arias put forward a complaint against Pablo García, claiming the latter had "perturbed" his marriage to Manuela Vásquez, a twenty-six-year-old Spanish woman (AGCA A2.2 Leg. 147 Exp. 2719). In fact, Manuel stated it was necessary to reprehend his wife on several occasions, but she had never listened to him because she had an *indomable genio* ("indomitable nature"). Concerned about their reputation, Manuel made Pablo his *compadre* "so that, in this manner, correction would be had with the contracted *parentesco*."[43] In other words, Manuel believed *compadrazgo* would provide a means to end the affair between his wife and Pablo. However, this strategy was apparently unsuccessful. Manuel alleged that Pablo continued to behave inappropriately even after becoming a *compadre* (and following various other measures). From Manuel's accounting of events, it appears that he and Pablo viewed *compadrazgo* differently. Whereas Manuel felt it conflicted with certain forms of intimacy, Pablo supposedly did not. As in cases of incestuous rape, appealing to incest codes to discourage sexual relations was only fruitful if all parties shared them and were willing to oblige them.

Manuela's story was different from that of her husband. When she was brought in for questioning, she denied any illicit involvement with Pablo. She said that he "is her *compadre* and would hardly be able to commit such a thing."[44] Hence, contrary to the allegations of her husband, Manuela insinuated that she and Pablo shared his sentiment that sexual relations between *compadres* and *comadres* were inappropriate, which ultimately testified to their innocence. The case record ends after her testimony, leaving the conclusion of the matter unknown.

Manuel's form of strategizing also appeared in a case from 1806 Quetzaltenango against Cosme Rivera, a *mestizo* blacksmith accused of *concubinato* with doña Crisanta Pardo, a local shop owner (AGCA A2.2 Leg. 219 Exp. 4574). Cosme's wife, Elorencia [sic] Gertrudis Monzón, explained the various reasons she had to suspect that something was going on between them. These included the amount of time Cosme spent at doña Crisanta's store, the physical contact between them, and Cosme's detachment from and later mistreatment of her. In order to see if with *honesto motivo* ("honorable cause") she could impede the involvement between Cosme and doña Crisanta, Gertrudis told her husband that she wanted doña Crisanta to become their *comadre* through the baptism of the child with whom she was pregnant. Like Manuel Arias above, Gertrudis thought entering into *compadrazgo* with doña Crisanta would put an end to her husband's infidelity.

Cosme refused to make doña Crisanta a *comadre*, even allegedly telling his mother-in-law that "he'd sooner go to hell than do that."[45] Ironically, in his mind, having doña Crisanta involved in their child's baptism would give further credence to his wife's (and mother-in-law's) suspicions of an *amistad* with her, a relationship which he denied. Following their statements, Gertrudis and Cosme were working with different assumptions about *compadrazgo*. While Gertrudis viewed sexual relations and *compadrazgo* as opposed to one another, Cosme apparently feared that one could imply the other. Yet, both approached the potential creation of such ties with particular goals in mind. Ultimately, Cosme and doña Crisanta were sentenced to the court fees and a cease of communication, which included a mandate for Cosme to relocate to an area distant from doña Crisanta.

Compadrazgo surfaced in a similar manner in an incest case from 1788 Petapa in which Eusebio Barillas accused his brother Josef Félix, a *mulato* farmer, of *ilícita amistad* with his wife, María Jacoba Suárez (Case 12). Initially, María Jacoba admitted to the *amistad*, stating that they carried it out at her parents' house. She went on to say that "in order to obviate this offense, she has urged [Josef Félix] to become her *compadre*."[46] Thus, María Jacoba (who was pregnant) seemed to think that entering into *compadrazgo* with her brother-in-law would make it less likely for them to continue their involvement with one another. Considering they were already brother- and sister-in-law, her approach suggests that, at least for her, spiritual kinship could provide a more effective obstacle to sexual relations than affinal kinship.

Later, María Jacoba denied any previous admission to the *ilícita amistad* with Josef Félix. She claimed that, on the contrary, she only testified to having asked her brother-in-law to enter into *compadrazgo* with her to temper her husband's jealousy. (Apparently, Eusebio once found her lying down naked with Josef Félix.) Even in her modified version of events, María Jacoba used a comparable logic. Being connected in this new way would automatically ease suspicion of their involvement, as sexual relations and *compadrazgo* were evidently more incompatible than sexual relations and siblings-in-law. For his part, Josef Félix stated that it was true María Jacoba encouraged him to become her *compadre*, but she did so because of his decision to marry her sister.[47]

The insinuation that spiritual incest was more unacceptable and improbable than affinal incest is consistent with evidence of the special place of spiritual kinship relative to non-spiritual kinship within and beyond the Iberian world. For example, Canon 53 of the Council in Trullo of 692 C.E. explicitly stated that "the spiritual relationship is greater than fleshly affinity" when outlawing marriage to a coparent (Percival 1916, 390). Also, using anthropological data primarily from Mexico and Guatemala, Benjamin D. Paul (1942) argued that "ritual kinship" (of which *compadrazgo* was a part) was modeled on, but more sacred than, consanguineous kinship (see Lynch 1986, 60–1). Further, Julian Pitt-Rivers (1958, 430) noted how in the Andalusian region of Spain, "the *compadrazgo* imposes the duty of cooperation in a way that kinship alone does not. It imposes a restraint in conduct, language, and feeling that is not to be derived from any other relationship." Thus, María Jacoba's comments were likely not unique to her.

Assumptions about sexual avoidance between spiritual kin and spiritual kinship's utility in managing social relations have present-day equivalents. For example, in modern Latin America, a spiritual kinsman is one of only a few adult males that can be trusted with a female relative (see Lynch 1986, 229). Also, Héritier (2002, 284–5) noted that women in Sicily sometimes choose a male member of their husband's social network who is sexually attracted to them to be the godfather of their child. This creates a sexual barrier but also allows for a continued intimacy between them. In colonial Guatemala, it was both women and men who used this form of strategizing. And considering *compadrazgo* can facilitate solidarity and alliance within and without families,[48] it is striking that these individuals potentially sacrificed more optimal candidates for *compadrazgo* in order to rectify the present state of their marriages.

Even though the previous cases did not center on spiritual incest per se, they show how regulations on sexuality between spiritual kin could infiltrate marital life and provide an avenue for resolving conflict within it. Of course, the success of such projects depended on a mutual agreement that spiritual kinship and sexual relations were incompatible.

Kin as Scapegoats

While many individuals refuted kin ties with sexual partners to lessen the charge against them, there were apparently also occasions on which alleging or admitting to sexual relations with a relative—as opposed to a non-relative—was preferable. The trial against Francisco de Paula Guerra, a *mestizo* hatter, for the forced deflowerment of his political niece Ciriaca serves as an example (Case 9, also in Chapter 2). Francisco's *defensor* argued it was reasonable that

> if [Ciriaca] is no longer a virgin like her mother says, another man is responsible, and, in saving this individual—who could have been a person of her affection—[Ciriaca] condemned Francisco by saying that her uncle was responsible in order to escape the punishment from her mother.[49]

That is, by blaming her uncle, Ciriaca would not only protect the man who took her virginity but herself as well. This argument implies that kin held women and girls less accountable for sexual relations with a (older) male relative. Indeed, there is not any mention of Ciriaca having been punished by her mother, though Ciriaca did state that her initial reserve to tell her mother about the incident was due to her anticipation of disciplinary action. And while the magistrate sentenced Francisco to a month of public works and the court fees, Ciriaca did not merit any legal penalty.

María Josefa García was also accused of falsely blaming her father for the loss of her virginity (Case 28). Despite María Josefa's father admitting to the crime, his legal representative proposed that she was not a virgin when it happened. First, he noted "the recklessness and temerity with which Josefa has attempted to make her father the author of her deflowerment and pregnancy."[50] He then suggested that "in order to conceal her fragility, she has tried to incriminate her father."[51] However, María Josefa's mother previously testified that she believed her daughter when she told her she was pregnant from her father because nobody ever came to their house. Her mother's statement hints at why women might escape blame for sexual violence executed by male kin—outsiders were easier to avoid than relatives. Surely, power imbalances between older male and younger female kin were also recognized as a contributing factor. Remember how María Josefa Dardón and her mother (Case 15, Chapter 4) used the concept of respect to make the former appear less culpable for the sexual encounters with her father.

Some individuals felt that male family members were easy targets when it came to accounting for a woman's loss of virginity or pregnancy. Arguments in the aforementioned case against Miguel Caixon, who was said to have fathered the two sons of his stepdaughter Juana, mirrored such concern (Case 19, also in Chapter 4). Miguel denied the relationship and identified Lorenzo Ratzal[52] as the true father of Juana's children. Supposedly, Miguel had previously caught Juana and Lorenzo "in the act" and the pair begged him to punish them instead of alerting the authorities. Miguel's *defensor*, José Antonio Godínez, argued,

> it would be more natural for [Juana] to say to my client, "My children are yours, not Lorenzo's," which is crucial evidence that they might belong to Ratzal—who confesses to his illicit sexual relations [with Juana]—and not to [Miguel].[53]

The "naturalness" to which Godínez referred is suggestive of a cultural environment in which men were thought to be in danger of false allegations related to their non-virginal or pregnant female kin. Of course, allusions to such "risk" may reflect concerns over preserving the male prerogative within the family more than anything else.

Assertions about sexual relations with a male relative were not necessarily malicious. Recall how Bernardo Quachita supposedly took responsibility for the pregnancy of his fiancée's sister to protect her from any dishonor that might come from her involvement with a *ladino* man (Case 54, Chapter 2). Nor was pinning sexual relations on a relative always on a woman's own initiative. For instance, María Basilia García argued that her father-in-law told her to blame her stepfather for her loss of virginity in order to cover up his own sexual relations with her (Case 65a).

Following these examples, male kin proved to be a useful scapegoat when a non-virginal status or pregnancy required explanation. What is especially intriguing in these cases is that this was considered a viable option even when both sexual partners would have been implicated in the crime of incest from a legal standpoint. Though references to this type of scapegoating could certainly serve to protect male privilege, perhaps there were also occasions when women were the primary beneficiaries of such strategies.

Conclusion

Overall, Guatemalan criminal records underline the subjective and relative nature of kin relations once sexual relations and the criminal process entered into the equation. While the exact nature of kin ties may have been relatively insignificant the majority of the time, potentially incestuous acts required their clarification. The importance of "real" kin to definitions of incest meant that individuals involved in incest trials could exploit ambiguities in relatedness created by kinship practices. It also placed women who were kin-like at greater risk of sexual violence than female kin. Those who did share kin ties with their rapists might stress these connections in hopes of deterring such violence. Still, stronger preoccupations with consanguineous incest (compared to affinal incest) could deflate such protests, leaving women connected through affinity more vulnerable to assaults from male relatives than those linked by blood ties.

Of course, the significance of incest models was not confined to the sphere of sexual violence. For example, colonial actors could draw from assumptions that sexual relations were more likely to manifest between non-kin and between affinal kin to conceal a consensual sexual relationship. They could also use their understandings of spiritual incest in their attempts to curb adulterous behavior, or at least, the perception of it. In short, the men and women of colonial Guatemala were adept at using kinship and incest codes to address a variety of problems in their daily lives and during run-ins with colonial authorities. This is not to say that such strategizing always required much forethought. Sometimes, it was nothing more than an intuitive response to a desperate situation.

Notes

1 An earlier version of this chapter appeared in Saffa, Sarah N. "'She Was What They Call a "Pepe"': Kinship Practice and Incest Codes in Late Colonial Guatemala." *Journal of Family History* 44 (2): 181–99. Copyright © 2018 (Sarah N. Saffa). DOI: 10.1177/0363199018818617.

2 *...á el Padre de la muchacha le crio de Pepe, p.r cuyo motivo las criaturas le intitulan de abuela.*

3 *...p.r la causa de haverla cricido, le disse Prima pero q.e no hay ningun parentesco.*

4 *...es hija de Ana Albarado y q.e esta la hubo antes de su primer matrim.o con Benito Berriondo quien trataba á esta muchacha con el cariño de una buerfana recojida, q.e algunos en el Pueblo creian ser hija de Benito y de Ana, otros q.e de esta solam.te y algunos q.e ni de uno ni de otro, sino q.e hera lo q.e llaman Pepe... f. 8v.*

5 *...pepe ó muchacha á quien su muger Ana Albarado havia recojido en su casa p.r caridad p.a criarla... f. 12.*

6 *...p.r su ignorancia y haver creido q.e hera muchacha á q.n su muger havia criado p.r huerfana ú otro motibo de caridad. f. 12v.*

7 *...por el respecto q tenia a su Madre Magdalena de Estrada y mied[o] grande a su tia Maria Phelipa permitio q esta su dha tia diera la criatura Gregoria Antonia hija suia a los dichos Narciso Gonzales y Petrona Quintanilla, su muger para q de charidad la crian. f. 17v.*

8 *...Yo y dho Narciso mi marido, somos sus Padres Lex.mos y q. como tal la criamos, y casamos; Dezpuez de q dho Narciso mi marido; la estrupo violentam.te sin atender q. era su P.e...de cuya Querella, no solo resulta la calumpnia Ynfamatoria contra la crianza, q nos deve, sino tambien el Despojo, q padesemos de ntros cortos vienes; Y siendo, siniestra la querella, ni concurrir la gravedad q. se supone de q. siendo Padre, huviese extrupado su hija; ni menos constarme á mi, q aun no siendo lo huviese executado; por tanto, recurro a Vm... f. 18–18v.*

9 *...si mediante á que la Dolores y su difunta muger no eran hermanas sino hijas ambas de Padres no conosidos, se podria casar con la Dolores para no dejarla desamparada... AGCA A2.2 Leg. 205 Exp. 4188 f. 8.*

10 *Estimada Prenda de mi Corazon, y todo mi consuelo Maria Gaitan...Hija esta solo sirbe de partisiparte como lla poco falta q.e quiten de las piedras y pongan en nosotros y por todas estas cosas y p.r bolber p.r tu credito y el mio te mando esta para q.e sepaz q.e la intension q.e llebo en el Dia es q.e nos pongamos en estado. esto bajo tu pareser pues me abis de mandar abisar si es tu gusto para segir la istansia. esto tanto lo ago p.r la Bolunta q.e te tengo como p.r bolber p.r tu onor y tapar tanta boca pues el termino con q.e nos llaman es tan grosero q.e nos llaman p.r inses.tos y asi solo tu repuesta espero para escribirle al Sor. Cura y correr las delijensias que llo te prometo portarme como ombre de bien y quidarte como bos mereses. lo q.e si te digo es q.e bien es q.e no ai ningun inconbiniente. pues piensan q.e bos sos mi Cuñada y no q.e podemos cazarnos y asi no dejes de responderme lo mas pronto q.e podas...Domingo Morales. AGCA A2.2 Leg. 205 Exp. 4188 f. 14-v.*

11 *...ha alegado verbalm.te q.e sin embargo de que se estimaban y reputaban en el concepto publico por tales hermanas, en realidad no lo eran, sino solo de leche, p.r q.e su muger havia sido unicamente expuesta á las puertas de dha Manuela de Leon, y de su marido Pantaleon Gaitan...y q.e la dha M.a Dolores es hija lexitima de los nominados consortes...* AGCA A2.2 Leg. 205 Exp. 4188 f. 16v.

12 *...p.a averiguarse con certeza de ser, ó no hermanas...* AGCA A2.2 Leg. 205 Exp. 4188 f. 16v.

13 *...haviendo muerto los legitimos padres desta muchacha, y quedado enteram.te huerfana, el Padre Zapata tomando prenda en su seguridad, la huviese entregado a su hermana de leche, como asi lo ha dicho ultimamente el mismo Domingo procurando dismentir el concepto comun de que la Ramona su muger y la Maria Dolores fuesen hermanas en realidad.* AGCA A2.2 Leg. 205 Exp. 4188 f. 25v.

14 *...p.r haver fallecido sus Padres, se havia venido la muchacha á buscarla y ella como Hermana mayor la havia recojido, y tenia en su poder...* AGCA A2.2 Leg. 205 Exp. 4188 f. 28.

15 *...los expuextos, del mismo modo llaman, y reverencian p.r padres a los q.e los crian y mantienen...* AGCA A2.2 Leg. 205 Exp. 4188 f. 29v.

16 *...dentro y fuera de casa se miran y tratan como hermanos.* AGCA A2.2 Leg. 205 Exp. 4188 f. 29v.

17 *Lo cierto es, q.e si Morales vivio en la duda de que propiam.te era cuñado de la Maria...desde luego no se le puede a Morales arguir de que cometiese incesto aun quando se le convenza de haver tenido trato ilicito con la Maria...* AGCA A2.2 Leg. 205 Exp. 4188 f. 30.-v.

18 *...efectivam.te no estaba en la creencia de que aquella era su Cuñada en realidad...* AGCA A2.2 Leg. 205 Exp. 4188 f. 30v.

19 *Si estaban en la intelig.a de q.e eran parientes tienen a su favor la presuncion mas fuerte y vehemente de honestidad. Si se tenian p.r libres de parentesco, no hai tal incesto, mayormente no haviendose probado el coito...* AGCA A2.2 Leg. 205 Exp. 4188 f. 33v.

20 *...no cabe en la cabeza su perpetrasion, pues la misma naturaleza lo repugna...* AGCA A1.15 Leg. 5390 Exp. 45725 f. 34v.

21 *...mirando el Amor q.e mi Marido, le tiene á sus Hijos como Padre al fin, me dijo, q.e á ella ce le ponia q.e mi Marido estava o tratava Ynlicitam.te con mi hija. respondiendole llo q.e no podia cer que ciempre era ací q.e p.a todos sus hijos era Amorozo.* AGCA A1.15 Leg. 5426 Exp. 46305.

22 *...tu heres la q.e mandas aqui, y no esa...* AGCA A1.15 Leg. 5425 Exp. 46287 f. 3v.

23 *...esta es Simona, esta sos vós...* AGCA A1.15 Leg. 5425 Exp. 46287 f. 4.

24 *...si era chucha, que si no era su Padre, y le respondia que no le hacia, que si le sucedia alguna cosa, que el respondia por todo, que no tuviera miedo.* A1.15 Leg. 2965 Exp. 28088 f. 4v-5.

25 *...las palabras que profirio para apagar el ardor de la pacion que le dominaba, y las contestaciones que la dió dirigidas á ablandar su constancia.* AGCA A1.15 Leg. 5390 Exp. 45733 f. 6.

26 *...aunque ella se resistio diciendole que si no beia que lo miraban como a Padre, que como queria aser esas cosas estando casado con su Madre...* AGCA A1 Leg. 2914 Exp. 27094 f. 10.

27 *...segura confianza del marido p.r aver este criado á la Juana aun desde pequeña y p.r esta razon tenerla p.r hija pues reciprocam.te assi le tratava en au[s]encia y pr[e]cencia de la madre. bastante fé era esta para no sospechar la mas Leve malicia.* AGCA A1 Leg. 2914 Exp. 27094 19.-v.

28 *...no era su madre que bien podian pecar...*

29 José denied that he told Anica he would marry her, as he was aware of the impediment that stemmed from their relationship to one another. Anica initially denied, but then conceded, that she knew they were unable to marry.

30 ...*pero luego que apagaron la candela se llegó [á] ella el dho Rivas á estarla forzando, y la declarante aunque se recistió con las reflexiones d[e] que habia comulgado aquel dia, que tenia amistad con su hermana, y que finalmente no era su gusto, le contestó Rivas no tenia animo de casarse con su hermana, y aunque ultimamente le manifestó lo odioso que le era su perzona logró Rivas sus torpes deceos, pues no tubo á bien evitarlos gritando porque temió escandalizar á los que dormian halli, y que su honor lo padeciese...* AGCA A2.2 Leg. 216 Exp. 4496 10v.

31 *Pero lexos Sor. de obserbar en el un christiano proceder ha llegado á tal modo su infamia, q.e sin temer á Dios, á la Justicia ni a mi á desflorado violentam.te haze pocas horas á una Muchacha Sobrina mia q.e vive vajo de mi amparo...* f. 1-v.

32 ...*le decia á su marido, sueltme, no sea indigno p.r Maria Santissima, mire q.e se lo digo a su Muger pues yo soi donzella, y sobrina de su Muger: á que le contextaba, q.e aunq.e fuera, q.e media vez q.e el metia el pie en el lodo, lo sabia sacar, y q.e si se lo decia á la q.e declara, la havia de matar...* f. 2.

33 ...*aunq.e estaba avierta la puerta, y su Marido con su Sobrina en la cama.* f. 2v.

34 ...*date prisa antes de que venga tu madre y tu muger...* f. 2.

35 ...*no queria de aquella suerte sino que subiese encima de ella...* f. 2.

36 ...*ponerla en la Casa nueva p.r q. no era su Padre sino su Cuñado y q. le consta de positivo q. viven juntos como marido y muger y que su tienda es una Sodoma p.r la aguard.te y concurrencia q. alli hay en perjuicio a la R.l Universidad...*

37 ...*la Agustina publica q. Cantarillas es su Padre y como este és ya hombre grande y ella muy moza respecto del por este motivo podrán crerlo algunas personas...*

38 ...*en realidad no son pariente[s] sino que el le trata a la declarante tia por, cariño q.e le tiene.*

39 See also AGCA A1.15 Leg. 2166 Exp. 15590. It includes an alleged (hyperbolic) comment about how one would find more than fifty women dressed as men in the convent of San Francisco de Guatemala at night.

40 ...*jamas ha tenido tal amistad, pues siempre ha tratado asi a la Ramona, como a sus otras Cuñadas, como hermanas....*

41 ...*el es temoroso de Dios, y sabe muy bien la gravedad del pecado q se le acomula, y nunca a tenido trato ilisito con ninguna de las dh.as sus dos nueras en obras ni en palabras por que siempre las á mirado, y atendido como a sus hijas propias...f. 7.*

42 Though occasions for sponsorship in Latin America today can be quite numerous (see Foster 1953, 8), it is likely that the *compadrazgo* referred to below was associated with the rites of baptism or confirmation.

43 ...*para q de esta suerte se esperimentase la ermienda con el parentesco contraido....*

44 ...*es su conp.e y mal pudiera comete tal....*

45 ...*primero se lo llevarian los diablos, antes que tal hiciese...f. 8v.*

46 ...*para obiar esta ofensa le á ynstado ál susodho á que encompadren. f. 2v.*

47 María de la Concepción Palacios also hinted at the incompatibility of *compadrazgo* and sexual relations during interrogation about Benito Guerén's involvement with both her and her sister (Case 8). She admitted to an *ilícita*

amistad with him in the past, "but year-to-date, she separated herself from it, making him a *compadre* through her son's confirmation."

48 See, for example, Foster (1953), Pitt-Rivers (1958), and Gudeman (1971).

49 *...si se halla (como dice dha su Madre estar violada) haver sido ótro el hechor; y dha Muchacha, por salvar al que fue, (que pudo ser Perzona de su cariño) haver condenado á dho Francisco, con el dicere, de que fue su tio, para evadirse del castigo de su Madre.* f. 7v.

50 *...la ligereza, y temeridad con q.e la Josefa ha querido constituir á su Pad.e autor de su desfloramiento, y preñez.* AGCA A2.2 Leg. 199 Exp. 4085 f. 7.

51 *...por encubrir su fragilidad, ha querido acriminar á su Pad.e...*AGCA A2.2 Leg. 199 Exp. 4085 f. 8.

52 Lorenzo's surname was also written as Ratzzal, Ratztzal, and Ratzab.

53 *...le seria mas natural desirle a mi parte son vuestros mis hijos y no de Lorenzo, relevante prueva és sean de del predho. Ratzal, q.e confiesa su ilisito trato, q.e no de q.n se infiere...*AGCA A1 Leg. 2914 Exp. 27094 f. 15v.

Bibliography

Brundage, James A. 1987. *Law, Sex, and Christian Society in Medieval Europe.* Chicago, IL and London: The University of Chicago Press.

Foster, George M. 1953. Cofradía and Compadrazgo in Spain and Spanish America. *Southwestern Journal of Anthropology* 9 (1): 1–28.

Gudeman, Stephen. 1971. "The Compadrazgo as a Reflection of the Natural and Spiritual Person." *Proceedings of the Royal Anthropological Institute of Great Britain and Ireland* 45–71.

Héritier, Françoise. 2002. *Two Sisters and Their Mother: The Anthropology of Incest.* Translated by Jeanine Herman. New York: Zone Books.

Herman, Judith Lewis. 2000. *Father-Daughter Incest.* Cambridge and London: Harvard University Press.

Jaffary, Nora E. 2007. "Incest, Sexual Virtue, and Mobility in Late Colonial Mexico." In *Gender, Race, and Religion in the Colonization of the Americas*, edited by Nora E. Jaffary, 95–107. Hampshire: Ashgate.

Lynch, Joseph H. 1986. *Godparents and Kinship in Early Medieval Europe.* Princeton, NJ: Princeton University Press.

Milanich, Nara. 2002. "The Children of Fate: Families, Class, and the State in Chile, 1857–1930." Ph.D. diss., Yale University.

Paul, Benjamin D. 1942. "Ritual Kinship: With Special Reference to Godparenthood in Middle America." Ph.D. diss., University of Chicago.

Percival, Henry R. 1916. *The Seven Ecumenical Councils.* Vol. 14. *A Select Library of Nicene and Post-Nicene Fathers of the Christian Church, Second Series.* New York: The Christian Literature Company. Kindle.

Pitt-Rivers, Julian. 1958. "Ritual Kinship in Spain." *Transactions of the New York Academy of Sciences* 20 (5): 424–31.

Rodríguez Jiménez, Pablo. 1988. "Matrimonio incestuoso en el Medellín colonial 1700–1810." *Revista Extensión Cultural* 24–25: 52–8.

Saffa, Sarah N. 2019. "'She Was What They Call a "Pepe"': Kinship Practice and Incest Codes in Late Colonial Guatemala." *Journal of Family History* 44 (2): 181–99.

Shelton, Laura. 2007. "Like a Servant or Like a Son?: Circulating Children in Northwestern Mexico (1790–1850)." In *Raising an Empire: Children in Early*

Modern Iberia and Colonial Latin America, edited by Ondina E. González and Bianca Premo, 219–37. Albuquerque: University of New Mexico Press.

Stern, Steve J. 1995. *The Secret History of Gender: Women, Men, and Power in Late Colonial Mexico*. Chapel Hill and London: University of North Carolina Press.

Yan, Yunxiang. 2001. "Practicing Kinship in Rural North China." In *Relative Values: Reconfiguring Kinship Studies*, edited by Sarah Franklin and Susan McKinnon, 224–45. Durham, NC and London: Duke University Press.

6 Incest and Indianness

Introduction

The experiences of Indians in colonial Guatemalan incest trials resonated with, but also differed from, the experiences of other colonial
actors. Records from these trials demonstrate the unique way in which
concepts of Indianness intersected with the crime of incest and notions
of criminality. Attention to such discourse allows for a more nuanced
examination of how the culturally informed attitudes of Spanish magistrates, legal advisors, and defense counsel conditioned their reactions
to individuals who knowingly or unknowingly, willfully or not, failed
to conform to Spanish laws governing kin relations. In the minds of
many Spaniards, Indians (or individuals like them) were ignorant of the
criminal nature of incest and tended to commit it. These stereotypes
began early in the colonial period and continued to be reproduced
through the early nineteenth century. Even when indigenous actors dis-
played a clear understanding of European definitions of incest, generalizations to this end remained in use, intensifying racial polarization
in the process.

Associations between Incest and Otherness

The link between incest and Otherness has a long history in the Western
world. Classical Greek and Roman writers associated incest with bar-
barians. Early Christians found themselves accused of incest by pagan
Romans, and they responded in kind (Archibald 2001, 17, 20–1; see also
Brundage 1987). In fourteenth- and fifteenth-century Christian Europe,
it was commonly held that indiscriminate sexual practices were specific
to heretics, who were either indifferent to or condoned sexual indulgence.
Crimes like incest, adultery, and sodomy were allegedly frequent among
them (Brundage 1987, 493). These generalizations bled into characterizations of populations outside the continent. Obviously, incest codes
among people of different cultural backgrounds will generally vary, even
when they do overlap. But accusations of incest were often not intended
to be merely descriptive. Instead, incest was one on a standard list of

practices of which Europeans might accuse Indian groups to demonstrate their inferior or barbarian nature (Wiesner-Hanks 2010, 213), and chroniclers of colonial Guatemala followed suit.

Francisco Antonio de Fuentes y Guzmán is perhaps best known among the colonial chroniclers for his reflection of Spanish attitudes towards the indigenous people of Guatemala. As Hill, II (2002, 24) noted,

> Like other *criollos*, Fuentes saw the Indians as a race to serve their conquerors, and he fully expresses all the stereotypes of Indians as lazy, drunken, only partly Christianized, and thus untrustworthy, which his class used to justify their exploitation.

In his *Recordación Florida* (1690), he maintained that beyond illness and injury, the continual drunkenness of the Indians of the Valley of Jilotepéquez had led not only sexual relations between men and their wives and concubines but also to those with their daughters, mothers, sisters, sisters-in-law, daughters-in-law, and girls of eight and nine years of age. Such behavior, Fuentes contended, was not uncommon (Fuentes y Guzmán [1690] 1882 v. 2, 101–2). Given precedents such as these, it is not surprising that similar themes surfaced in late colonial incest trials.

Indianness in Colonial Incest Cases

Courts typically work within implicit categories of race and gender that they can then reproduce or challenge (Merry 1994, 42). Indeed, Spanish legal professionals in colonial incest trials regularly drew upon a discourse of Indianness when formulating their arguments. *Ignorancia* ("ignorance")—often coupled with *rusticidad* ("rusticity")—formed a core component of Indianness. As we have seen, ignorance had an important role in the criminal context because individuals viewed as ignorant theoretically acted with less ill intent and were, therefore, deserving of more lenient treatment by Spanish authorities. Tailoring the handling of a criminal based on their mental and moral state was rooted in the ritual of penance within the Church and introduced into Western criminal law by church courts in the Middle Ages (Wiesner-Hanks 2010, 49–50).

The discourse of Indianness formed a part of the 1803 incest case against Anica Lantán and her stepson, José Hernández, whose involvement began following the death of José's father (Case 38, also in Chapter 5). In defending Anica, don José María Pozo cited "the rusticity and ignorance of the Indians, especially of the women," and how, "for this reason, [Indians] do not have the same ill intent and malice to commit crime as [*ladinos*]." He then continued,

> in conformity with that laid out in law, Indians should not have the same penalty as *ladinos* imposed on them. Rather, they should be

judged with *equidad* [fairness] and not with the rigor that the same laws allow for [*ladinos*].[1]

In other words, Indians should be treated with a degree of leniency, not with the full rigor of the law.

José's legal representative drew upon similar themes, but in more vivid language. In discussing how Anica allegedly went to José's bed to make him "fall" with her, don Mateo de la Canal said,

> Thus, an extraordinary force and action out of the goodness and power of God would have been necessary to sustain [José] Hernández in a provocation as singular as this, especially when they lived together, wherein he would be unable to bear the pleas and tears of a jealous and afflicted stepmother, who would even deny him going to Mass because she thought that he would go look for another woman. What, then, could be expected of a poor Indian in whom ignorance and rusticity go hand-in-hand? The greatest saint would have fallen with such provocation.[2]

These characterizations were used despite the fact that both Anica and José testified that they understood the impediment that prevented them from marrying one another (and, presumably, the illicit nature of their relationship). In the end, authorities determined they merited release due to a general royal pardon, but they were to cease communication with one another.

Some individuals were willing to qualify the alleged ignorance of Indians. Such was the case for don José del Valle (an *asesor*) in his comments to the *alcalde mayor* in the 1806 case against Guillermo Lázaro and his sister-in-law, María Andrea de la Cruz, who had sexual intercourse together on three occasions (Case 47). Like defense counsel in the case above, Valle initially argued that it seemed the otherwise serious crime of incest "should be viewed with some *equidad* when committed by Indians, whose ignorance establishes in their favor the presumption of a lack of malice, which is assumed of those of other *castas* [i.e. socioracial categories]."[3] He cited as precedent Book VI, Title 1, Law IV of the *Recopilación de leyes de los reynos de las Indias* (1680), which stated that Indians were not to be punished for bigamy—a crime more severe than incest—prior to two warnings.[4] Still, Valle claimed, the Indians of his day did not deserve the same degree of *equidad* as prescribed in past laws because "it should be assumed their civilization is now more advanced (at least with respect to Christian religion) than right after the Conquest."[5]

The notion that Indians did not understand the gravity of incest seems to have translated into a stereotype that individuals so identified tended to commit it. This sentiment emerged in the comments of the *fiscal* in an 1806 case from Las Monjas against Domingo Mariano Mejía and

Juana Crisostoma Bajal (or Bajan)—political uncle and niece—whose sexual involvement may have begun prior to the former's marriage to the latter's aunt (Case 46).[6] In forwarding his legal opinion of the case, Fiscal Silva said that "the licentiousness of the Indians and indifference with which they regularly view the crime of incest makes them fall into it whenever the occasion presents itself."[7] Mariano had the opportunity to deflower Crisostoma because her aunt regularly sent her to the countryside to take Mariano his lunch, and he would continue to pursue her until his (by then) wife happened to learn about it, kicking Crisostoma (and her infant) out of the house. Ultimately, the *fiscal* took into consideration "the rusticity of the Indians and the few scruples with which they commit crimes of this sort" [8] and the fact that Mariano's wife had forgiven him for the offense when suggesting a sentence.

This view was also expressed in the 1815 criminal proceedings against José María Gómez and María Baltazara Gómez for father-daughter incest (Case 66, also in Chapter 4). Don Vicente Arrazola, defense counsel for the father, stated,

> It has been said that the delinquents are Indians, which is all that needs to be said regarding the matter, considering that the manner in which they comport themselves in relation to sex is consistent with what Ovid sang of other peoples very similar to our natives, among whom fathers indifferently 'mixed' with their daughters, and sons with their mothers.[9]

The case concluded with the release of both father and daughter due to a general royal pardon and an order for the separation of María Baltazara from her father.

Based on the case sample for this study, Indians accounted for a little over half of the individuals who were involved in incest trials when analysis is limited to actors whose *calidad* was identified. Out of the eighty-six individuals whose *calidad* was recorded, forty-six were Indian, or approximately 53 percent. However, population estimates for the late colonial period suggest that Indians constituted around 70 percent of the total population (see Lovell and Lutz 1994, 135), making the number of Indian defendants lower than what might be expected. Thus, the notion that Indians were more likely to engage in incest (by Spanish standards) than their non-Indian counterparts is not substantiated by the case sample. Further, legal professionals chose to use stereotypes of Indians even when Indian actors clearly shared their values.

Challenges to and Reinforcements of Colonial Discourse: A Case from Mixco

Since an ignorance defense theoretically had the power to aid the accused, it potentially worked against Indian plaintiffs using the legal system to seek justice for incestuous crimes. The case against Vicente Fuentes, an Indian farmer from Mixco whose trial began this study, provides detailed insight into this dynamic (Case 61). In 1810, Vicente was accused of sexual violence against his daughter-in-law Rosalía by his son and her husband, José Rumualdo Fuentes. Appearing before the *alcalde mayor*, José said,

> even though he is my father, he will not for this reason get away with the deed, as it would not be Christian, nor would we profess the faith of Jesus Christ. Therefore, I denounce Vicente Fuentes for having annulled my marriage and his, having had a forced sexual act with my wife on two occasions. Thus, in merits of justice, I request exile for his whole life...I not reuniting with her by any means because there is no reason for I myself to seek that salt country. The Señor General knows well the crime that it is, as he is my father, and I would not be a Christian if I did not do so. And in merits of justice, I request that he be banished for his whole life to a *castillo* [fort or prison].... If he is here, I will not reunite with her regardless of any punishment executed on him on the Señor General's order....[10]

Through his petition, José indicated that his Christian identity took precedence over any loyalty to his father and that his father's incestuous actions were incompatible with this identity. In fact, he elsewhere described the deed as having "offended God and me." To be sure, the Church had long been concerned with how the claims of kin could compete with the claims of God (see Herlihy 1985, 114), and José's statements show that he was more concerned with fulfilling the latter than the former.

Despite not explicitly using the term "incest," José demonstrated a clear understanding of the special nature of the crime, including the need for married couples to maintain a degree of separation (i.e. abstain from sexual intercourse) after an incestuous encounter until measures had been taken to absolve the sin and "habilitate" the marriage.[11] Knowing that he would be committing a sin should he behave otherwise, he phrased his decision to abstain from Rosalía in terms of avoiding "that salt country." While salt can have positive connotations in Christian discourse, it can also have negative ones. For example, Alonso de la Peña Montenegro, Bishop of Quito during the late seventeenth century, mentioned in his *Itinerario para párrocos de indios* ([1668] 1771, 317) that eating too much salt was a mortal sin because of the ill effects it had on one's health. It is also possible that "salt country" referred to salted earth in which no vegetation can grow, an apt agricultural metaphor for the threat of such actions to one's salvation.[12] Whatever the case, José clearly wanted his father banished so that it would be impossible for him to violate Rosalía again, thereby ensuring no further risk to himself.

In later testimony, José described how he learned about the sexual assaults on Rosalía. He had been absent from home for a period a time and discovered his wife was pregnant upon his return. Because the timing did not line up, he interrogated Rosalía about it,

> thinking she had mixed carnally with another *hombre extraño* ["strange or unfamiliar man," i.e. a non-relative], and it turned out that his own father, Vicente Fuentes, was who committed this crime, because of which he came to the authorities so that he be disciplined.[13]

From his statement, it is apparent that José automatically assumed that a non-relative was at fault for his wife's pregnancy and that he was surprised to discover the contrary. Thus, like Spanish authorities, he viewed sexual intercourse between his father and his wife as extraordinary and criminal, and he looked to the legal system to enact justice.

Rosalía elaborated on the nature of Vicente's assaults, emphasizing her lack of consent like her husband had done. Rosalía claimed the first incident occurred when Vicente offered to accompany her on an errand to prevent her getting lost. After traveling a distance, he grabbed her against her will in a *milpa* and penetrated her. He was slightly tipsy at the time. On another occasion, when Vicente was sober, he signaled to her with his hat to come over, but she did not comply. He then followed her to a ravine where she was doing laundry and raped her a second time. After the incidents, she allegedly found herself pregnant, though this was later disproved.

Vicente initially denied the accusation, making it necessary for the court to convene a *careo* between him and Rosalía. As discussed in the previous chapter, Rosalía took this opportunity to remind her father-in-law about how he called her a "bitch" and claimed he was not her father during an assault and how she responded that there would be consequences anyway. Don José Baucello, Rosalía's initial *curador*,[14] elaborated on this interchange. He called attention to how Rosalía

> tried to persuade her father-in-law to contain his drive, making him understand that she was his political daughter, and that such behaviors were for the *irracionales* ["irrationals"] and not observed among Christians...But despite this, Fuentes did not heed such natural assurances and, on the contrary, insisted that she not be afraid.[15]

Hence, Rosalía apparently understood the illicit nature of sexual relations with one's father-in-law among Christians and tried to discourage Vicente by reminding him of their relationship and professed religion.

In fact, even though Rosalía initially claimed that she was unaware of the particular sin that she and her father-in-law committed, after being pressed following the *careo* (which suggested otherwise), she admitted she was conscious of it. Vicente, on the other hand, deemphasized the nature of their kin tie and disregarded the warning about the negative repercussions that would result from sexual intercourse with his daughter-in-law.

Following Rosalía's remonstrations during the *careo*, Vicente admitted that he became aware of his crime after the two sexual encounters with her and, consequently, told her to stay quiet about them. Still, Vicente maintained that, at the time of the crime, "he did not know what he was doing, nor the gravity of the sin that he was committing, and he asked to be viewed with compassion."[16] Thus, in contrast to his son and daughter-in-law, Vicente insisted on his ignorance of the criminal nature of his actions, at least at the time he committed them.

Like Vicente, his initial *curador*, don Félix de Salazar, drew on assumptions of ignorance. However, the latter linked it directly to *calidad*. He argued that, if Vicente had been a *persona de algún cultivo* ("a cultured person"), he would have deserved the suitable consequences of the crime, but his client was no such person. While conceding that the incest was proven, Salazar argued that the violent nature of it was not because it would not have occurred twice had Rosalía actually been unwilling the first time. She could have removed herself from the situation or reported her father-in-law. "But," he continued, "what do we want from uncultured, stupid peoples without fear of, nor respect for, God? As it is said that no matter how much effort their priests put into instructing them, the Indians are yet to be conquered."[17] In other words, Salazar contended that both Vicente and Rosalía were willing parties to the incest, but as Indians, they did not understand its criminal nature and thus did not deserve rigorous penalties.

Joaquín Eduardo Mariscal, the *procurador de pobres* and second legal representative for Vicente, made arguments similar to those of the first. He asserted that his client, "being deficient in rational principles, was resolved to sin,"[18] and he contended that Vicente's success in the act depended on Rosalía's consent. He then went on to say,

> Even though Vicente is a rustic Indian and lacks the requisite lights of religion, he came to know his crime and infer its gravity following its commission. He thereby imposed perpetual silence on his daughter-in-law, believing that, with this, all was finished and buried and that he would comply with God and the loyalty that he owes his son by not returning to solicit her further. Such are the simple and never malicious sentiments of the Indians of this area, as in them the lights of religion and charity do not glow, which in the *cultos* ["learned, civilized individuals"] move believers to commiseration.[19]

In short, Vicente did not know that what he was doing was sinful until after the fact, and once knowledgeable of its criminal nature, he desired to rectify the situation, albeit incorrectly. Thus, both of Vicente's legal representatives argued that he *and* Rosalía were consenting parties to the incest and that the authorities should excuse such behavior with stereotypes of Indians as ignorant of, and lacking in, Christian virtues, completely ignoring how other members of Vicente's own family situated the crime within a Christian framework.

Whereas Vicente and his legal representatives used ignorance as a defense strategy, Rosalía's defense counsel attempted two different approaches. As alluded to above, Baucello advocated for her innocence by highlighting her knowledge of Christian concepts and her employment of them to discourage her father-in-law's sexual advances. Notably, he omitted discussion of her *calidad*, which becomes significant when his lines of argumentation are compared with the strategies of her second legal representative, Juan José León.

León initially argued in a parallel fashion to Baucello. He focused on evidence that suggested Rosalía was an unwilling participant in the incest, knowledgeable of its deviant nature, and innocent of any wrongdoing. Regarding her chastity, he rhetorically asked,

> How many examples are read in stories of women, who, having cared extraordinarily about purity, have fallen into the cunning traps of a licentious man in the end? And who does not note that, even though their bodies were stained, their virtues have become all the more admirable?[20]

Further, Rosalía's repugnance towards her father-in-law's behavior was evidenced by her having told him "that the corporal union between fathers and daughters was the most monstrous—seen only among animals."[21] León also pointed out that one could only imagine how surprised and afflicted Rosalía would have been as a result of "the unexpected movements of her father-in-law," "the strange inclination of which he was possessed," and "the improper solicitation of her father."[22] In arguing that Rosalía would have been caught off guard by such behavior, León implied she was aware that his comportment was abnormal and inappropriate. Thus, like Baucello, León initially stressed how Rosalía's understanding of kinship norms was in accordance with those deemed proper under Spanish law, and here again, there was no mention her *calidad*.

However, León explored two hypothetical scenarios in case it was determined that Rosalía consented to the act. It is in these two hypothetical scenarios that León utilized the ignorance defense for the first time and demonstrated its intersection with *calidad*. In the first scenario,

Rosalía neglected to resist Vicente despite not wanting to have sex with him. In this case, León contended,

> Respect for her father and fear of raising a hand to him would have prevented her from making any possible efforts in her defense, just like when a child, unjustly scolded by their father, does not dare to contradict him nor make use of their rights for fear of committing an offense. There is also no doubt that Rosalía Surqueah is imbued with the common error of idiotic peoples—that fathers should be obeyed even in sinful commands—whose condition and principles of governance do not allow for anything else.[23]

Hence, León began his argument with kin norms familiar to the Hispanic tradition, but he then proceeded to distinguish Rosalía's situation by pointing out how she would have experienced them in a particularly exaggerated form due to her alleged "idiocy."

The source of Rosalía's supposed ignorance surfaced in León's discussion of the second hypothetical scenario. León maintained that Rosalía merited lenient treatment even if she happily committed adultery with her father-in-law, which he found unlikely since he was a *hombre decrépito* ("decrepit man") with respect to her. (Vicente was 39 years old, whereas Rosalía was 18.) He argued,

> sensuality is the passion that is the most difficult to overcome, for which reason I will assert, without fear of erring, that it is the most trying form of passion for the *justos* [those who live by faith] who continually drill their bodies with harsh penitence, and that it has been the cause of confusion among learned minds…And causing so much harm, and in such people, what can be expected of a rustic Indian without principles of religion, who does not have other prescript to act than her own will?[24]

Suddenly, then, Rosalía's *calidad* became an essential component of her defense.

Overall, León took two distinctive approaches in defense of his client. First, he omitted discussion of Rosalía's *calidad* and focused instead on her moral uprightness and unwillingness to engage sexually with her father-in-law. It was only when he entertained the idea of her showing no resistance to her father-in-law either out of fear or due to her consent that he used stereotypes of her *calidad* and rusticity to excuse her behavior. In other words, if Rosalía had been afraid of offending her father-in-law through disobedience, her association with "idiotic peoples" was at fault. If she had wanted to have sexual intercourse with him, who could blame an *india* from the countryside when even the most pious and educated individuals struggled with sensuality?

The arguments from the respective legal counsels of Vicente and Rosalía demonstrate how negative stereotypes of Indians were employed as a means to alleviate blame in crimes of incest. It was not until a second appeal (following a reduced sentence) that Mariscal admitted that "it is well known that among the Indians there are some who have more malice than others,"[25] but he, of course, suggested that Vicente was not one of them. And comparisons between defense strategies reveal that an indigenous identity had no relevance when an accused person behaved in a manner consistent with norms laid out by Spanish legal and ecclesiastical authorities. Indeed, when portrayed in this fashion, Rosalía's *calidad* was ignored, almost as if it would have been incompatible with such a depiction.[26] According to Philip J. Deloria (2004, 5), "To assert that a person or an event is anomalous cannot help but serve to create and to reinforce other expectations." Even though Rosalía's defense counsel did not explicitly identify her as an Indian anomaly, they did so implicitly when placing her actions within a Hispanic moral framework. Vicente, on the other hand, always represented the rule, not the exception. In either case, the association between incest and Indianness was strengthened.

Severo Martínez Peláez (2009) noted a similar phenomenon in his analysis of the aforementioned *Recordación Florida*. He found a divergence between the *criollo* author's opinions on Indian matters and the actual information contained within the text, contradictions which he attributed to class prejudice. According to Martínez Peláez (2009, 126), a social class gradually comes to take its prejudices as absolute truths, blinding its members to reason and the fallacies inherent in them. Portrayals of Indianness in the case against Vicente Fuentes (and others) that ran contrary to the actions of actual Indian actors reflect the attitudes of Spanish legal professionals who seem to have been generally unable (or unwilling) to acknowledge similar values and attitudes between Indians and themselves. Obviously, there were legal and economic reasons to keep these distinctions in place, but, perhaps, they also speak to a deeper anxiety about maintaining boundaries between ethnic and racial groups. As Deloria (2004, 45) noted of assimilation policy in the United States, white Americans often found the possibility of a strong likeness between Indians and non-Indians disturbing.

In sum, even though portrayals of Indianness in incest cases were especially negative and often contrary to the actions of the individuals involved, they theoretically offered a silver lining for accused persons in the form of more lenient sentencing. As a result, this type of discourse was not limited to the ethnic Spaniards who staffed the colonial courtrooms. It was also employed by members of the same marginalized class.

Self-Description and Indianness

In critiquing James C. Scott's (1990) work on domination and resistance, Don Kulick (1996) discussed how transgendered sex workers in

Brazil (*travestis*) "appropriate the language of the dominant" and use it to their own advantage. Even though this form of resistance reproduces the structures that subordinate *travestis*, it is still a means to survive, and even prosper, in a society where they are marginalized. Indians in colonial Guatemala were also adept at using the language of the dominant to their own advantage,[27] and this type of linguistic appropriation can be found in incest cases as well.

During the legal proceedings against Vicente Fuentes, Andrea Sotoc (his wife)[28] petitioned for his sentence of four to five years of imprisonment at Omoa (in present-day Honduras) to be converted to public works. (He had also been sentenced to twenty-five lashes.) According to her plea, she feared that he would die there because of its harsh reputation and that, as a result, she and her children would suffer. To further support her request, she pointed out "the lack of education and less malice that ordinarily or generally is observed in those of our kind."[29] In so doing, Andrea employed the same concepts of Indianness as her husband's legal representatives in the hope of having his sentence commuted. However, in the end, Vicente's sentence was not commuted beyond the twenty-five lashes and four years of imprisonment (originally eight) at Omoa.

Indian defendants from Ciudad Vieja also utilized the ignorance defense in Case 54, which related to the supposed involvement of Bernardo Quachita with two sisters (also in Chapters 2 and 5). María de los Ángeles Sánchez, sister of Bernardo's fiancée, shared the moments surrounding Bernardo's alleged solicitation of her. She said that

> even though she told him she knew he was in *ilícita amistad* with her sister [María Germana] under *palabra de casamiento* [verbal promise of marriage], Quachita responded that it did not matter, that if she turned out pregnant, he would take the child to be raised at his house, and, for this reason, she fooled around with him from which she has become pregnant.[30]

In her *confesión*, she explicitly blamed Bernardo for the incest since he continued to pursue her even after she reminded him about his relationship with her sister (cf. Case 45). And despite her apparent hesitation to engage with him, she testified that "because of her ignorance, she did not comprehend the crime that she committed nor that it would cause an impediment to the marriage that Quachita had proposed to her sister."[31] Thus, María de los Ángeles was not at fault because she did not instigate but rather was hesitant about sexual relations with Bernardo. Further, she was unaware of the offense she committed by indulging him.

Bernardo spoke in like manner. When he was charged with committing the "enormous crime" of having had "*concubinato incestuouso* with the two Marías...knowing for certain that they are sisters"[32] and scolded that "such excesses are only seen among the irrationals," he responded that "as a fragile man, and without these Christian sentiments, he did not gauge the enormity [of the crime] that he was committing in these excesses of which he is charged."[33] Despite these admissions of guilt, both Bernardo and María de los Ángeles ultimately denied ever having had sexual intercourse together, and it will be recalled that legal counsel argued their alleged relationship was intended to cover up María de los Ángeles relationship with a *ladino* man. While Asesor Zelaya was not convinced of their innocence, he proposed their release since "the criminality and gravity [of the incest] is greatly lessened by their *calidad* and ignorance."[34] The *alcalde ordinario* presiding over the case took his advice.

Reference to a deficiency in Christian principles appeared in the case against José María Gómez and his daughter María Baltazara as well (Case 66, also in Chapter 4). Another daughter named Juana Josefa, who was identified as "very *castellana*," brought forward the accusation. She was not sworn in prior to formalizing her accusation "because of not being instructed in the Christian doctrine." Juana Josefa claimed that her father had been involved with her sister for a year and that she had caught them fornicating together on three occasions, once in the stubble field and twice behind their home. Being

> fearful that her father would do the same with [her]...she told the *alcalde* of the area, not having done so sooner because of her lack of instruction. And she is presently residing in another house in which they are teaching her the catechism since her father was not doing it.[35]

It was important for Juana Josefa to clarify why she had not informed authorities immediately about her father's sexual activity with her sister to avoid a charge of consent to the crime. Thus, the plaintiff of this case, like the defendants above, used the ignorance defense to protect herself during her encounter with authorities. Notably, when Juana Josefa's father initially denied the crime, he argued that "he would have to be a brute to commit such a sin. His parents raised him and educated him with the fear of God."[36]

Two Indian defendants called themselves *tontos* ("fools") during their trials (cf. Sousa 1997, 203–4). The first was Andrés Victorio, a widower who in 1794 was reported for having lived in a marital fashion with his sister-in-law, María Anastacia Vásquez (Case 17a). According to Andrés, his involvement with María Anastacia had been under the pretext of marriage, and they had two children together (one of which survived). However, when the priest told him he could not marry her—presumably because of the affinal impediment—he separated from her. When the magistrate asked Andrés what *parentesco* he had with María Anastacia, he said that "there is none. She is *hermana de madre* of Petrona Martel, who was his legitimate wife, but they had different fathers" (cf. Case 39).[37] Remonstrated as to how he could say he did not have any *parentesco* with María Anastacia when she was *hermana de madre* of his wife, he responded that "like the fool that he is, he does not know."[38] Charged with living with his sister-in-law in *mala vida* [i.e. in an illicit manner], he replied that "he did so with the objective of getting married, and as a fool, he did not know what he was doing."[39] Don Mateo de la Canal, legal counsel for both Andrés and María Anastacia, followed suit. He said that their ignorance regarding their *parentesco* was apparent in their testimonies, which should not be surprising, "considering the idiocy that is so characteristic of those of their kind and quality."[40] The pair was arrested again in 1797 (Case 17b).

Juana Crisostoma Bajal from Case 46 above described herself in the same manner as Andrés Victorio. Charged as guilty of *ilícita amistad* with her political uncle—committing incest in the process and making him commit adultery—she said that "it is all true, but that, as a fool, she did not know the ill that she was doing until now that they have told her."[41] Regardless of whether Andrés Victorio and Crisostoma Bajal truly felt foolish about their actions or not, their use of the self-deprecating "fool" label would have played right into stereotypes of Indianness.

Importantly, ignorance of incest was not a viable defense for everyone. For example, when Manuel Aldana (Case 44), a *mestizo* from Cobán living in Nueva Guatemala, claimed he did not realize he was committing incest through his sexual involvement with two "carnal" sisters (i.e. whole sisters), the *alcalde ordinario* retorted that

> he cannot be ignorant of it, for it is well known among even the coarsest of peoples that licentious union between one man and two carnal sisters is a crime beyond that of fornication alone, and considering his circumstances—he knows how to read and write and has not been isolated—the ignorance that he feigns cannot be assumed.[42]

In short, Aldana's urban lifestyle and education betrayed him. His identification as non-Indian, and *mestizo* in particular, also likely worked against him.

Overall, the ignorance defense—whether in terms of general ignorance or a matter more specific to the crime of incest—was intimately linked to the indigenous population. Indians constituted 78 percent of the individuals of known *calidad* on whose behalf the ignorance defense was utilized by legal professionals and/or defendants themselves (25 of 32 records).[43] Indian men accounted for 80 percent of male defendants of known *calidad* who were accompanied by an ignorance defense (12 of

15 records), and two-thirds of these *indios* used ignorance in their own defense (8 of 12 records) (see Table 6.1). Indian women represented 76 percent of female defendants of known *calidad* who were accompanied by an ignorance defense (13 of 17 records), and 77 percent of these *indias* used ignorance on their own behalf (10 of 13 records) (see Table 6.2). While this defense theoretically benefitted an accused person, it also served to perpetuate a colonial discourse that reinforced hierarchical structures in colonial society.

To the extent that this approach succeeded, it would have also worked against indigenous plaintiffs and victims of sexual violence. In cases where the ignorance defense intersected with sexual violence or intimidation, 9 out of 12 cases involved an Indian man and an Indian woman (see Table 6.3). This suggests that cases carried out in Spanish courts could contribute to an environment in which indigenous women in particular were at risk of sexual violence from male kin. That being said, only two Indian men accused of incestuous violence—Pedro Castellanos from Case 26 and Josef Silverio Ampérez from Case 65a—escaped penalty, and the ignorance defense only appeared during the trial of the latter. Further, Indian

Table 6.1 Male Defendants and the Ignorance Defense

Case Number	Male Defendant	Calidad	Agent
28	Josef Eustaquio Garcia	*indio*	self
65a/65b	José Silverio Ampérez	*indio*	self
65b	Manuel Cornel	*indio*	self
17a	Andrés Victorio	*indio*	self; defense counsel
46	Domingo Mariano Mejía	*indio*	self; *fiscal*
47	Guillermo Lázaro	*indio*	self; *asesor*
54	Bernardo Quachita	*indio*	self; defense counsel; *asesor*
61	Vicente Fuentes	*indio*	self; wife; defense counsel; *fiscal*
2	Domingo Álvez	*indio*	defense counsel
21	Hipólito Cojulum	*indio*	defense counsel
38	José Hernández	*indio*	defense counsel
66	José María Gómez	*indio*	defense counsel
44	Manuel Aldana	*mestizo*	self
37	Patricio de León	*mestizo/mulato*	*asesor*
10	Esteban Quiñones	*pardo libre*	defense counsel
3	Pedro Monzón	n/a	self
58	Felipe Gil	n/a	self
36	Mariano Donis	n/a	defense counsel

Table 6.2 Female Defendants and the Ignorance Defense

Case Number	Female Defendant	Calidad	Agent
1	Madalena Velasco	*india*	self
2	Isabel Matul	*india*	self
65a	María Basilia García	*india*	self
65b	María Leandra Ampérez	*india*	self
65b	María Manuela López	*india*	self
17a	María Anastacia Vásquez	*india*	self; defense counsel
38	Anica Lantán	*india*	self; defense counsel
46	Juana Crisostoma Bajal	*india*	self; *fiscal*
54	María de los Ángeles Sánchez	*india*	self; defense counsel; asesor
61	María Rosalía Surqueah	*india*	self; defense counsel; *fiscal*
54	María Germana Sánchez	*india*	defense counsel
66	María Baltazara Gómez	*india*	defense counsel (for male)
47	María Andrea de la Cruz	*india*	asesor
62	doña María Salomé Soto	*española/criolla*	self
3	Francisca de Escudero	*española*	self (through defense counsel)
48	Manuela Antonia González	*mestiza*	self
29	Josepha Mejía	*mulata/parda libre*	self; *fiscal*
44	doña Feliciana Rivas	n/a	self
58	Petrona Alvarado	n/a	self
64	Alejandra Vidal	n/a	self

Table 6.3 Incestuous Rapists, Victims, and the Ignorance Defense

Case Number	Male Actor	Calidad	Female Actor	Calidad
2	Domingo Álvez	*indio*	Isabel Matul	*india*
2	Domingo Álvez	*indio*	Isabel Cox	*india*
21	Hipólito Cojulum	*indio*	María Mercedes Quemé	*india*
28	Josef Eustaquio García	*indio*	María Josefa García	*india*
38	José Hernández	*indio*	Anica Lantán	*india*
61	Vicente Fuentes	*indio*	María Rosalía Surqueah	*india*
65a	José Silverio Ampérez	*indio*	María Basilia García	*india*
65b	José Silverio Ampérez	*indio*	María Leandra Ampérez	*india*
66	José María Gómez	*indio*	María Baltazara Gómez	*india*
37	Patricio de León	*mestizo/ mulato*	Francisca de León	n/a
10	Esteban Quiñones	*pardo libre*	Secundina Hernández	n/a
58	Felipe Gil	n/a	Petrona Alvarado	n/a

defendants generally had lower acquittal rates than other socioracial groups (see Chapter 3). Thus, the effectiveness of this form of defense was apparently limited. In either case, Indian women and girls stood to suffer most. Should the ignorance defense succeed, rapists would surely count among its beneficiaries and be emboldened by a sense of impunity. Should it not be effective, victims of sexual violence would likely find themselves subject to more rigorous sentences. Of course, there were certainly times when an injured party might actually want their offenders to be viewed with compassion for emotional or practical reasons. This turned out to be the case for José Fuentes from Case 61 above, who eventually requested the release of his father because of the hardship his absence had created for his mother and siblings.

Indianness as a Tool of Comparison in Incest Cases

Colonial concepts of Indianness also emerged in incest trials as a tool of comparison. In these cases, comparisons of the defendants with Indians served as a tactic to either excuse the incestuous behavior of an accused person or highlight the especially deviant nature of it. The 1804 case against Patricio de León, who was interchangeably identified as *mestizo* and *mulato*, serves as an example (Case 37, also in Chapter 4). Patricio was charged with *haver querido usar torpemente de su hija* ("having tried to use his daughter in a lewd manner"). Juan José Pisabaj,[44] an Indian man who was the only eye witness to the crime, testified that on his return from an errand he came across a man, who was drunk and in a sexual position with a young child underneath him. This man asked the child, "Does it hurt you?", and she responded, "Yes." Knowing who they were, he interrupted by asking Patricio, "*Hombre*, what is this? We are Christians. As such, the law of God is observed, as this is with your daughter."[45] Patricio retorted that the girl was his wife—not his daughter—yet another example of how kin might be strategically relabeled. When Juan José tried to get Patricio to come with him to the resident priest, he refused and said, "You'd better make me a noose and hang me here."

Even though Patricio was not an Indian, the *asesor* drew from Indianness in his commentary. He underlined Patricio's *rusticidad* and how "among the Indians and those who are raised like them, the crime of incest, like inebriation—following Father Avendaño and Mr. Solórzano—is not a sin of great gravity because they do not comprehend its malice."[46] Here, stereotypes about Indians served as a point of reference for determining accountability in an incest case in which the accused was not himself identified as Indian. That is, because of Patricio's supposed association with Indians, the *asesor* felt he should be treated more leniently.

It is significant that this nineteenth-century *asesor* cited two seventeenth-century writers. Juan de Solórzano Pereira was a Spanish jurist who became a judge in the Audiencia of Lima in the early seventeenth century and wrote on law in the Western Indies (e.g. *Política Indiana* ([1647] 1703)). Father Diego de Avendaño was a Jesuit priest whose works included the *Thesaurus Indicus* (1668), which addressed legal and moral concerns in Spanish America. In referring to these writers, the *asesor* carried forward stereotypes of Indians and those associated with them into his own century. Simultaneously, he completely disregarded the fact that it was an Indian man who reproached Patricio when he discovered him with his daughter and reported the crime to the authorities. The actions of the *asesor* demonstrate some of the ways that stereotypes of Indians could survive in the legal arena. Generalizations from past centuries could be cited uncritically, while information that contradicted them was ignored.

While the cases thus far have shown how Indianness could be employed to the benefit of a defendant, records of incestuous crime also reveal how such discourse could work against them. In 1804 Verapaz, Manuel and Manuela Salvatierra, father and daughter, were charged with incest (Case 41). Their *calidades* were not explicitly stated, but they seem to have been Indian. According to the interim *fiscal*, "the incest committed by Manuel Salvatierra with his legitimate daughter is one of the most abominable crimes that can be counted among *lascivos* ['lewd persons'], as even nature itself is horrified by them."[47] In other words, it was unnatural. Citing the aforementioned Solórzano and Montenegro, he asserted that "the sin of incest is almost as common among Indians as drunkenness. But that which is committed in the first degree of father with daughter was viewed with repugnance even among the *indios gentiles* [Indians unexposed to Christianity]."[48] Such fathers were cruelly punished, while the daughters were treated with great compassion because of their compromised ability to defend themselves from "a man one should naturally respect and fear."[49] In contrasting the incestuous behavior of the accused with that of *indios gentiles*, the *fiscal* emphasized the particularly abhorrent nature of the crime, which was undoubtedly meant to injure the accused. Thus, allusions to Indianness had the potential to work for or against a defendant, and its use as a reference point in discussions of incest had the effect of reinforcing an association between Indians and this particular crime.

Alcohol and Ignorance

While ignorance and inebriation had strong associations with Indianness, inebriation was a tool available to the population at large to excuse one's incestuous actions. Like the ignorance defense, inebriation spoke to one's state of mind and influenced the perception of one's criminal actions. As noted by William B. Taylor (1979, 64, 104), colonial courts often viewed drunkenness as a mitigating factor—a principle termed *excepción de ebriedad*, or drunkenness as mitigator. Case 61 against

Vicente Fuentes and Rosalía Surqueah is representative of court interest in the state of mind of incestuous offenders. During the trial, the magistrate asked Rosalía whether her father-in-law "was drunk in terms of not knowing what he was doing"[50] on the two occasions that he raped her. She answered that he was slightly tipsy the first time, but in his right mind the second time.

Defendants might also comment on their state of mind during incestuous crime, or at least, the state of mind required for it. When Vicente initially denied raping Rosalía, he said that "he has not committed such crime unless he did so drunk and forgot."[51] In like fashion, don Juan Manuel Dardón argued during a *careo* with his daughter that *estaría loco o ebrio* ("he would have to be crazy or drunk") to have committed the crime of which she accused him (Case 15, also in Chapter 4). She countered that "he was never drunk, even though he sometimes drank liquor, and that he has never suffered from madness, nor any other lack of his senses."[52]

Drunken confusion could allegedly lead to a mistaken identification of kin. Josef Eustaquio García—the Indian bricklayer from Chapter 4 who arrived home drunk one night and had sex with his daughter in her bed—claimed that "he had a carnal act with his daughter thinking she was his wife, for which he repented the next day"[53] (Case 28). In his defense, the *procurador de pobres* argued,

> It is evident that García had a single sexual act with his daughter, but also that he was out of his mind, or such that he did not know what he was doing, because he was possessed of inebriation...which circumstance is sufficient in legal opinion to excuse him from the ordinary penalty.[54]

This latter statement in particular highlights the legal import attributed to state of mind. But given that a drunken state was obviously relevant to criminality, authorities were cautious when it came to inebriation as an excuse. In Case 37 above, where Patricio de León also identified his daughter as his wife while drunk, the magistrate alleged that Patricio only admitted to inebriation, a crime in and of itself, to cover for the other one—incest with his daughter.

The 1798 case against Hipólito Cojulum for the rape and deflowerment of his young sister-in-law shows how an inebriation defense and an Indianness defense could be combined in incest cases (Case 21). Initially, Hipólito admitted to grabbing and deflowering María Mercedes Quemé, causing her to spill blood. However, he did so "because he was drunk and did not know what he was doing." Later, through an interpreter likely translating from K'iche', Hipólito said that even though he was drunk, he now remembered that the act was not violent but rather María Mercedes had consented to his request. When questioned about the inconsistency in his statements, he said that "at the time of the incident he was not completely drunk but rather partially drunk, and thus, he remembers that the girl agreed to the act."[55] María Mercedes, for her part, denied that she consented to it and argued that "she would never have been able to agree to it because she would not know—due to her status [virgin]—what he was asking of her."[56]

Don Juan José Gutiérrez Marroquín, Hipólito's first *defensor*, explained that the only arguments on which to base his defense were the *calidad* of his client and the (drunken) state in which he was when he committed the crime. He claimed that among Indians,

> crude education does not remove them from but rather further establishes them in an idiocy of the first order that absolves them of the ordinary penalty of the laws...This mitigating circumstance is preponderated in *excesos de torpeza* [i.e. sexual crimes], in which fragility works in proportion to the little resistance that it finds in the face of a lack of education and recognition of religion and its sacred laws.[57]

Further, Hipólito's inebriation at the time would have led to unintentional actions and compromised his ability to combat his presumed weakness and fragile resistance. Hence, inebriation could act as a compounding factor on an individual already at risk for committing sexual crimes (cf. Taylor 1979, 105). Hipólito's second defense counsel compared his drunken incestuous behavior to the experience of Lot from the Old Testament, who had sex with his daughters while drunk on wine. Hipólito's true crime, he maintained, was inebriation.

References to alcohol did not speak solely to one's state of mind during a sex act. Some individuals used inebriation to argue that they would have been physically incapable of having sex in the first place. This was seen in the case against don Apolinario Rivas, who argued he was so drunk the night of the alleged rape of doña Teodora Bocanegra that he did not even get undressed (Case 45, also in Chapter 5). Therefore, he believed the accusation of rape was unlikely.

Overall, the use of intoxication to excuse incestuous behavior was not as strongly associated with concepts of Indianness as the ignorance defense. Still, colonial actors might frame inebriation as exacerbating Indians' alleged weakness to sexual crimes, reinforcing the association between Indians and deviant sexual behavior in the process.

Conclusion

Filtering records of incestuous crime through the lens of Indianness reveals cultural assumptions on the part of colonial authorities and legal

professionals that individuals identified as Indian—or Indian-like—
were ignorant of what constituted incest and the severity of this crime.
This, in turn, fueled expectations that such individuals would commit
it. While the ignorance defense was not wholly dependent on references
to Indianness, they were often intertwined. Much of Indianness had its
roots in the early colonial period, and these stereotypes continued to be
employed by actors in the late colonial legal arena with little room for
counternarratives. Since references to Indianness could theoretically aid
defendants, it potentially worked against individuals who felt wronged
and were seeking justice in the Spanish courts. The implications of the
ignorance defense were the greatest for Indian women and girls, whose
sexual assaulters could expect more lenient treatment when it was effective, and who would have found themselves held more accountable
for incestuous violence when it was not. Further, the use of Indians as
points of reference in criminal proceedings related to incestuous crime—
whether as a means to condemn or acquit a defendant—again had the
effect of linking this sector of the colonial population to this particular
crime. Indeed, legal proceedings undoubtedly provided an arena for the
perpetuation of colonial discourse that would function on some level to
further cement the subordinate and marginalized position of indigenous
peoples in colonial Guatemalan society.

Notes

1 *...la rusticidad, é ignorancia de los Indios; principalm.te de las Mugeres...
p.r esta razon no hay en los de esta clase el mismo dolo y malicia q.e en los
de la otra para delinquir...conforme á lo prebenido p.r las Leyes, no debe
imponerse la misma pena á los Indios, q.e a los Ladinos, sino q.e aquellos
deben ser jusgados con equidad, y no con el rigor, q.e disponen las mismas
Leyes se jusgue á estos...*

2 *Era pues presiso un impulso, y movimiento, extraordinario de la bondad, y
poder de Dios, p.a sostener á Hernandes en una provocacion tan singular
como esta; y mas viviendo junto[s] en donde no podia resistir a los ruegos,
y lagrimas, de una Madrastra zelosa, y afligida, q.e hasta la salid[a] á Misa
le negaba, p.r pareserle, q.e iba a buscar otr[a] Muger. ¿Que podia pues
esperarse de un Pobre Yndi[o]; en quien la ignorancia, y rustisidad caminan
juntas? El mayor santo huviera caido; co[n] semejante provocacion...*

3 *...parece que debe mirarse con alguna eguidad quando se comete por Yndios, cuia ignorancia funda á su favor la presuncion de no proceder con la
malicia que se supone en los de las otras castas. f. 7v.*

4 Reference to this law also surfaced in Case 54.

5 *...deb[e] suponerse mas adelantada su sivilizacion (á lo menos respecto de
la Religion Cristiana) q.e en los immediatos á la Conquista... f. 7v.*

6 It is noteworthy that Mariano identified himself as *mestizo*, yet he was elsewhere described as *indio tributario* and evidently treated as if he were Indian.

7 *...la torpeza de los Yndios, é indiferencia con que regularm.te ven el delito
de incesto, les hace caer en el, q.do la ocasion se les presenta. f. 10.*

8 *...de la rusticidad de los Yndios y del poco escrupulo con que cometen delitos de esta clase... f. 10v.*

9 *Se ha dicho ser Ynd.s los delinquentes, con lo q. se dijo todo sobre esta par-*
ticular, combiniendo el modo con q.e se portan en q.to al sexto, con lo q.e
cantó Ovidio de otras gentes muy parecidas á nros. naturales entre las q.e
indiferentem.te se mesclaban el Padre con la hija, y el hijo con la madre... f.
13.

10 *...aunque es mi padre pero no por eso a de salirse con el echo pues no sera*
cristiandad ni profesaremos la fe de Jesucristo por lo que pido contra Bis-
ente Fuentes por aber anulado mi matrimonio y el suyo abiendo yegado a
tener auto fordadamente con mi muger por dos veses por lo que en meritos
de Justicia pido un destierro para toda su bida...prosediendo yo a no jun-
tarme con eya por ninguna manera por que no sera rrazon que yo mismo
Busque esa sal pais. Bien sabe el Senor General el delito que se tiene pues
es mi padre, y faltara yo a ser cristiano si n[o] lo hiziera asi y en meritos
de Justici[a] pido que lo destierren para toda su bida a un castiyo...que yo
estando el no me junto con eya aunque egecuten en si el quastigo que el
Senor General mandara... AGCA A1.15 Leg. 2965 Exp. 28088 f. 1-v.

11 When José said he would "not reunite with her by any means," he used the
verb *juntarse*, which also referred to sexual intercourse (see *Diccionario de
Autoridades* 1726–1739 v. 4).

12 Thomas Gage ([1648] 1958, 204) used the term "salt earth" when discussing
salt production in Amatitlán, noting how mules were brought there to feed
on the "salt earth."

13 *...pensando se huviese mesclado con otro hombre estraño carnalmente, y*
resultó que su mismo Padre del que expone Vicente Fuentes, fue el que
cometió este crimen, por lo qual se presento a la Justicia para que se le es-
carmiente. AGCA A1.15 Leg. 2965 Exp. 28088 f. 3v.

14 Following an appeal, Vicente and Rosalía were assigned new legal
representatives.

15 *...procuró persuadir a su Suegro a fin de que contubiese su impetu, hacien-*
dole ver que era su hija politica, y que semejantes procedimientos quedaban
para los irracionales, y no se obcerbaban entre Cristianos...pero a pesar de
esto Fuentes no hiso caso de estos combencimientos tan naturales, y por el
contrario la insistia a que no tubiese miedo... AGCA A1.15 Leg. 2965 Exp.
28088 f. 8.

16 *...no supo lo que se hiso, ni la gravedad del pecado que cometia, y pide se*
le mire con conmiseracion. AGCA A1.15 Leg. 2965 Exp. 28088 f. 6v.

17 *Pero que queremos que practiquen unas jentes yncultas, unas jentes yn-*
brutesidas, unas jentes sin temor, ni respeto á D.s pues Esta En desir, que
los Yndios p.r mas cognato q.e pongan sus Curas en ynstruirlos, Estan
hasta El dia por conquistar... AGCA A1.15 Leg. 2965 Exp. 28088 f. 9v.

18 *...falto de los principios racionales se deliberó á pecar...* AGCA A1.15 Leg.
5390 Exp. 45733 f. 3v.

19 *Aunque Yndio rustico Vicente, y sin las luces necesarias de religion, despues*
de cometido su delito, lo conoció, é infirió su gravedad, y p.r esto impuso
á su nuera perpetuo silencio, creyendo q.e con esto todo se havia conclu-
ido, y hechadosele trra y q.e con no bolverla á solicitar mas, cumpliria con
Dios, y con la lealtad q.e debia guardar á su hijo: tales son los sentimientos
sencillos, y nada maliciosos de los Yndios en esta parte, pues como en ellos
no resplandecen las luces de religion y caridad, q.e en los cultos, se hacen
acrehedores á la conmiseracion. AGCA A1.15 Leg. 5390 Exp. 45733 f. 18.
Charity is a theological virtue that refers to loving God above all things
for his sake and loving others for God's sake. Religion, a moral virtue with
which God is revered, is born from the theological virtue of Charity. See, for
example, *Diccionario de Autoridades* (1726–1739 v. 2, v. 5).

20 *Quantos exemplos se leen en las Historias, de Mugeres que habiendo cuidado extrahordinariamente de la pureza, han caido por ultimo en las artificiosas trampas de un disoluto; y quien no advierte, que aunque sus cuerpos quedaron manchados, sus virtudes se han hecho mas admirables.* AGCA A1.15 Leg. 5390 Exp. 45733 f. 5v-6.

21 *...la union corporal de Padres é hijas era la mas monstruosa, vista solamente entre los animales.* AGCA A1.15 Leg. 5390 Exp. 45733 f. 7.

22 *...los inesperados movimientos de su suegro...la extraña inclinacion de que estaba poseido...la necia pretencion de su Padre.* AGCA A1.15 Leg. 5390 Exp. 45733 f. 7-v.

23 *Los réspetós de su Padre, y él temór de no levantar la la mano contra el, la impedirian hacer los esfuerzos posibles en su défénsa; asi como quando un hijo es reprendido de su Padre injustamente, no se atreve á contradecir, ni usar de sus derechos, por el miedo de incurrir en alguna falta. No debe dudarse tampoco que la Rosalia Surquiah esta imbuida en el érror comun de las gentes idiotas, que á los Padres debe obedecerse hasta en los mandatos pecaminosos; por que su condicion, y principios de govierno no pronostican otra cosa.* AGCA A1.15 Leg. 5390 Exp. 45733 f. 7v.

24 *...la sensualidad es la pacion que mas dificilmente se vence; por cuyo motivo aseverare, sin temor de errar, que es el escalon mas trabajoso para los justos, que continuamente exercitan su cuerpo con asperas penitencias, y q.e ha sido la causa del trastorno de ilustratos entendimientos... Y haciendo tantos extragos, y en tales Personas. ¿Que se debe esperar de una Yndia rustica sin principios de Religion, que no tiene otra regla para obrar que su propia voluntad?* AGCA A1.15 Leg. 5390 Exp. 45733 f. 8.

25 *...es bien savido que entre los Yndios ay unos que tienen mas malicia que otros...* AGCA A1.15 Leg. 5390 Exp. 45733 f. 14.

26 Compare with Lewis's (1995) analysis of a witchcraft case involving two free black women. Lewis found that, to her benefit, the defendant and her defenders were able to portray her as "not black" and "not female," two characteristics typically associated with witchcraft and viewed as inferior following racial and gender hierarchies that privileged Spanish and male statuses.

27 See, for example, Bertrand 1989, 163.

28 Her surname was also written as Sotoh and Tzoh.

29 *...la falta de instruccion y menos malicia q.e ordinariam.te o por lo comun se advierte en los de nuestra clase...* AGCA A1.15 Leg. 5390 Exp. 45733 f. 20v.

30 *...aunque le dijo q.e savia que estava con su ermana en ilicita amistad con palabra de casamiento, le respondio Quachita, q.e no le asia, q.e si resultava preñada se llevaria la criatura a criar a su casa, y con este motivo se metio con él, de q.e a resultado embarasada...* f. 3.

31 *...p.r su ig[no]rancia nunca penetró el delito q.e cometio n[i] que fuese motibo de q.e se impidiese el casamiento q.e Quachito tenia propuesto a su hermana...* f. 5v-6.

32 Though Bernardo had said that he was not sure whether they were whole sisters or not.

33 *...enorme delito...en haver mantenido concubinato incestuoso con las dos Marias...sabiendo de positivo q.e son ermanas...semejantes exésos solo entre los irracionales se ven...como hombre fragil, y sin estos sentimientos cristianos, no graduó la enormidad q.e cometia en estos exésos de q.e se le hace cargo...* f. 5.

34 *...por su calidad é ignorancia se disminuye mucho su criminalidad, y gravedad...* f. 17v.

35 *...temerosa de que su Padre hiciese lo mismo con la que declara lo haviso al Alcalde del lugar, no habiendolo hecho antes por falta de advertencia,*

y se halla en el dia entregada en otra casa en donde le estan enseñando la doctrina pues su Padre no lo hacia...

36 *...si acaso es bruto para haber hecho semejante pecado, que sus Padres le criaron, y educaron con temor á Dios... f. 2.*

37 *...ninguno Que es hermana de Madre, de Petrona Martel, q.e fue su muger lexitima pero q.e heran hijas de distintos Padres. f. 5v.*

38 *...como tonto q.e es, no save. f. 5v.*

39 *...lo hizo con el fin de casarse y como tonto no savia lo q.e hacia. f. 5v.*

40 *...lo que no deve hacer fuerza, si se considera el Idiotismo que es tan proprio en los de su clase, y calidad. f. 8.*

41 *...todo és verdad; pero q.e como era tonta, no sabia lo mal q.e hacia, hasta ahora q.e se lo han dicho. f. 8.*

42 *...no puede ignorarlo, p.r ser cosa muy sabida aun entre las gentes mas burdas q.e el trato torpe de un mismo hombre con dos hermanas carnales es un nuebo delito, á mas de el de la simple fornicacion, y q.e en el p.r sus circunstancias de saber leer y escribir, y la de haverse rosado con gentes no se puede suponer la ignorancia q.e aparenta...*

43 This does not include incidents where individuals were unaware due to intoxication, did not realize their relatives had a sexual relationship with the same person as them, or misunderstood the nature of a relationship like when Domingo Morales from Chapter 4 did not believe his deceased wife was the sister of the woman he wanted to marry.

44 Juan José's surname was also spelled Pisabah, Pixavag, and Pixabah.

45 *...hombre q.e es esto somos cristianos asi se cumple la Ley de Dios como es esto con tu hija...* AGCA A1.15 Leg. 3028 Exp. 29261 f. 2v.

46 *...entre los Yndios y los que se crian a estilo de ellos, el delito de incesto, lo mismo q.e la embriaguez (como dice el P.e Avendaño, y apunta el S.or Solo[r]zano) no es de los pecados de mayor gravedad, por no tener la comprehension de su malicia...* AGCA A1.15 Leg. 3028 Exp. 29261 f. 11.

47 *...el incesto cometido p.r Manuel Salvatierra con su hija lexitima Manuela es uno de aquellos delitos mas avominables q. puedan contarse entre los lacibos pues aun la misma naturaleza se orroriza de ellos.*

48 *...el pecado de insesto es casi tan comun entre los Yndios como el de la embriaguez; pero el q. se comete en el primer grado de Padre con hija aun entre los Yndios gentiles se vio con repugnansia...*

49 *...un hombre á quien naturalm.te debe respetar y temer.*

50 *...estava ebrio en terminos de no saver lo que hacia.* AGCA A1.15 Leg. 2965 Exp. 28088 f. 3.

51 *...no ha cometido tal delito, a menos que lo haya executado bolo, y no se acuerde.* AGCA A1.15 Leg. 2965 Exp. 28088 f. 4v.

52 *...nunca estaba ebrio, aunque algunas besses havia tomado águardiente, y q.e nunca há padecido de locura ni de ótra falta de sentidos... f. 10v.*

53 *...pensando que era su muger tubo acto carnal con su hija de lo que se arrepintio al dia siguiente.* AGCA A2.2 Leg. 199 Exp. 4085 f. 4v.

54 *Es constante, que Garcia tuvo un simple acceso con su hija; pero igualm.te lo es, q.e fué estando fuera de si, ó en terminos, q.e no sabia lo que hacia; p.r q.e se hallaba poseido de la ebriedad...cuya circunstancia es bastante en el concepto legal p.a escusarle de la pena ordinaria...* AGCA A2.2 Leg. 199 Exp. 4085 f. 8.

55 *...quando el suceso no estava bolo p.r entero sino es medio tomado, y p.r eso se acuerda que la muchacha le dio palabra en aquel acto... f. 9v.*

56 *...nunca pudiera haver condesendido siendo hasi que no savia por razon de su estado p.a que pudiera combidarla... f. 9.*

57 *...la tosca educasion, no los saca y antes los establese mas, en una estuticia de prim.a orden, q.e los dispenza de la pena ordinaria de las Leyes...*

cuia execpcion se prepondera en los exesos de torpeza donde la frajilid[ad] obra á proporcion de la poca resistencia q.e encuentra, respecto á la ninguna educasion, y falta de reconocim.to de la Religion y sus sagradas Leyes. f. 11-v.

Bibliography

Archibald, Elizabeth. 2001. *Incest and the Medieval Imagination.* Oxford: Clarendon Press.

Avendaño, Diego de. 1668. *Thesaurus Indicus.* Antwerp, Belgium: Collegÿ Societatis Jesu Monachÿ.

Bertrand, Michel. 1989. "La tierra y los hombres: la sociedad rural en Baja Verapaz durante los siglos XVI al XIX." In *La sociedad colonial en Guatemala: estudios regionales y locales,* edited by Stephen Webre, 141–87. Antigua, Guatemala: CIRMA.

Brundage, James A. 1987. *Law, Sex, and Christian Society in Medieval Europe.* Chicago, IL and London: The University of Chicago Press.

Deloria, Philip J. 2004. *Indians in Unexpected Places.* Lawrence: University Press of Kansas.

Diccionario de Autoridades. 1726–1739. 6 vols. Madrid: Real Academia Española. http://web.frl.es/DA.html.

Fuentes y Guzmán, Francisco Antonio de. (1690) 1882. *Historia de Guatemala: ó Recordación Florida,* edited by Justo Zaragoza. Madrid: Luis Navarro.

Gage, Thomas. (1648) 1958. *Thomas Gage's Travels in the New World,* edited by J. Eric S. Thompson. Norman: University of Oklahoma Press.

Herlihy, David. 1985. *Medieval Households.* Cambridge and London: Harvard University Press.

Hill, II, Robert M. 2002. *Colonial Cakchiquels: Highland Maya Adaptation to Spanish Rule, 1600–1700.* Belmont, CA: Thomson Wadsworth.

Kulick, Don. 1996. "Causing a Commotion." *Anthropology Today* 12 (6): 3–7.

Lewis, Laura A. 1995. "'Blackness,' 'Femaleness' and Self-Representation: Constructing Persons in a Colonial Mexican Court." *Political and Legal Anthropology Review* 18 (2): 81–9.

Lovell, W. George, and Christopher H. Lutz. 1994. "Conquest and Population: Maya Demography in Historical Perspective." *Latin American Research Review* 29 (2): 133–40.

Martínez Peláez, Severo. 2009. *La patria del criollo: An Interpretation of Colonial Guatemala,* edited by W. George Lovell and Christopher H. Lutz. Translated by Susan M. Neve and W. George Lovell. Durham, NC and London: Duke University Press.

Merry, Sally Engle. 1994. "Courts as Performances: Domestic Violence Hearings in a Hawai'i Family Court." In *Contested States: Law, Hegemony and Resistance,* edited by Mindie Lazarus-Black and Susan F. Hirsch, 35–58. New York and London: Routledge.

Montenegro, Alonso de la Peña. (1668) 1771. *Itinerario para párrocos de indios, en que se tratan las materias mas particulares tocantes á ellos para su buena Administración.* Madrid: En la oficina de Pedro Marín. Google Books.

Scott, James C. 1990. *Domination and the Arts of Resistance: Hidden Transcripts.* New Haven, CT and London: Yale University Press.

Solórzano Pereira, Juan de. (1647) 1703. *Política Indiana*. Belgium: Henrico y Cornelio Verdussen. Google Books.

Sousa, Lisa Mary. 1997. "Women and Crime in Colonial Oaxaca: Evidence of Complementary Gender Roles in Mixtec and Zapotec Societies." In *Indian Women of Early Mexico*, edited by Susan Schroeder, Stephanie Wood and Robert Haskett, 199–214. Norman and London: University of Oklahoma Press.

Taylor, William B. 1979. *Drinking, Homicide, and Rebellion in Colonial Mexican Villages*. Stanford, CA: Stanford University Press.

Wiesner-Hanks, Merry. 2010. *Christianity and Sexuality in the Early Modern World: Regulating Desire, Reforming Practice*. London and New York: Routledge.

7 Conclusion

Guatemalan criminal records show how incest codes and the criminal process spurred divisions within kin networks and encouraged racialized views of kin behavior. The presence of these variables transformed households into a series of concentric circles in which more nuclear members were assumed to be more loyal and sexually off-limits than those positioned farther out. It also prompted Spanish legal professionals to differentiate indigenous kinship models from Hispanic ones despite contradictions to this logic, giving the impression of a general incommensurability between an indigenous identity and Hispanic kin norms on their part. Colonial actors of all sorts were proficient at using these types of distinctions as they negotiated various crises within and outside the courtroom. Ultimately, the models of relatedness created within incestuous crime foreshadowed changes in marriage proscriptions and continued racial polarization following independence.

One theme that stands out within these records is the role of kinship malleability and notions of "real" kin in the manifestation of, and response to, incestuous crime. For example, the regular practice of incorporating non-biological children (occasionally termed *pepes*) into kin networks could make the exact nature of a kin tie unclear. Recall Case 39 against Domingo Morales and Dolores Gaitán. Domingo wished to marry Dolores and was adamant that she and his deceased wife were not (real) sisters but rather maternal half-sisters (like he first claimed) or milk sisters (as he came to argue). In the face of evidence to the contrary, the malleable nature of kinship—or rather, the confusion that could ensue from it—was mobilized for his defense since ignorance of kin ties could lessen culpability. Undoubtedly, there were individuals who exploited this potential during criminal proceedings, where defendants and their legal representatives were often desperate to make the former appear innocent before the magistrate.

Distinctions between (real) kin and kin-like individuals had implications for sexual violence and the legal proceedings surrounding it. Because "adopted" children were set apart from the biological children of oneself or one's spouse, some colonial actors viewed them as potential sexual partners. Felipe Gil from Case 58 courted his stepdaughter under the belief that she was merely a girl his wife had in her care—not her daughter. Petrona Quintanilla from Case 5 made clear that sexual violence against an "adopted" child was not as deviant as that executed by a father on his daughter. Thus, to the extent that incest codes impeded sexual relations with biological and stepchildren, "adopted" children were more likely to be subject to sexual attention and violence than other children in the home. These children could also have their loyalty to the family called into question as don Juan Manuel Dardón in Case 15 made evident. This suggests that identification as a *pepe* was not only a means to distinguish membership within the household—it could also be a form of discrimination. Such prejudice, in turn, might affect how testimony from a *pepe* was received in the courtroom.

On the whole, incest codes and the courtroom environment would have contributed to the ongoing significance of "real" kin (versus other types of individuals) and shaped perceptions of relatedness. They forced such distinctions to be made even though these differences could have been relatively insignificant in other contexts. Clearly, men were in a more powerful position when it came to making these decisions, using sexual coercion to impose their own understandings of "real" kin on the women in their lives. Further, some colonial actors were apparently unaware of the "reality" of kinship even when there was no debate about genealogical origins. One cannot forget how widower Andrés Victorio from Case 17 erroneously stated (from the court's perspective) that there was not any kin tie between him and the *hermana de madre* of his wife and the remonstration that followed. If the records allow, it would be beneficial to examine whether individuals ever identified paternal half-siblings as non-siblings, considering the patrilineal bias noted for some indigenous groups in the area and apparent in Western kinship models at this time.

In terms of consanguineous versus affinal incest, it appears that the latter tended to be more culturally acceptable. The overwhelming majority of incest cases involved affinal kin (through sexual intercourse or formal marriage), affinal incest cases enjoyed a slightly greater acquittal rate (understood as an absence of major penalties), and affinal incest was less likely to be associated with rape than consanguineous incest. A higher tolerance for affinal incest would theoretically translate into a higher absolute number of sexual assaults on female affinal kin compared to their consanguineous counterparts, and female affinal kin did, in fact, represent nearly 75 percent of the rape victims in the case sample. These discrepancies are compatible with qualitative data from the case sample that attributed particular importance to consanguineous kin. Rosalía Surqueah's father-in-law rejected her identification of him as her father to justify the sexual violence he ultimately perpetrated on her (Case 61), and Rosalío Yescas claimed he always treated his sisters-in-law as sisters in contesting the alleged relationship he had with one of them (Case 73). As seen in Case 11, degree of relatedness was also a factor, with legal counsel using the idea that (first-degree) mother-son incest was more unnatural than (second-degree) incest between an aunt and nephew, or between cousins, in defense of his client.

Indeed, colonial actors were adept at using kinship and incest codes in a myriad of strategic ways. Beyond their utility in justifying sexual relations and defending an individual on trial, they could also conceal and prevent illicit sexual behavior. Agustina from Case 68 supposedly referred to her brother-in-law as her father to ward off any impression of a romantic relationship between them. Perhaps even the way in which Manuela González from Case 48 reportedly glossed over a shared mother during sexual intercourse with her brother was significant to the moment between them. Various individuals tried to take advantage of *compadrazgo* to curb adulterous behavior, or at least, to ease suspicion of it. Testimony from María Jacoba Suárez from Case 12 insinuated that spiritual kinship was more powerful in this regard than affinal kinship. In addition, one needed only to create (or feign) affinal ties to impede the realization of an undesired marriage. Case 45 was suggestive in this regard. And on some occasions, male kin may have served as a preferred scapegoat for a loss of virginity or pregnancy.

Guatemalan records dealing with incestuous violence confirm what might be expected in an atmosphere in which a culture of honor and religious doctrine promoted male dominance—victims were always women and girls. As seen in Chapters 2 and 4, sexual violence against female kin was most often perpetrated by father-types—fathers, stepfathers, and fathers-in-law—and concepts like *respeto* could make female kin feel like they had no other choice than to give in to the sexual appetites of these men. Undoubtedly, many who experienced incestuous violence stayed silent out of respect for, or fear of, their perpetrators. In fact, the only victim of incestuous violence who denounced the crime to authorities on her own was Gregoria Gonzales from Case 5. Some victims even feared sharing episodes of sexual violence with other kin. Remember Ciriaca from Case 9 who was afraid that informing her mother of the rape by her uncle would result in her own punishment. Colonial authorities, for their part, apparently took sexual violence into some consideration during incest trials. Not only could the violent nature of an incestuous encounter merit comment and condemnation, but it also seems to have influenced acquittal rates. Like we saw in Chapter 3, there was a rise in acquittal rates for women when sexual violence or intimidation was involved, whereas men saw a decline under these circumstances.

As discussed in Chapter 5, victims of incestuous violence often stressed kin ties to discourage their rapists, whereas their attackers chose to disregard such ties to excuse the sexual encounter between them. These tendencies had parallels in other types of scenarios, suggesting they fit into larger patterns of gendered relations. One example comes from a case involving María Agustina Vásquez, an Indian *molendera* (tortilla maker) from Chinautla who was stabbed by her husband (AGCA A1.15 Leg. 4293 Exp. 34344). When asked about the motivation behind her injury, she said she was unaware of it because she had not given her husband any incentive to do so. She recounted how he lay down on the ground away from her after returning early in the morning from sleeping in the *milpa*. She "began to call to him affectionately, telling him, 'Come here, Tata, don't stay over there.'"[1] Seeing he did not want to move, she went over to him and lay down. Shortly after, he sat up, took the blanket from her, and stabbed her with a knife. Francisco said that he did not have any reason to stab her—he just felt like it. In fact, he reported that they had gotten along fine. Thus, here again, a woman reiterated her relationship to a man—in this case using a term of endearment to coax her aloof husband to bed—only to be dismissed and assaulted by him shortly after.

Incestuous crime in Guatemala also sheds light on how a culture of honor that encouraged male sexual rivalries created an environment in which formal incest codes were bound to be broken. Like we saw in Chapter 2, male sexual rivalries motivated by cuckoldry could easily result in three-party incest should more than one female relative of a rival become a sexual target. Further, some men evidently used female adultery to justify sexual relations with their own daughters. Aquilina Maquín from Case 55 and Leandra Ampérez from Case 65b essentially became pawns in their fathers' attempts to salvage their manhood. While it is unclear to what degree Aquilina and Leandra's fathers might have intended to injure their wives through their actions, these episodes do invite us to think about how children figured into the politics of marriage and the ways in which the politics of marriage shaped the parent-child bond.

Another avenue for future research would be to examine criminal records that include instances of sexual relations between male kin and between female kin. Because incest trials dealt exclusively with relations between men and women, sexual encounters between male relatives and between female relatives were absent. Investigation of the latter will show whether the patterns that surfaced in incest trials also manifested when family members shared a gender, allowing for a more holistic analysis of sexual intimacy and violence within the family. For instance, would men and boys have responded to rape by a male relative like the women in Chapter 5? What about women and girls who faced sexual assault at the hands of a female relative?

While some patterns in incestuous crime transcended socioracial categorization, incestuous crime also played into colonial discourse on Indianness. Spanish legal professionals often drew from assumptions that Indians were ignorant of incest and had a tendency to commit it.

Indians did represent over half of the defendants (of known *calidad*) in incest trials, but this is actually lower than what might be expected since Indians constituted the majority of the colonial Guatemalan population. Moreover, the language that surfaced in these cases was not so much an exercise in cultural relativism as it was an attempt to highlight Indians' inferiority to Spaniards, and thereby excuse their behavior. Needless to say, Spaniards were not the only ones who employed the ignorance defense in the courtroom. Indians recognized its utility as well. Regardless of whether ignorance of incest was sincere, this defense contributed to the survival of negative stereotypes of Indians among their Spanish contemporaries. Further, comparisons between incestuous criminals and Indians made for the benefit of, or in detriment to, a defendant served to further associate Indians with this particular crime.

Of course, individuals like Rosalía Surqueah and José Fuentes from Case 61 clearly conceived of incest in terms comparable to colonial authorities, but such similarities were glossed over in various ways. And individuals wronged by incestuous crime and anxious to find justice in the court system were potentially disadvantaged when aspects of Indianness were harnessed in defense of their offender. The degree to which this form of argumentation succeeded had the greatest implications for Indian women, who might see their sexual offenders treated more leniently when legal officials were moved by it, or find themselves held more accountable for an assault when they were not. Though the strength of this defense was evidently limited, the apparent need to distinguish between indigenous and Hispanic familial life—even when doing so contradicted the evidence at hand—served to fuel racial polarization in the area, which would ultimately seep into the post-independence era.

Obviously, incest codes were not homogenous across society, nor were all forms of incest viewed in the same way. Such heterogeneity is intriguing because it allows room for culture change. It would be worth investigating incest trials from the early post-independence period to see what types of narratives emerge because prohibitions on civil marriages between relatives had been modified by the late nineteenth century.[2] The *Código Civil de la República de Guatemala* (1877) included a list of relatives between whom marriage was proscribed. Book 1, Title 4, Articles 119–120 forbade marriage with consanguineous relatives in the direct line *infinitum* regardless of whether such relatives were legitimate. Affinal relatives in the direct line were similarly prohibited. Marriage proscriptions also applied to siblings and half-siblings and to adoptive parents[3] and their adopted children (*Código Civil* 1877, 8). Thus, kin ties associated with the direct line of descent—whether through blood, marriage, or adoption—were of particular concern within marriage law at this time, whereas collateral ones beyond the sibling pair had apparently lost their relevance. These developments would have been in opposition to policies within canon law, where, for example, marriage to a sibling-in-law (following the death of a spouse) was prohibited until the late twentieth century (Héritier 2002, 107). The 1877 proscriptions also did not address unions between spiritual kin, even though it was not until 1917 that canon law abolished many of the marital consequences related to sponsorship (Lynch 1986, 18). A loosening of restrictions on collateral and first-degree affinity unions and a disregard for those between spiritual kin is consistent with precedents noted for the colonial period. As we have seen, direct relatives could benefit from a greater presumption of honesty than collateral ones, affinal incest was more acceptable than consanguineous incest, and dictionary definitions of incest did not include sexual relations between spiritual kin, nor did any of the cases brought before the secular courts focus on spiritual incest per se. In short, late-nineteenth-century marriage law in many ways resonated with incest codes from the colonial period.

While incest may at first come across as a peripheral subject, this study has shown how approaching topics like kinship, gender, and race through this lens can add further nuance to our understanding of social relations in a given area. Latent divisions between kin suddenly bubble to the surface once sexual relations come on the scene, revealing pseudo-kinship categories like that of the *pepe* in the process. Also, incest codes can provide individuals with multiple avenues to creatively manage interpersonal relationships and skirt the law, thereby yielding insight into how individuals use cultural resources to their own ends. Further, incest often intersects with and reinforces social inequalities in society, making it useful for understanding power dynamics in the family and beyond. Finally, incestuous crime can spark conversation and debate about relatedness and sexual relations within the family, rendering it a fruitful arena in which to explore mechanisms of culture change.

Notes

1 *...comenzó a llamarlo carinosamente, diziendole veni tata quitate de ay.* f. 2.
2 In Guatemala, civil marriage and divorce was formalized in 1836 and 1837 only to be returned to ecclesiastical jurisdiction a few months later following a rebellion that ousted the liberal government. It was not until 1877 that the state was again granted shared jurisdiction over marriage and divorce (Komisaruk 2013, 248–9).
3 This included the wife of an adoptive father and, presumably, the husband of an adoptive mother.

Bibliography

Código civil de la república de Guatemala, 1877. 1880. Madrid: F. Gongora y Compañia. https://catalog.hathitrust.org/Record/100352263

Héritier, Françoise. 2002. *Two Sisters and Their Mother: The Anthropology of Incest*. Translated by Jeanine Herman. New York: Zone Books.

Komisaruk, Catherine. 2013. *Labor and Love in Guatemala: The Eve of Independence*. Stanford, CA: Stanford University Press.

Lynch, Joseph H. 1986. *Godparents and Kinship in Early Medieval Europe*. Princeton, NJ: Princeton University Press.

Appendix

Incest Case Log

1 AGCA A1 Leg. 2890 Exp. 26609

Year: 1682
Location: Jurisdiction of Totonicapán
Relationship(s): stepfather/stepdaughter
Participants: Pedro Cardona (*indio*, age n/a); Madalena Velasco (*india*, age n/a)
Penalty: Cardona: to be taken through the public streets on a horse with a town crier announcing the legal proceedings and crime, to receive one hundred lashes, to be banished twenty leagues from his town, and to be placed in a home with a shackle on his foot "like a slave" for two years. He was to pay for his tribute, clothing, and court fees from what he received monthly.

2 AGCA A1.15 Leg. 3024 Exp. 29166

Year: 1710
Location: Jurisdiction of Totonicapán
Relationship(s): father-in-law/daughter-in-law (x2)
Participants: Domingo Álvez (or Álvarez) (*indio*, 55 years old); Isabel Matul (*india*, 18 years old); Isabel Cox (*india*, 15 years old)
Penalty: D. Álvez: paraded through the streets of his town and given 200 lashes accompanied by a town crier, a trumpet, and a drum. Matul: paraded through the streets of her town and given one hundred lashes accompanied by a town crier, a trumpet, and a drum. Cox: absolved.

3 AGCA A1.15 Leg. 2893 Exp. 26711

Year: 1730
Location: Jurisdiction of Totonicapán
Relationship(s): uncle/niece
Participants: Pedro Monzón (*español*, age n/a); Francisca de Escudero (*española*, age n/a)

Penalty: Monzón: warned that future communication with Escudero would result in two years of banishment with his wife and children; habilitation of marriage. Escudero: ordered to move to Quetzaltenango; warned that future communication with Monzón would result in two years of *recogimiento* in the Casa Nueva.

4 AGCA A1 Leg. 5452 Exp. 46780

Year: 1743
Location: Jurisdiction of Verapaz
Relationship(s): father/daughter
Participants: Bernardino Muños (*calidad* n/a, age n/a, but an older man); María de la O Muños (*calidad* n/a, age n/a)
Penalty: n/a

5 AGCA A2 Leg. 142 Exp. 2597

Year: 1749
Location: Jurisdiction of Sacatepéquez
Relationship(s): father/daughter
Participants: Narciso Gonzales (*mulato libre*, age n/a); Gregoria Antonia Gonzales (*mulata libre*, 15 years old)
Penalty: N. Gonzales: n/a beyond initial sequestration of assets as he was never obtained. G. Gonzales: n/a.

6 AGCA A1.15 Leg. 5405 Exp. 46063

Year: 1762
Location: Jurisdiction of Escuintla
Relationship(s): stepfather/stepdaughter
Participants (of the crime of incest): Miguel Vásquez (*indio*, age n/a)
Penalty (for the crime of incest): A priest originally sentenced Vásquez to fifty public lashes, but Vásquez got him to change it to one hundred pesos. The priest also obtained an additional sixty-two pesos, a large pot, and an untamed mule from Vásquez's wife. Everything was ordered to be returned to Vásquez.

7 AGCA A2 Leg. 153 Exp. 2909

Year: 1773
Location: Jurisdiction of Sacatepéquez
Relationship(s): one man/mother and daughter
Participants: Josef María Grajeda (*calidad* n/a, age n/a); María Michaela Chinchilla (*calidad* n/a, age n/a); Ana de los Dolores Tortola (*calidad* n/a, 24 years old)
Penalty: n/a

8 AGCA A2.2 Leg. 153 Exp. 2914

Year: 1773
Location: Jurisdiction of Sacatepéquez
Relationship(s): one man/two sisters
Participants: Benito Montes de Oca (or Benito Guerén) (*mestizo*, 24 years old); María de la Concepción Palacios (*calidad* n/a, 20 years old); María Ignacia Palacios (*calidad* n/a, 16 years old)
Penalty: n/a

9 AGCA A2.2 Leg. 154 Exp. 2976

Year: 1775
Location: Jurisdiction of Sacatepéquez
Relationship(s): (political) uncle/(political) niece
Participants: Francisco de Paula Guerra (*mestizo*, 22 years old); Ciriaca (no surname) (*calidad* n/a, 11–12 years old)
Penalty: Guerra: time served; one month of public works; fees. Ciriaca: no penalty.

10 AGCA A1 Leg. 159 Exp. 3122

Year: 1784
Location: Jurisdiction of Sacatepéquez
Relationship(s): stepfather/stepdaughter
Participants: Esteban Quiñones (*pardo libre*, over 40 years old); Secundina Hernández (*calidad* n/a, 15 years old)
Penalty: Quiñones: fifty lashes at an exterior post of the prison; three hours of *argolla* (public shaming with an iron collar around the neck) with a sign stating his crime; six months of service in the royal prison; habilitation of marriage. Hernández: no penalty.

11 AGCA A2.2 Leg. 160 Exp. 3162

Year: 1785
Location: Jurisdiction of Sacatepéquez
Relationship(s): mother/son
Participants: Manuela Antonia Hernández (*mestiza*, 60 years old); Josef María Santa Cruz (*mestizo*, 20 years old)
Penalty: Santa Cruz: six months of service in the San Carlos prison of Nueva Guatemala. Hernández: freed, considering the time she spent in prison as time served.

12 AGCA A1 Leg. 2934 Exp. 27550

Year: 1788
Location: Jurisdiction of Sacatepéquez

Relationship(s): brother-in-law/sister-in-law; one man/two sisters
Participants: Josef Félix Barillas (*mulato*, 26 years old); María Jacoba Suárez (possibly *castiza*, 25 years old); María de los Santos Suárez (*calidad* n/a, 13 years old)
Penalty: J. F. Barillas: court fees totaling thirty-eight pesos and four reales; to avoid communication with M. J. Suárez as much as possible. M. S. Suárez: no penalty.

13 *AGCA A1.15 Leg. 5475 Exp. 47033*

Year: 1791
Location: Jurisdiction of Totonicapán
Relationship(s): n/a
Participants (in incest): Manuel Arriaga (*calidad* n/a, age n/a); Dominga Estrada (*calidad* n/a, age n/a)
Penalty: Estrada: two years of reclusion. Arriaga: n/a.

14 *AGCA A1.15 Leg. 4070 Exp. 32149*

Year: 1791
Location: Jurisdiction of Sacatepéquez
Relationship(s): n/a
Participants: don Manuel Inocencio Rodríguez (*calidad* n/a, age n/a); Paula Rodríguez (*calidad* n/a, age n/a)
Penalty: n/a

15 *AGCA A1.15 Leg. 2910 Exp. 27017*

Year: 1793
Location: Jurisdiction of Totonicapán
Relationship(s): father/daughter
Participants: don Juan Manuel Dardón (*español*, 43 years old); María Josefa Dardón (*calidad* n/a, 19 years old)
Penalty: J. M. Dardón: n/a, he escaped from prison. M. J. Dardón: n/a, but to be removed from *depósito* to be treated for an illness and then returned.

16 *AGCA A1 Leg. 4301 Exp. 34446*

Year: 1794
Location: Jurisdiction of Sacatepéquez
Relationship(s): one woman/father and son
Participants: Ana María Turcios (*calidad* n/a, age n/a); Tomás Castellanos (*calidad* n/a, age n/a); Mariano Castellanos (*calidad* n/a, 18 years old)
Penalty: Turcios: to be sent to the location of her husband. The authorities were to keep an eye on her conduct, she was to live a marital life, and

she was not allowed to go to Nueva Guatemala without permission from the tribunal of the Real Audiencia. T. Castellanos: responsible for paying the fees of the case which totaled twenty-three pesos and seven reales.

17 AGCA A2 Leg. 175 Exp. 3475/AGCA A2.2 Leg. 183 Exp. 3652A

Year: 17a: 1794; 17b: 1797
Location: Jurisdiction of Sacatepéquez
Relationship(s): brother-in-law/sister-in-law
Participants: Andrés Victorio (*indio*, 37 years old in 1794); María Anastacia Vásquez (*india*, 30 years old in 1794)
Penalty: Victorio (17a): six months of public works. Vásquez (17a): six months of reclusion in the Casa de Recogidas. Victorio (17b): no communication with Vásquez even in licit things. (He was to be turned in to the Indios Justicias of Ciudad Vieja, putting them in charge of looking after his conduct and keeping him from communicating with his sister-in-law.)

18 AGCA A2.2 Leg. 181 Exp. 3594

Year: 1796
Location: Jurisdiction of Sacatepéquez
Relationship(s): (political) uncle/(political) niece
Participants: Josef Teodoro Juárez Coronado (alias Masate) (*mulato*, 19 years old); María Cecilia Mangoche (*calidad* n/a, 15–16 years old)
Penalty: Masate: included in a royal pardon and ordered not to live nor communicate with M. C. Mangoche. The case was to be continued against M. E. Mangoche for perjury.

19 AGCA A1 Leg. 2914 Exp. 27094/AGCA A1.15 Leg. 4339 Exp. 35071

Year: 1797
Location: Jurisdiction of Totonicapán
Relationship(s): stepfather/stepdaughter
Participants: Miguel Caixon (*indio*, 51 years old); Juana Velasco (*india*, 25 years old)
Penalty: Caixon: fifty lashes at the whipping post and one year of public works in the *cabecera* of San Miguel Totonicapán. Velasco: one year of reclusion in the Casa de Recogidas in Nueva Guatemala.

20 AGCA A1.15 Leg. 5495 Exp. 47259

Year: 1798
Location: Jurisdiction of Quetzaltenango
Relationship(s): one man/mother and daughter

Participants: Gerónimo Chávez (*indio*, age n/a); Catalina Soltano (or Solórzano) (*india*, age n/a); María Francisca Trullo (*india*, age n/a)
Penalty: Chávez: four years of public works and fifty lashes at the public post with sign in front announcing his crimes. Soltano: two years of service in the church of San Marcos. Trullo: two years of service in the church of San Marcos.

21 AGCA A1.15 Leg. 5495 Exp. 47260

Year: 1798
Location: Jurisdiction of Quetzaltenango
Relationship(s): brother-in-law/sister-in-law
Participants: Hipólito Cojulum (*indio*, 26 years old); María Mercedes Quemé (*india*, 13 years old)
Penalty: Cojulum: For incest: twenty-five lashes at the *picota* and six months of service in the public works of that *cabecera*. (He was absolved of the crime of *abortos*.) Quemé: no penalty.

22 AGCA A2.2 Leg. 187 Exp. 3765

Year: 1798
Location: Jurisdiction of Sacatepéquez
Relationship(s): (political) first cousins
Participants: Manuel Matute (*mulato*, 23 years old); Eusebia Escalante (*calidad* n/a, 11–14 or more years old)
Penalty: Matute: freed with time served and to split the fees with E. Escalante. E. Escalante: four months of reclusion because of perjury.

23 AGCA A1.15 Leg. 5390 Exp. 45734/AGCA A1.15 Leg. 5387 Exp. 45682

Year: 1799
Location: Jurisdiction of Sacatepéquez
Relationship(s): n/a, but related in the first degree
Participants: Manuel de Jesús López (*indio*, age n/a)
Penalty: n/a, he escaped from prison.

24 AGCA A2.2 Leg. 191 Exp. 3873

Year: 1799
Location: Jurisdiction of Sacatepéquez
Relationship(s): stepfather/stepdaughter
Participants: Francisco López (*indio*, over 60 or 70 years old); Manuela Boche (*india*, 21 years old)
Penalty: López: six months of service in public works. Boche: six months of reclusion in the Casa de Recogidas. The *alcalde* was to take care that

after López and Boche completed their sentences they separate from one another so that they not commit the crime again, putting Boche in a *casa de honradez*.

25 AGCA A1.15 Leg. 5538 Exp. 47872

Year: 1800
Location: Jurisdiction of Suchitepéquez
Relationship(s): father/daughter
Participants: Feliciano Calito (*calidad* n/a, age n/a); Ildefonsa Timotea Calito (*calidad* n/a, 8 years old)
Penalty: F. Calito: not enough evidence so he was absolved and freed. I. T. Calito: no penalty.

26 AGCA A2.2 Leg. 194 Exp. 3962

Year: 1800
Location: Jurisdiction of Sacatepéquez
Relationship(s): brother-in-law/sister-in-law
Participants: Pedro Atanacio Castellanos (*indio tributario*, 20 years old); Josefa Mata: (*calidad* n/a, 14–15 years old)
Penalty: Castellanos: released pending further evidence. J. Mata: no penalty.

27 AGCA A1.15 Leg. 5423 Exp. 46273

Year: 1801
Location: Jurisdiction of Escuintla
Relationship(s): n/a, but presumably through affinity
Participants: Manuel Hércules y Canales (*calidad* n/a, age n/a); Sabina Villegas (*calidad* n/a, age n/a)
Penalty: Hércules y Canales: two years of public works. Villegas: deceased.

28 AGCA A2.2 Leg. 199 Exp. 4085/AGCA A1.15 Leg. 4381 Exp. 35730

Year: 1801
Location: Jurisdiction of Sacatepéquez
Relationship(s): father/daughter
Participants: Josef Eustaquio García (*indio*, 35 years old); María Josefa Canuto García (*calidad* n/a, 16 years old)
Penalty: J. E. García: two years of public works; habilitation of marriage. M. J. García: n/a, proceedings were to be carried out once she had the child.

150 *Appendix*

29 *AGCA A1.15 Leg. 4385 Exp. 35825*

Year: 1802
Location: Jurisdiction of Sacatepéquez
Relationship(s): one woman/two brothers
Participants: Josepha Mejía (*mulata* or *parda libre*, 18 years old); Bartolomé Monterroso (*mulato* or *mulato blanco*, 17 years old); Manuel Monterroso (*mestizo*, 21 years old)
Penalty: J. Mejía: one year of reclusion in the Casa de Recogidas; six pesos and five and a third reales in court fees. B. Monterroso: six pesos and five and a third reales in court fees. M. Monterroso: six pesos and five and a third reales in court fees.

30 *AGCA A1.15 Leg. 4386 Exp. 35841*

Year: 1802
Location: Jurisdiction of Sacatepéquez
Relationship(s): one man/mother and daughter
Participants: Luís Toscano (*calidad* n/a, 16 years old); Máxima Morales (*calidad* n/a, age n/a); Josefa Morales (*calidad* n/a, age n/a)
Penalty: Luís Toscano: to be freed and handed over to his mentor prior to getting married. J. Morales: to be freed and to take the necessary steps so she and Toscano could marry. M. Morales: released.

31 *AGCA A1.15 Leg. 5425 Exp. 46287/AGCA A1.15 Leg. 5426 Exp. 46305*

Year: 1802
Location: Jurisdiction of Escuintla
Relationship(s): father/daughter
Participants: Simón Hernández (*indio*, over 60 years old); María Josefa de la Cruz (*india*, 25 years old)
Penalty: Hernández: time served and freed. Cruz's husband was to be found (if not deceased) and reunited with Cruz, and they were to live separately from Hernández.

32 *AGCA A2.2 Leg. 203 Exp. 4147*

Year: 1802
Location: Jurisdiction of Sacatepéquez
Relationship(s): brother-in-law/sister-in-law (they are also cousins)
Participants: Teodoro Rebolorio (*mulato libre*, 26 years old); Cornelia Váldez (*calidad* n/a, but her brother was *mulato*, 25 years old)
Penalty: Rebolorio: freed and warned to avoid communication with Váldez when possible. Váldez and her brothers were jointly sentenced to

the fees of the case for the reckless nature of their conduct. (However, it may have been Rebolorio who ultimately had to pay the fees.)

33 AGCA A1.15 Leg. 4391 Exp. 35952

Year: 1803
Location: Jurisdiction of Sacatepéquez
Relationship(s): one man/mother and daughter
Participants: Gregorio Solórzano (*mulato* or *pardo libre*, 22 years old); Eustaquia Betansos (*mulata libre*, 50 years old); Lucía Ansueto (*calidad* n/a, age n/a)
Penalty: Solórzano: freed; court fees which totaled thirteen pesos and two reales; no communication with Lucía Ansueto even in licit matters. Betansos: freed.

34 AGCA A1.15 Leg 5426 Exp. 46332

Year: 1803
Location: Jurisdiction of Escuintla
Relationship(s): stepfather/stepdaughter; father/daughter
Participants: José Bernabé Polanco (*calidad* n/a, age n/a); Juana de Dios Flores (*calidad* n/a, age n/a); Petrona Polanco (*calidad* n/a, age n/a)
Penalty: J. B. Polanco: included in royal pardon; court fees, which he was unable to pay because of his extreme poverty; habilitation of his marriage was ordered, but his wife had died. Flores: ordered to not live with her stepfather but rather with her most immediate relative, who would watch after her conduct. P. Polanco: no penalty.

35 AGCA A1.15 Leg. 4392 Exp. 35971

Year: 1803
Location: Jurisdiction of Sacatepéquez
Relationship(s): brother-in-law/sister-in-law
Participants: Domingo Rodríguez (*mulato*, 22 years old); Antolina Castellanos (*calidad* n/a, 20–21 years old)
Penalty: Rodríguez: freed and warned to not communicate with A. Castellanos for any reason.

36 AGCA A1.15 Leg. 5427 Exp. 46342

Year: 1803
Location: Jurisdiction of Escuintla
Relationship(s): one man/mother and daughter
Participants: Mariano Donis (*calidad* n/a, 15 years old); María del Rosario (*calidad* n/a, age n/a); María Simeona Palacios (*calidad* n/a, age n/a)

Penalty: Mariano Donis: included in royal pardon; court fees. María Simeona Palacios: not allowed to live with her mother and was to be placed in a *casa de confianza y satisfacción*.

37 AGCA A1.15 Leg. 3028 Exp. 29261/ A1.15 Leg. 5475 Exp. 47050

Year: 1803
Location: Jurisdiction of Totonicapán
Relationship(s): father/daughter
Participants: Patricio de León (*mestizo* or *mulato*, 56 years old); Francisca de León (*calidad* n/a, 9–11 years old)
Penalty: P. de León: six months of public works; twenty-five lashes at the *picota*. It appears F. de León was removed from her father's house at least temporarily.

38 AGCA A2.2 Leg. 205 Exp. 4206

Year: 1803
Location: Jurisdiction of Sacatepéquez
Relationship(s): stepmother/stepson
Participants: Anica Lantán (*india*, 30 years old); José Hernández (*indio*, 22–24 years old)
Penalty: They were included in a royal pardon and told not to communicate even in licit things. Officials were to keep an eye on their behavior.

39 AGCA A2.2 Leg. 205 Exp. 4188/ AGCA A1.15 Leg. 4391 Exp. 35964

Year: 1803
Location: Jurisdiction of Sacatepéquez
Relationship(s): brother-in-law/sister-in-law
Participants: Domingo Morales (*mulato libre*, 52 years old); María Dolores Gaitán (possibly *mestiza*, 40 years old)
Penalty: Morales and M. D. Gaitán were ordered to not communicate with one another. She was to be sent to her hometown and put under the care of her relatives. Morales was not to visit this town and M. D. Gaitán was not to visit the capital in which Morales resided.

40 AGCA A2.2 Leg. 57 Exp. 1134

Year: 1804
Location: Jurisdiction of Sacatepéquez
Relationship(s): stepfather/stepdaughter

Participants (of incest): José Luis Faxardo (*mulato*, over 40 years old); Serapia Rodríguez (*calidad* n/a, age n/a)
Penalty: n/a beyond mention of an order for the sequestration of Faxardo's assets because Faxardo's case was to be continued under ordinary jurisdiction, while the rest of this document, which contained a copy of the initial proceedings of Faxardo's case, dealt with individuals under military jurisdiction.

41 AGCA A1.15 Leg. 5458 Exp. 46834

Year: 1804
Location: Jurisdiction of Verapaz
Relationship(s): father/daughter
Participants: Manuel Salvatierra (*calidad* n/a, age n/a); Manuela Salvatierra (*calidad* n/a, age n/a)
Penalty: Manuel Salvatierra: fifty lashes at the *picota* with a sign in front that read *por incestuoso con su hija*; four years of imprisonment at Omoa. Manuela Salvatierra: attendance at the punishment of her father with another sign that said *por incestuosa*; one month of reclusion in the prison; one year of service in her parish.

42 AGCA A1.15 Leg. 5427 Exp. 46349/AGCA A1.15 Leg. 5427 Exp. 46352

Year: 1804
Location: Jurisdiction of Escuintla
Relationship(s): n/a
Participants: José Benito Avila (*calidad* n/a, age n/a)
Penalty: Avila: included in royal pardon.

43 AGCA A1 Leg. 5428 Exp. 46383

Year: 1804
Location: Jurisdiction of Escuintla
Relationship(s): n/a
Participants: José Onorato Zamora (*calidad* n/a, age n/a); Eustaquia Rivera (*calidad* n/a, age n/a)
Penalty: Zamora: included in the royal pardon; court fees totaling fourteen pesos and five and a fourth reales; no further communication with Eustaquia Rivera even in licit things.

44 AGCA A2.2 Leg. 211 Exp. 4368

Year: 1805
Location: Jurisdiction of Sacatepéquez

Relationship(s): one man/two sisters
Participants: Manuel Aldana (*mestizo*, 28 years old); doña Feliciana Rivas (*calidad* n/a, 20 years old); doña Casilda Rivas (deceased) (*calidad* n/a, age n/a)
Penalty: Aldana: six years of armed service and court fees. F. Rivas: freed and handed over to her father so that he could keep a watchful eye on her conduct.

45 AGCA A2.2 Leg. 216 Exp. 4496/AGCA A2.2 Leg. 57 Exp. 1154

Year: 1805
Location: Jurisdiction of Sacatepéquez
Relationship(s): one man/two sisters
Participants: don Apolinario Rivas (*español*, 25–26 years old); doña Isidora (or Decidora) Bocanegra (*española*, 26 years old); doña Teodora Bocanegra (*calidad* n/a, but presumably *española*, 24 years old)
Penalty: Apolinario Rivas: six years of armed service. I. Bocanegra: six months of reclusion. T. Bocanegra: doña Francisca Bocanegra and the *alcalde de barrio* were to keep an eye on her conduct, and she was warned so she could correct her conduct in the future.

46 AGCA A1.15 Leg. 5387 Exp. 45675

Year: 1806
Location: Jurisdiction of Sacatepéquez
Relationship(s): (political) uncle/(political) niece
Participants: Domingo Mariano Mejía (*indio* or *mestizo*, but *indio* identification more heavily emphasized in the case, 38 years old); Juana Crisostoma Bajal (or Bajan) (*india*, 20 years old)
Penalty: Mejía: six months of public works; no further communication with Bajal; an ecclesiastical judge also made him perform public penance to revalidate his marriage. Bajal: service in a *casa de honra*.

47 AGCA A1.15 Leg. 5387 Exp. 45657

Year: 1806
Location: Jurisdiction of Sacatepéquez
Relationship(s): brother-in-law/sister-in-law
Participants: Guillermo Lázaro (*indio*, 25 years old); María Andrea de la Cruz (*india*, 20 years old)
Penalty: Lázaro: six months of public works; habilitation of marriage. M. A. de la Cruz: six months of reclusion (fled from hospital where she was treated for illness and died before her capture).

48 AGCA A2.2 Leg. 219 Exp. 4575

Year: 1806
Location: Jurisdiction of Sacatepéquez
Relationship(s): brother/sister
Participants: Vicente Martir González (*mestizo*, 23 years old); Manuela Antonia González (*mestiza*, 30 years old)
Penalty: V. M. and M. A. González were released. They were to pay fees totaling nineteen pesos and two and a half reales. They were warned to refrain from living alone together in the future. V. M. González was to seek a reunion with his wife.

49 A1.15 Leg. 5431 Exp. 46459

Year: 1806
Location: Jurisdiction of Escuintla
Relationship(s): stepfather/stepdaughter
Participants: Juan de Mata (*calidad* n/a, age n/a); Juana Alvina Pineda (*calidad* n/a, 12 years old)
Penalty: Mata: six years of armed service. Pineda: no penalty.

50 AGCA A1.15 Leg. 5430 Exp. 46449

Year: 1806
Location: Jurisdiction of Escuintla
Relationship(s): brother-in-law/sister-in-law
Participants: Andrés Palomo (*calidad* n/a, age n/a); Luciana Josefa Niño (*calidad* n/a, age n/a)
Penalty: Palomo: n/a. Niño: ordered to be freed because she was engaged to be married.

51 AGCA A1.15 Leg. 5477 Exp. 47089

Year: 1806
Location: Jurisdiction of Totonicapán
Relationship(s): brother-in-law/sister-in-law
Participants: Leandro Estrada (*calidad* n/a, age n/a)
Penalty: Estrada: eight years in the armed services.

52 AGCA A1.15 Leg. 5387 Exp. 45682

Year: 1807
Location: Jurisdiction of Sacatepéquez
Relationship: n/a
Participants: Andrés Gómez (*indio*, 40 years old)
Penalty: n/a

53 *AGCA A1 Leg. 2959 Exp. 27999/AGCA A1.15 Leg. 5387 Exp. 45682*

Year: 1807
Location: Jurisdiction of Sacatepéquez
Relationship(s): one man/mother and daughter
Participants: Pedro Martir Osorio (*mulato*, 56 years old); María Macedonia (*calidad* n/a, age n/a); Juana Bautista Sánchez (*calidad* n/a, 19 years old)
Penalty: Macedonia and Sánchez were released because the former was nursing and the latter was about to give birth. Osorio was also released.

54 *AGCA A2.2 Leg. 223 Exp. 4723*

Year: 1807
Location: Jurisdiction of Sacatepéquez
Relationship(s): one man/two sisters
Participants: Bernardo Quachita (*indio*, 46 years old); María Germana Sánchez (*india*, 20 years old); María de los Ángeles Sánchez (*india*, 30 years old)
Penalty: All were considered as time served. No fees. Their local authorities were to keep an eye on them and ensure that the offense was not repeated.

55 *AGCA A1 Leg. 2959 Exp. 27997/AGCA A1.15 Leg. 5390 Exp. 45725/ AGCA A1.15 Leg. 5390 Exp. 45734*

Year: 1807
Location: Jurisdiction of Sacatepéquez
Relationship(s): father/daughter
Participants: Marcos de la Cruz Maquín (or Maquís) (*indio*, 30–33 years old); Aquilina de Terso Maquín (or Maquís) (*india*, 12–14 years old)
Penalty: M. Maquín: one hundred lashes; two years of public works; habilitation of his marriage. A. Maquín: no penalty.

56 *AGCA A1.15 Leg. 4427 Exp. 36740*

Year: 1807
Location: Jurisdiction of Sacatepéquez
Relationship(s): first cousins
Participants: Vicente Quintanilla (*castizo*, 28 years old); María Enrríquez Gonzales (*calidad* n/a, 26 years old)
Penalty: Quintanilla: released; court fees. M. E. Gonzales: no penalty.

57 *AGCA A1.15 Leg. 5390 Exp. 45730*

Year: 1809
Location: Jurisdiction of Sacatepéquez

Relationship(s): n/a, but related in the second degree
Participants: Felipe Gámez or Gómez (*calidad* n/a, age n/a); Petronila Estrada (*calidad* n/a, age n/a)
Penalty: Gámez: two years of public works. Estrada: six months in service to the sick at the hospital.

58 AGCA A1.15 Leg. 5522 Exp. 47691

Year: 1810
Location: Jurisdiction of Sololá
Relationship(s): stepfather/stepdaughter
Participants: Felipe Gil (*calidad* n/a, 40 years old); Petrona Alvarado (*calidad* n/a, 19 years old)
Penalty: Gil: included in royal pardon; fees totaling seventeen pesos and five and a half reales; habilitation of marriage. P. Alvarado: included in royal pardon; to live with her grandfather.

59 AGCA A2.2 Leg. 234 Exp. 4982

Year: 1810
Location: Jurisdiction of Sacatepéquez
Relationship(s): one man/mother and daughter
Participants: Bartholomé Álvarez (*mulato*, 20 years old); Pía Ramírez (*mulata*, 30 years old); Ignés Ramírez (*mulata*, 16 years old)
Penalty: Álvarez: included in royal pardon; fees. P. and I. Ramírez: no penalty.

60 AGCA A1.15 Leg. 2965 Exp. 28089

Year: 1810
Location: Jurisdiction of Sacatepéquez
Relationship(s): brother-in-law/sister-in-law
Participants: Roberto Figueroa (*calidad* n/a, age n/a); Josefa Turcios (*calidad* n/a, age n/a)
Penalty: J. Turcios: to be reunited with her husband and warned to not cause suspicion. Figueroa: reprimanded to calm his wife and to not give her *motivos de sentir* ("cause for regret").

61 AGCA A1.15 Leg. 2965 Exp. 28088/AGCA A1.15 Leg. 5390 Exp. 45733/AGCA A1.15 Leg. 5390 Exp. 45734

Year: 1810
Location: Jurisdiction of Sacatepéquez
Relationship(s): father-in-law/daughter-in-law
Participants: Vicente Fuentes (*indio*, 39–40 years old); María Rosalía Surqueah (*india*, 18 years old)

Penalty: V. Fuentes: four years of imprisonment at Omoa; twenty-five lashes; habilitation of marriage. Surqueah: two months interior service in the Beaterio de Indias; spiritual exercises; habilitation of marriage.

62 AGCA A1 Leg. 2967 Exp. 28123

Year: 1810
Location: Jurisdiction of Sacatepéquez
Relationship(s): brother-in-law/sister-in-law
Participants: don Manuel de la Trinidad Mayén Catalán (*español/criollo*, 53 years old); doña María Salomé Soto (*española/criolla*, 40–45 years old)
Penalty: Considered as time served due to statute of limitations. Catalán was to perform spiritual exercises and a general confession before reuniting with his wife. Catalán and his wife were not to communicate with M. S. Soto in the future.

63 AGCA A2.2 Leg. 238 Exp. 5104

Year: 1811
Location: Jurisdiction of Sacatepéquez
Relationship(s): stepfather/stepdaughter
Participants: Pedro Pablo Calderón (*mulato*, 38 years old); María Petrona Nolasca Calderón (*calidad* n/a, 13 years old)
Penalty: P. Calderón: included in royal pardon; legal fees; officials were to keep an eye on his conduct. M. Calderón: no penalty.

64 AGCA A1.15 Leg. 2966 Exp. 28115

Year: 1811
Location: Jurisdiction of Sacatepéquez
Relationship(s): stepfather/stepdaughter; (political) uncle/(political) niece
Participants: Manuel Rodenas (*mulato*, 40 years old); Josefa Gavina Aguilar (*calidad* n/a, age n/a); Alejandra Vidal (*calidad* n/a, 23 years old)
Penalty: Rodenas: included in pardon. Aguilar and Vidal: no penalty.

65 AGCA A2.2 Leg. 237 Exp. 5068/AGCA A1.15 Leg. 5461 Exp. 46857

Year: 1811
Location: Jurisdiction of Verapaz
Relationship(s): 65a: stepfather/stepdaughter; (future) father-in-law/ (future) daughter-in-law; 65b: father/daughter; one man/mother and daughter

Participants: 65a: Felipe Vásquez (*indio castellano*, 38 years old); María Basilia García (*india castellana*, 14–15 years old); José Silverio Ampérez (*indio castellano*, 40 years old). 65b: José Silverio Ampérez (*indio castellano*, over 40 years old); María Leandra Ampérez (*india*, 16–18 years old); Manuel Cornel (*indio*, over 30 years old); María Manuela López (*india*, over 30 years old).
Penalty: J. S. Ampérez (65a): freed without fees because he was included in the royal pardon and was *indio*. J. S. Ampérez (65b): escaped. B. García: died before conclusion of the case. F. Vásquez: died before conclusion of the case. M. M. López: escaped. M. L. Ampérez: escaped. Cornel: escaped.

66 AGCA A1.15 Leg. 2985 Exp. 28388

Year: 1815
Location: Jurisdiction of Sacatepéquez
Relationship(s): father/daughter
Participants: José María Gómez (*indio*, 35 years old); María Baltazara Gómez (*india*, 22 years old)
Penalty: J. M. Gómez: included in royal pardon. M. B. Gómez: included in royal pardon; she was to be kept separated from her father.

67 AGCA A1.15 Leg. 2985 Exp. 28390

Year: 1815
Location: Jurisdiction of Sacatepéquez
Relationship(s): one man/mother and daughter
Participants: Marto Gallardo (*calidad* n/a, age n/a); Teodora Paz: (deceased) (*calidad* n/a, age n/a); Diega Paz (*calidad* n/a, age n/a)
Penalty: n/a

68 AGCA A1.15 Leg. 4470 Exp. 37705

Year: 1815
Location: Jurisdiction of Sacatepéquez
Relationship(s): brother-in-law/sister-in-law
Participants: José María Díaz (alias Cantarillas) (*calidad* n/a, age n/a); Agustina (no surname) (*calidad* n/a, age n/a)
Penalty: They were told to separate their residences and to stop selling alcohol, from which resulted the gathering of people of both sexes.

69 AGCA A1.15 Leg. 3005 Exp. 28771

Year: 1820
Location: Jurisdiction of Sacatepéquez
Relationship(s): father/daughter

Participants: Tomás Pérez (*indio*, 51–100 years old); María Catalina Pérez (*india*, 20 years old)
Penalty: T. Pérez: handed over to the Indios Justicias of Santo Tomás. M. C. Pérez: to be placed in "a house of good conduct."

70 AGCA A1.15 Leg. 5543 Exp. 48019

Year: 1820
Location: Jurisdiction of Chiquimula
Relationship(s): stepfather/stepdaughter (x3)
Participants: Felipe de la Cruz Flores (*calidad* n/a, age n/a); Aureliana Velásquez (*calidad* n/a, 13–14 years old); Encarnación Velásquez (*calidad* n/a, age n/a); Antonia Velásquez (*calidad* n/a, 7–8 years old)
Penalty: Flores: included in royal pardon. Velásquez sisters: ordered to be removed from the house of Flores.

71 AGCA A1.15 Leg. 5450 Exp. 46739

Year: 1820
Location: Jurisdiction of Chiquimula
Relationship(s): brother-in-law/sister-in-law
Participants: don Manuel Castañeda (*calidad* n/a, age n/a); doña María Antonia Canales (*calidad* n/a, age n/a)
Penalty: Castañeda: included in the royal pardon except for the *derecho de tercero*. Canales: no penalty. Measures were to be taken by the *corregidor* to make sure it did not happen again.

72 AGCA A1.15 Leg. 5543 Exp. 48013

Year: 1820
Location: Jurisdiction of Suchitepéquez
Relationship(s): n/a
Participants: Juan José Álvares (*calidad* n/a, age n/a)
Penalty: n/a

73 AGCA A1.15 Leg. 3007 Exp. 28829

Year: 1821
Location: Jurisdiction of Sacatepéquez
Relationship(s): brother-in-law/sister-in-law
Participants: Rosalío Yescas (*mulato*, 26 years old); María Ramona Álvarez Román (*ladina*, 24 years old)
Penalty: Yescas and Román were freed, but they were to pay court fees and appear if summoned regarding the case.
Note: Location refers to where a case was tried. Relationships reflect accusations or the types of relationships being scrutinized.

Index

Note: Page numbers followed by "n" denote endnotes.